I0156127

Memories
of the
Dakota Sioux War, 1862

Respectfully
O.G.Wall

Memories of the Dakota Sioux War, 1862

Two Eyewitness Accounts of the Uprising in Southwest Minnesota

ILLUSTRATED

Recollections of the Sioux Massacre

Oscar Garrett Wall

Reminiscences of the Little Crow Uprising

Asa W. Daniels

LEONAUR

Memories of the Dakota Sioux War, 1862
Two Eyewitness Accounts of the Uprising in Southwest Minnesota
Recollections of the Sioux Massacre
by Oscar Garrett Wall
and
Reminiscences of the Little Crow Uprising
by Asa W. Daniels

FIRST EDITION

ILLUSTRATED

Leonaur is an imprint of Oakpast Ltd

Copyright in this form © 2021 Oakpast Ltd

ISBN: 978-1-78282-948-5 (hardcover)
ISBN: 978-1-78282-949-2 (softcover)

http://www.leonaur.com

Publisher's Notes

The views expressed in this book are not necessarily
those of the publisher.

Contents

My Excuse

As rise the glorious achievements of man upon the ruins of convulsed Nature, or upon the landscape desolated by war, so out of that night of blood that hung like a pall over the Minnesota frontier in that fateful month of August, 1862, has grown in all essentials except form of government, a mighty empire.

Before the Sioux tragedy was enacted, the pioneer had come, and on the borders founded his home in a land of promise. Clustered about him were dear ones who, in this land of freedom and health, shared the joys and hopes that pervaded every breath inhaled. Here was the opportunity for willing hands and honest hearts—the one place where the shackles of poverty could never enslave those willing to work. Gradually the "covered wagon" gave way to the "shack" as a temporary abiding place, and the latter to the more comfortable yet modest home of the settler.

Small fields gave forth bountiful harvests; gardens were rich with their treasures, or aglow with fragrant flowers; schools were being founded, and churches organised, though widely scattered; herds were increasing from small beginnings, and for the first time in life the dream of an independent home, with its comforts and promises, was being realised. But intrigue had secretly and systematically laid the foundation of wrongs which should overthrow these bright hopes; which should rob these new homes not only of all their possessions, but of life itself, and leave blackened ruins, the skulls and crossbones of erstwhile happy homes, where, at intervals over vast prairies, the new dwellings had glistened in the golden sunlight. The grafter in the Indian department, entrusted with power and authority, was willing to imperil the whole frontier for the sake of plundering the Indian, who was no match for the conspirators acting as the servants and servants' servants of the government.

Thus, the Indian was taught to look upon the white race as his conniving, secret enemy, willing to violate sacred pledges and solemn obligations, and ready to take, under one pretence or another, the

7

lion's share of the sums pledged to him by the government. In fact, for these acts of bad faith and the repeated disappointments resulting, the government itself had come to be regarded by the red man as unworthy of confidence. Worst of all, white people indiscriminately had been brought under the ban by the misdeeds of government *employés* and avaricious traders, who had sown the wind that ripened into the whirlwind with which the border was swept without distinction.

But the savage tide was turned back by force of arms, and was so broken and scattered in the campaigns that followed, that confidence was for all time restored along the frontier.

The "prairie schooner" set sail again, and a tide of humanity followed in the wake of the soldiery, until at length perfect civilization marked, not alone the wilds of western Minnesota, but the vast plains that now constitute the Dakotas as well; and, what a transformation to be witnessed in a single lifetime!

A member of Captain Marsh's company, stationed at Fort Ridgely, at the time of the massacre in 1862, and in the service in 1863, on the Sibley expedition throughout what is now that portion of North Dakota east of the Missouri River, I witnessed, from beginning to end, the stormy scenes attending the outbreak and its suppression, and from contact and observation became very familiar with the history of the Sioux Massacre. But even these facts were but a slight incentive to assume the arduous task of preserving to North-western annals, many incidents forever lost, unless passed to the pages of history ere the final departure of the rapidly vanishing participants in those scenes of nearly fifty years ago; for assuredly the waves of time must soon forever close over the unspoken and unwritten of that tragic period.

Though yet in my "teens," I kept faithfully each day a diary of events, getting information when necessary, from the highest sources of authority, and no day was allowed to pass without the record being preserved. No matter what my tasks, I would keep my diary. I had no special future purpose in this, and placed no value upon the book after being mustered out of the army and reaching home, but carelessly left it with other relics and memories of a by-gone day, and in the changes that followed, never saw it again for over twenty years, when, on a visit to my mother, she presented it to me, having carefully preserved it. I had supposed it lost, and never regarded it as of enough value to merit an inquiry as to what might have become of it. In the light of the mature present, however, I find its pages full of interest and an ample reward for my painstaking.

In addition to this I had a messmate and intimate companion during the campaign of 1863, John McCole, who originally belonged to and was an officer of the Renville Rangers, and whose acquaintance I made during the siege of Fort Ridgely in 1862. Only a few days before the outbreak he had enlisted at Redwood, having up to that time for several years been a clerk and an accountant in one of the stores of the agency. He knew personally and well nearly every Indian on both the Upper and Lower reservations, and spoke the Sioux language fluently. He knew intimately all the Indian scouts, over sixty in number, on the Sibley expedition of 1863, and through him I had several extended interviews with the scouts, and particularly with Chaska, between whom and McCole there was a strong bond of friendship.

Chaska had throughout remained loyal to the whites, even at the risk of his own life; yet he knew the history of the massacre from the standpoint of the Indians, and was most interesting in his narrations, and particularly interesting in explaining how lack of discipline caused Little Crow's plans to miscarry immediately after the massacre at the agency, to the great advantage of Fort Ridgely and the whites generally.

Forty-seven years having elapsed, and no one thus far having cared to incur the expense and risks or assume the labour necessary to publishing much of interest thus far unwritten, and which is an important part of North-western history, and possessing an accumulation of matter and information as stated herein, I give to the public without apology or further excuse, the succeeding pages, conscious that among other things they contain the only detailed historical account of the Sibley Expedition of 1863 ever published.

O. G. W.

Cause of the Outbreak

The impositions perpetrated on the Indians, if not by the government agents, at least by their approval, were monumental. The Indians, instead of being put in possession of their own, and given protection, were plundered on every hand, and the gross injustice inflicted as inevitably adjusted itself at the doors of the government officials as the detached leaf adjusts itself to the law of gravitation.

A thousand lives having been blotted out by methods horrible to contemplate, and a vast area of beautiful country having been made barren and desolate, friends sought to mitigate the sins of derelict officers when the angry clouds of responsibility gathered about their heads, and strove to break the force of the awful consequences of their official sins, by belittling troublesome truths and pointing alone to the depravity of the savage race; but that the Sioux Massacre of 1862, was due to official chicanery there is little doubt, and fortunate was the official whose good name saved him blameless for acts open to suspicion or criticism. To merely perpetuate these facts, is not the object of their recital in this book. My preference was to omit this chapter; but, to judge the Indian fairly, and by the standard we ourselves would be judged, a hint at the great wrongs done the Sioux, should live in the ages to come, along with the history of their revengeful deeds.

To go to the beginning of corruption and intrigue in the Indian department, would be to penetrate the dim and dusty mists of the musty past, which is no part of the mission of this book. We need turn no farther than to the treaty of Traverse des Sioux (Saint Peter) of 1851, to have our eyes opened to the methods in which the Sioux massacre had its conception and in which, continued, it had its birth.

The crimes committed against the red race, in what assumed to be honourable treaties, and in the carrying out of the terms of those treaties, would not have been tolerated for a day by white men. The whites would have put the treaty-makers and treaty-breakers to flight or to death. With treaties fairly obtained, and their terms honourably administered, there would, it is reasonable to assume, have been no Sioux massacre.

When the Traverse des Sioux treaty was consummated it was supposed by the Indians, they would receive the purchase price of their lands, but to their consternation the traders gathered like vultures and presented claims for goods sold to the Indians on credit for nearly $400,000, or a sum considerably in excess of the amount the Sioux were to receive, and the monstrous claims of the traders were recognised by the Indian authorities. Added to these were charges for removing the Indians from the lands they had ceded by treaty to within new boundaries.

Claims for depredations upon traders or settlers by lawless Indians had been filed with the Indian department, and on *ex-parte* evidence or none at all, were allowed, and the amount ordered deducted from the sum total of payments to be made, thus robbing the law-abiding to make good for alleged offenses committed by lawless Indians. The policy was first to secure the signatures of the chiefs to a sale of tribal lands, frequently by doubtful methods, in payment for which hundreds of thousands of dollars were provided from the United States treasury; but the enormous sums of gold were swept from the pay-table by questionable claims, and the Indian found himself possessed of neither land nor money.

The indignation of the Indians was such that violence to the officials of the government in attendance, was imminent. Hon. Alexander Ramsey, as Superintendent of Indian Affairs, and a member of the Treaty Commission, in attendance at the great council of December, 1852, at Traverse des Sioux, sought to discipline Red Iron, chief of the Sissetons, because of his indignation at what he pronounced high-handed methods on the part of representatives of the government. Gov. Ramsey deposed Red Iron from his chieftainship, and had him arrested by the soldiery in attendance, and brought before the commission in irons, when the following colloquy took place, Red Iron being commanded to arise.

RED IRON

Gov. Ramsey, with a sternness for which he was noted, addressed the deposed chief as followg "What excuse have you for not coming to the council when I sent for you?"

Red Iron, stately in stature and in the maturity of middle age, nonchalantly met the issue without a suspicion of embarrassment, amid the profound silence his calm demeanour commanded, with not even a scowl, fixing his eye sternly on his interlocutor, he replied: "I started to come, but your braves drove me back."

Governor Ramsey: "What excuse have you for not coming the second time I sent for you?"

Red Iron: "No other excuse than I have given you."

Governor Ramsey: "At the treaty I thought you a good man, but since, you have acted badly, and I am disposed to break you; I *do* break you."

Red Iron, with emphasis: "You break me! My people made me a chief. My people love me; I will still be their chief. I have done nothing wrong."

Governor Ramsey: "Red Iron, why did you get your braves together, and march around here for the purpose of intimidating other chiefs, and prevent them coming to the council?"

Red Iron: "I did not get my braves together; they got together themselves to prevent boys going to council to be made chiefs to sign papers, and to prevent single chiefs going to council at night to be bribed to sign papers for money we never received. We have heard how the M'dewakantons were served at Mendota—that by secret councils you got their names on paper and then took their money. We don't want to be served so. My braves want to come to council in daytime, when the sun shines, and we want no council in the dark. We want all our people to counsel together, so that we can all know what was done."

Governor Ramsey: "Why did you attempt to come to the council with your braves when I had forbidden your braves coming to council?"

Red Iron: "You invited the chiefs only, and would not let the braves come too. This is not the way we have been treated before; this is not according to our customs, for, among the Dakotas, chiefs and braves go to council together. When you first sent for us there were two or three chiefs here, and we wanted to wait until the rest would come, that we might all be in council together, and know what was done, and so that we might all understand the papers, and know what we were signing. *When we signed the treaty the traders threw blankets over our faces and darkened our eyes, and made us sign papers we did not understand, and which were not explained or read to us.* We want our Great Father at Washington to know what has been done."

Governor Ramsey: "Your Great Father has sent me to represent him. What I say he says. He wants you to pay your old debts in accordance with the papers you signed when the treaty was made (the papers signed when the Indians were blindfolded), and to leave that money in my hands to pay these debts. If you refuse to do that, I will take the money back."

Red Iron: "You take the money back. We sold our land to you and you promised to pay us. If you don't pay us, I will be glad, for we will have our land back if you don't give us the money. That paper was not explained to us. We are told it gives about $300,000 of our money to some of the traders. We don't think we owe them so much. We want to pay our debts. We want our Great Father to send three good men here to tell us how much we do owe, and whatever they say we will pay," and, turning to his assembled people, "that is what these braves say. Our chiefs and all our people say this."

"*Ho, ho,*" responded the chiefs and braves.

Governor Ramsey: "That can't be done. You owe more than your money will pay, and I am ready now to pay your annuity, and no more, and when you are ready to receive it the agent will pay you."

Red Iron: "We will receive our annuity, but we will sign no papers for anything else. The snow is on the ground, and we have been waiting a long time to receive our money. We are poor. You have plenty. Your fires are warm; your *tepees* keep out the cold. We have nothing to eat. We have been waiting a long time for our moneys. Our hunting season is past. A great many of our people are sick from being hungry. We may die because you won't pay us. We may die, but if we do, we will leave our bones on the ground, that our Great Father may see where his Dakota children died. We have sold our hunting grounds and the graves of our fathers. We have sold our own graves. We have no place to bury our dead, and you will not pay us for our lands."

Red Iron was removed under guard and locked up, and the $300,000 treaty money was paid to the traders. The Indians were wild with indignation, and it was with difficulty they were restrained from slaughtering the officials and the traders.

Thus, the seeds of hatred were newly sown, and offenses revived and set ablaze. Time rolled on. The policy was perpetuated. The offenses of the officials and the traders were made the offenses of the whole white race. If the servants of the people were the enemies of the red men, was it not evident by this same token that the power that created these officials, the white race, was an enemy? So, these simple people reasoned.

One of the claims allowed by these officials out of the treaty fund at this council was that of $55,000 to Hugh Tyler, a man utterly unknown to the Indians, "*for assisting to get the treaty measure through the United States Senate, and for necessary disbursements.*" Thousands of dollars were thus absorbed, as history testifies.

Referring to these crimes and the resulting massacre of 1862, the Right Reverend Bishop Whipple, a man of temperate language and a high authority, spoke as follows after the Minnesota frontier had been made desolate:

> There is not a man in America, who ever gave an hour's calm reflection to the subject, who does not know that our Indian system is an organised system of robbery, and has been for years a disgrace to the nation. It has left savage men without governmental control; it has looked on unconcerned at every crime against the laws of God and man; it has fostered savage life by wasting thousands of dollars in the purchase of paint, beads, scalping-knives and tomahawks; it has fostered a system of trade which robbed the thrifty and virtuous to pay the debts of the indolent and vicious; it has squandered the funds for civilization and schools; it has connived at theft; it has winked at murder, and at last, after dragging the savage down to a brutishness unknown to his fathers, it has brought a harvest of blood to our own door.

Yellow Medicine

In accordance with the terms of the treaty of 1851, the Indians concerned in that treaty assembled at the Yellow Medicine Agency about the first of July, 1862, to receive their annuities.

As a precautionary measure, in view of the thousands of Indians to be assembled, fifty men of Co. C, of the Fifth, stationed at Fort Ripley, were sent forward by Captain Francis Hall as a reinforcement to Co. B, which constituted the garrison at Fort Ridgely. This detachment left Fort Ripley under First Lieutenant T. J. Sheehan, June 19, 1862, marching by way of Elk River, Henderson, etc., for want of a good road more directly connecting in that day the two forts. Lieutenant Sheehan's march covered a distance of two hundred miles, his destination being reached on the evening of the ninth day, or June 28th.

There were three companies of the Fifth stationed on the frontier—B at Fort Ridgely, C at Fort Ripley, on the Mississippi River, and D at Fort Abercrombie, on the Red River of the North. The detachment from Co. C, and a like number from Co. B were dispatched on the 30th day of June, 1862, to Yellow Medicine, where the payment was to be made, leaving Fort Ridgely under command of Lieutenant Sheehan as ranking officer, the command arriving at the Upper, or Yellow Medicine Agency, on the 2nd day of July.

All was expectancy among the thousands of Indians, and added to anticipation were the combined elements for making the occasion a heyday most enjoyable. The seasons had unfolded their wealth of luxuries; the redolent hills and plains, with their wild flowers and carpet of native green, were little less than enchanting, even to other than the "children of Nature;" the wooded glens of the beautiful streams that near this spot unite their waters, were suggestive of happiness; Nature had solved the baffling enigma that gave the world once more, with its varied species, hues and forms, the tranquil summertime.

Each day witnessed the influx of large bands of Indians, until all had reached this modern Mecca. The great gathering was a sight to behold, with its confusion of strange humanity, wolf-eared dogs and pot-bellied ponies, and its vast array of *tepees* that sheltered the six thousand or more nomads.

Dreaming not of disappointment, happiness reigned throughout the great throng. But a single foreboding disturbed the spirits of these wanderers of the plains, and that was, that the hated, grasping traders would intervene to rob them of their annuities. The trader, who always "stood in" with the agents and other Indian officials, was the bogie of the red man. As the anticipated day of payment drew near, the Indian dread of his time-honoured enemy increased, this dread finally manifesting itself in a request that Lieutenants Sheehan and Gere, the latter of Co. B, meet the chiefs and braves in council. The lieutenants acceded to the request, and entering the council circle, were regaled with Indian oratory and the formality common to such councils.

Confiding their misgivings to the young officers, they besought their intervention at the making of the payment. The speeches were all of one purport, prefaced with a bit of self-aggrandizement, and then they impressively proceeded to remind the officers that the traders were always allowed to sit at the pay-table and take the money of the Indians; this the council implored the officers to prevent, and the savages were manifestly disappointed when told by the officers that the soldiers were powerless to restrain the traders without authority to do so from the agent.

Days ripened into weeks, but the promised annuities came not. The civil war was at white heat. Gold was in great demand, and paper money fifty *per cent*, below par. Indian superintendents and agents were not above temptation. There was a fortune in the clever conversion of the gold provided, into paper, or more familiarly, greenbacks, and it was said the gold was converted into currency at a handsome profit. The treaty called for specie payment, and as the Indians knew nothing of paper, it was pointed out they would scorn it with disappointment and indignation.

Re-conversion, the story ran, was attended with much loss of time, as well as financial sacrifice which the parties to the transaction sought industriously but unsuccessfully to avoid, as gold was constantly seeking the coffers of hoarders, while paper money was continually depreciating in value. That the fatal delay in making the Indian payment was due to speculation, was oft asserted, never denied and generally believed at the fort and the agencies. To this delay, whatever may have been its cause, was the outbreak largely attributable.

Hunger hears excuses impatiently at best. Broken promises and hunger together, when an Indian is the victim, will undo more confidence in a day than many earnest missionaries could inspire in a year. The assembled Indians were kept in waiting for several weeks, during which time hunger became widespread, and starvation actually threatened. In fact, famine was only averted by the killing of dogs and ponies, and the digging of roots with which to stay this hunger. Indian children were actually reported to have starved to death as a result of the dalliance in making the payment and issuing the provisions.

While authorities assign various reasons for the Sioux Massacre of 1862, no doubt had the gold payment been promptly made in good faith at the appointed time, the murdered settlers and the hapless traders would have been spared to work out the ordinary problems of life undisturbed.

On the 14th of July, a tour of inspection was made of the monstrous Indian camp to ascertain if it was true, as rumoured, that a large number of Sioux were present who were not entitled to annuities. The rumour was well-founded, there being several hundred Yanktonais and Cut-heads, who were merely hopeful visitors. Such a gathering of Sioux has never since taken place on Minnesota soil, and its like will never be witnessed again. This city of the plains numbered seven hundred and seventy-nine lodges, and was imposing both for its vastness and for the thousands who made up the aggregate of its inhabitants.

The policy of dalliance went heedlessly on. The Indians were known to be destitute. The surrounding country had been swept bare of nearly every available living creature which would serve them as food. There were provisions in abundance in the government warehouse, belonging to the Indians, but they were withheld to be delivered at the time of payment. It would not do to go through the farcical form of making the annual payment and have the money swept from the pay-table by the traders with no provisions on hand with which to appease the wrath of the disappointed Indians; so, these provisions must be held. It would be safe to sweep the pay-table if only at the opportune moment the hungry stomachs of the Indians could be flattered with enough bacon and flour for a few meals. Not to observe this precaution might be hazardous to the hopes of men to whom longevity had its fascinations.

On the 18th, the Indians reported their condition unendurable from lack of food. Starvation, they said, was in their midst. Agent Galbraith thought there was no occasion for alarm, but Lieutenant Sheehan, reasoning from the temper of a hungry man, sent to Fort Ridgely, fifty-two miles away, for a second twelve-pound mountain howitzer.

Lieutenants Sheehan and Gere, conscious that conditions existed that should be logically met, from at least a humanitarian standpoint, advised the issuing of provisions to the famishing people assembled in such vast numbers. On the 21st of July, Agent Galbraith assured these officers he would arrange to count the Indians, issue the provisions and send the assembled Sioux back to their hunting-grounds. On the 26th of July, the Indians were counted, more than twelve hours being required in which to make the enumeration. Even up to ten days after this preparatory enumeration no provisions had been issued. At last starvation forced a crisis.

On the morning of August 4th, two Indian messengers entered the little military camp and informed the soldiers the Indians were coming down to make a demonstration; that they would come armed, but they wished the soldiers to understand there was no premeditated hostility in this visit. A moment later there came like the wind a thousand warriors, firing their guns wildly and yelling like demons. (It was precisely two weeks from the very hour that the massacre began at the Redwood Agency.) No oracle was needed to warn the little band of soldiers, just one hundred strong, that a climax had at last been reached, and that their lives were in peril.

The hundreds of horsemen were but little in advance of the fleet warriors on foot. They completely encircled the little military camp, and could have crushed it at a single blow. The clicking of their gun-locks showed they were ready, with pieces cocked, should a soldier fire a shot. The starving Indians had come, not to make war, but to forcibly take what they had peaceably pleaded for in vain for nearly two weeks—provisions, of which they knew there was an abundant supply, belonging to them. Mah-ka-tah, the chosen leader of the raid, rushed to the warehouse and struck the door a ringing blow with his tomahawk. Like clockwork the soldiery was brought into line with a promptness that even the Indians contemplated with a look of envy.

But the Indians themselves had acted with a promptness and coolness in carrying out their design, as unexpected as it was daring. It became apparent their demonstration was made with a view of overawing the soldiers while a party of warriors should break down the warehouse door and take possession of the stores. They quickly effected an entrance to the building and were removing flour. Lieutenant Gere ordered his men to remove the tarpaulin that sheltered the howitzers, and quickly trained a gun on the warehouse door. If there is anything for which an Indian shows a wholesome respect, it is a cannon. Those who were removing the sacks of flour were warned of their danger, and glancing at the big gun, fell back to the right and left in haste and confusion, leaving an opening down through which Lieutenant Sheehan and Sergeant S. A. Trescott marched with a squad of sixteen men.

Lieutenant Sheehan proceeded to the office of Agent Galbraith for a conference. Trescott, a man of resolution and coolness (who, by the way, was killed at the ferry just two weeks from this date, whither he had gone with Captain Marsh on the ill-fated march to the Lower Agency), cleared the warehouse of the Indians. He and his men having accomplished this task, stood defiantly at the entrance of the building. Every fibre of manhood was now at its extremest tension. The Indians were wrought to the highest pitch of excitement and determination. A spark would have exploded the savage wrath that had at last reached the limit of suppression. The miracle is that the massacre that was deferred just two weeks to a day was not here and now begun.

Two of Sergeant Trescott's men were stationed at the warehouse entrance, one on either side of the door, with their guns crossed to bar entrance to the building. The ejected Indians hurled themselves back at the entrance, and in an instant the gun of James Foster, one of the guards, was covered from lock to muzzle with the hands of the warriors who sought to wrest the weapon from him. In this struggle the gun was discharged, but fortunately without injury to anyone. All eyes were on this struggle, and it was plain the discharge of the musket was accidental, though the men, red and white, were writhing in an encounter of desperation which threatened instantly to involve every element present.

On the one hand were officers of courage, judgment and coolness, with men at their command as true in pluck and discipline as were ever lined up. On the other hand, were savages tortured with hunger, and whose families were in distress, but who were determined not to be the first to shed blood in open conflict if avoidable, be it said to their credit.

Realising the gravity of the situation and the dire consequences of the step from which there could be no recession, there was mutual relaxation in deference to reason at an instant when the taking of life seemed inevitable.

The chiefs plead the necessities of their people, and urged that the provisions stored in the warehouse belonged to the Indians, and that they were unjustly withheld from distribution at a time of great suffering. The officers, now that a lull had succeeded the white-heat of excitement, advised the Indian Agent to make an issue of provisions. He hesitated, explaining that he doubted the effect upon the Indians from a disciplinary point of view, but realising the moment was one of great danger he acted upon the suggestion, but the issue was wholly inadequate to the occasion, and the Indians did not disperse until the military assumed a threatening attitude by forming a line of battle for the protection of the warehouse. There was now left to the Indians but one of two alternatives—that of beginning hostilities or withdrawing peaceably to their camp. They chose the latter, but sullenly.

The Indians were displeased and angry, and held a stormy council after their withdrawal to their lodges. A widespread feeling of hostility prevailed, and excitement was again in the ascendant, fiery speeches calling forth the approving "Ho, ho," on every hand. Delay, hunger and broken promises had disarmed those chiefs who had preached the virtues of patience and forbearance, and they received scant courtesy in this turbulent conclave of maddened warriors.

Among those who stood for peace and forbearance was Standing Buffalo, chief of one of the Sisseton bands. The decision of the council favoured immediate hostilities, amid the wildest excitement, the entire council being committed by the action of the majority. Under the license of such a vote it is a matter of wonder the massacre was not at this time precipitated. That it was not was due to the dogged persistence of Standing Buffalo and his friends and supporters, whose course, though unpopular, had a restraining influence over chiefs and warriors of the more conservative type, who, in turn, after the decision of the council, were nonconcurrent, even if silent.

The council at an end, Standing Buffalo repaired to the military camp and reported that war had been decided upon; that he had opposed the result, but having participated in the deliberations of the council, was bound by the decision. He warned the military to be on the alert.

The troops were put in the best possible condition for defensive purposes, while the citizens at the agency, together with all available means of defence took refuge in the government warehouse. There was a feeling of the greatest apprehension, with good reason for it. As a result of this apprehensiveness Lieutenant Gere was dispatched to Fort Ridgely on the 5th, to confer with Captain Marsh. This young officer was at all times equal to the demands made upon him. Means for conveyance were not of the best, but leaving Yellow Medicine at four o'clock in the afternoon, and passing through the Redwood Agency at midnight, he reached Fort Ridgely at three o'clock in the morning of August 6th, where he called Captain Marsh from his slumbers, and acquainted him with the dangerous condition of affairs at the Upper Agency.

After a brief conference Captain Marsh joined Lieutenant Gere, and they set out at once for the Yellow Medicine Agency, which they reached at 1:30 o'clock in the afternoon of August 6th. After the arrival of these officers, the hand of violence having been stayed, a council of the Indians was secured by Agent Galbraith and Captain Marsh, at which it was agreed that the stock of annuities, consisting of provisions and other stores, should be issued at once; that the Indians should repair, after receiving their allotments, to their homes or to the great hunting-grounds to the westward, to be recalled again on the arrival of their money. The issue began on the afternoon of August 7th, and continued for two days thereafter, the Indians breaking camp as rapidly as they could be reached in regular order, so that by the time the last of the supplies were issued, the great camp had disappeared.

Never was calamity more narrowly averted; and did not the success attending this adjustment lead Captain Marsh into the very jaws of death ten days later?

Smarting under their hardships and the long succession of broken promises and disappointments, the Indians spread away to repeople the vast plains, but they were filled with wrath.

The military detachment withdrew from the agency on the 11th of August, and arrived at Fort Ridgely on the evening of the next day, and nothing being heard of the Indian superintendent and the long-promised money, Captain Marsh issued an order for the return of Lieutenant Sheehan and detachment to their company headquarters at Fort Ripley. Lieutenant Sheehan set out on his march on the 17th, the very day upon which occurred the massacre at Acton. He was unconscious of this fact however, until a courier, dispatched after him by Captain Marsh on the 18th, overtook him at dusk of that day as he had gone into camp between New Auburn and Glencoe.

He had made forty-two miles in the two days' march from Fort Ridgely, but immediately struck camp and retraced his steps with great energy, marching all night and covering the forty-two miles' distance by the early forenoon of the next day, his continuous march from the morning of the 18th until the morning of the 19th, being over sixty miles, without rest. The battle at the Redwood Ferry had been fought, and Captain Marsh and a large number of his men had gone down to death. Lieutenant Sheehan thus became the ranking officer, and hence the commander of Fort Ridgely.

Beginning of the Outbreak

From what, frivolous acts matters of the gravest consequence may flow, was well illustrated by the folly which immediately precipitated the Sioux Massacre. Lack of mental breadth and the absence of fundamental principles upon which to found character, charitably interpose themselves as an argument of extenuation in behalf of the vagabond savage. There was lurking in the Indian heart a vengeful spirit. He had been wronged and he knew, it. He had been robbed by the traders through the connivance of dishonest agents. He had this year been called from his hunting-grounds to receive his annuities, and after being kept in waiting until starvation invaded his lodges, was turned back to the plains empty-handed and gaunt.

Stung with bitter disappointment he nursed his wrath sullenly. He believed his people the victims of premeditated fraud, and judged the whites as a race by those with whom he had come in contact about the agencies. Notwithstanding all this, the Sioux Massacre might have been avoided but for a senseless controversy over the trivial matter of a few eggs. It was not likely that up to this time the killing of a settler had been resolved upon. There were vicious Indians who delighted at all times in doing lawless things. They were always a source of trouble among their own people, even on ordinary occasions, just as there are "black sheep" in nearly every white community, who are pestilential.

A nest of eggs and the bad disposition of one of these Indians proved to be the touch-and-go that fired the whole Minnesota frontier, resulting in a thousand murders and horrors indescribable.

In the fall of 1861, while hunting along the Crow River, near Forest City, Meeker County. Chief Mak-pe-ya-we-tah, of one of the Lower Agency bands, purchased a sleigh of George Whitcomb with which to return to Redwood, having been caught in winterish weather. The chief was unable to pay for the sled, but left his wagon to secure the debt. On the 10th of August, 1862, with a party of twenty Indians, the chief started to Forest City, intending to redeem his wagon and spend a season in deer-hunting. Nearing their destination, the chief and four members of his band separated from the main body and proceeded on to Whitcomb's, several miles north-eastward, the fifteen stopping, intending to engage in hunting.

Among the latter were some of the most notorious malcontents of the Lower Agency. Some six miles from Acton a member of this latter party found a hen's nest, and proposed to eat the eggs. It was urged by a law-abiding Indian that he had no right to do this; that the eggs were those of a white farmer, and should not be taken or destroyed, as such an act might get them all into trouble. The law-abiding Indian was accused of cowardice, and with the accusation the finder of the nest destroyed the eggs. The Indian of conscientious scruples denounced this act as contemptible, and as showing neither courage nor good sense. His courage questioned, the malcontent drew up his rifle and shot an ox, boasting of this as an act of defiance confirming his courage, but the law-abiding Indian remonstrated in stronger terms than ever, and denounced the breaking of eggs and the shooting of oxen as very cowardly.

By this time the whole party was rent with dissension. Four of the Indians stood up for the whites and good order, while the other eleven became more contemptuous as the quarrel progressed. Each party accused the other of cowardice, the eleven claiming the four feared the whites, while the four ridiculed the eleven for their acts. Violence among themselves seemed imminent, when they finally separated, the eleven saying they would show that they were brave, for they proposed to kill a white man.

Singularly, after the quarrel and separation, the four who stood for law and order were the first to kill a white man and bring on the crisis. Not long after the parting they heard the ring of the rifles of the eleven some distance away in the settlements. They felt sure this meant that the whites were being killed, and that now their velour would be forever questioned unless they joined in the horrible work. Two of the four still protested against violence, and even yet all might have turned favourably except for an unwise and ill-timed quarrel precipitated by a white man, who was noted for bad temper and not the best for good faith in his dealings with the Indians,

This man was Robinson Jones, at whose house the four Indians called near the middle of the day of Sunday, August 17th. The Indians here asked for liquor, not an uncommon thing to do, but were refused. Jones was a man of powerful physique, and was courageous and aggressive. He thought he recognised in the quartet an Indian who had borrowed a gun from him some months previously, that had not been returned, and took the suspected delinquent hotly to task. The Indian positively denied the accusation. A quarrel ensued and Jones, in his violent way drove the Indians from the house. They went to the home of Howard Baker, eighty rods away.

At Baker's house were a Mr. Webster and wife, who had just arrived that day in their immigrant wagon from Michigan, seeking a home on the Minnesota frontier. At Baker's the Indians asked for water and tobacco, and were accommodated. They drank, and filling a pipe sat down and smoked. They were friendly and good-humoured. Unfortunately however, Jones and his wife came to the Baker home. Baker being a son of Mrs. Jones by a former husband. Here Jones renewed his quarrel with the Indian about the gun. The Indians finally grew very angry, and Mrs. Baker, in her alarm, asked Mrs. Jones if they had given the Indians liquor. She replied that they had not, and that "they had no liquor for such black devils as these."

This added fuel to the flame, for the Indians apparently understood the language, and the spirit in which it was uttered. Here, without question, was the shedding of blood first fully decided upon. The Indians bantered the white men to shoot at a mark with them, Jones replying with an oath that he was not afraid to shoot "with any dammed redskin." Having emptied their guns, the Indians reloaded, but the whites, not believing the Indians dared to commit an act of violence, or premeditated it, did not reload their pieces. This was the opportunity for which the Indians had made their play, and they fired, Jones, his wife. Baker and Webster each receiving a shot, the last three being killed or mortally wounded.

Jones attempted to escape to the cover of timber, but was felled by another shot. He clung to life tenaciously, and died in great agony, having, in his final struggle, filled his mouth with handful of earth, and dug holes in the compact ground with his boot-heels. The Indians could not have inflicted, had they tried, greater suffering upon the man they intensely disliked, than he endured until mercifully relieved by death.

Mrs. Webster was in their covered wagon getting some things to pass out to her husband when the Indians opened fire, and was not sought out or disturbed. Mrs. Baker, shocked and unnerved at what had occurred, stumbled and fell down cellar with a child in her arms, both escaping uninjured in the fall; nor were they molested by the Indians, who immediately repaired to the house of Jones, upon which they seemed to centre their vengeance, where they killed a Miss Clara D. Wilson, a young lady whose home was in the Jones family.

Having inaugurated the horrible Sioux Massacre, in the town of Acton, Meeker County, the four Indians hastened to a neighbour of the Jones family, a Mr. Eckland, where they took two horses and fled, mounted double, for the vicinity of the Redwood Agency. They reached their own camp, four miles above Redwood, near daylight on Monday morning, August 18th. Rousing their tribesmen and relating what had happened, all was consternation. A council was called, and it was immediately foreseen that the four Indians must be turned over to the white authorities, or the whole band of Rice Creek Indians, to which the four belonged, be held as accomplices in the crimes committed. There was but little time in which to choose a course.

Many of the band were opposed to making war on the whites. Only the previous evening in fact it had been decided at a meeting to start on Monday morning (this fatal Monday morning) for Fort Ridgely to make a demand for their annuities, and if unsuccessful, then to proceed on to St. Paul. In view of this previous plan and of the aversion of friends and relatives to surrender the four to be dealt with for the murder of the whites at Acton, it was decided to hasten down to the Lower Agency, lay the matter of a decision before Little Crow and other Agency Indians.

To portray the wild excitement and frenzied condition of the Indian village in the early dawn of that August morning is not a pen-possibility. Only on the previous night, be it remembered, the wrongs of the agents and traders had been rehearsed, and the disappointments and the sufferings of the Indians dwelt upon. Longer patience had ceased to be a virtue. Disappointment had been piled upon disappointment until the limit of endurance had been reached, and a final trip, first to the fort, and then to St. Paul if necessary, for redress, had been planned for this very morning. In this acute condition of mind, the news of the outbreak at Acton produced consternation, and dis-

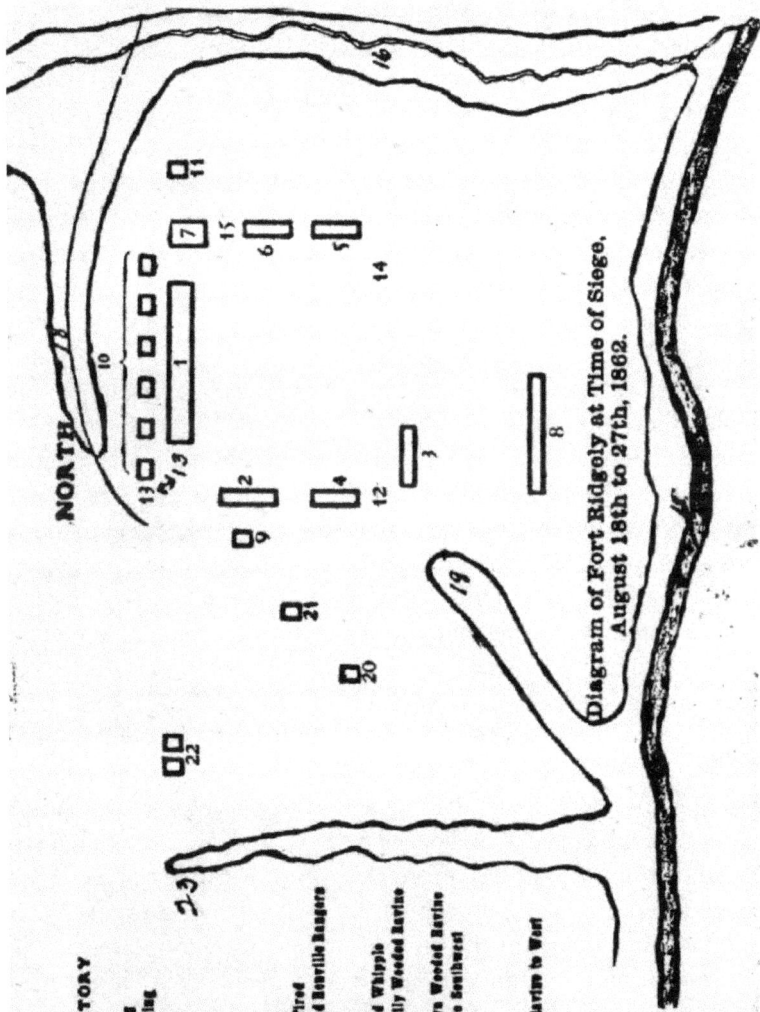

Diagram of Fort Ridgely at Time of Siege,
August 18th to 27th, 1862.

NORTH

EXPLANATORY

1 — Barracks
2 — Commissary Building
3 — Headquarters Building
4 — Officers' Quarters
6 — Laundry
7 — Large Barn
8 — Blacksmith Shop
9 — Old Log Quarters
10 — Building Whipple Fired
11 — Position of Jones and Renville Rangers
12 — Position of McGrew
13 — Position of Bishop
15 — Position of Gere and Whipple
16 — Fort Creek in Heavily Wooded Ravine
17 — Minnesota River
18 — St. Peter Road, Down Wooded Ravine
19 — Depressed Ground to Southwest
20 — Sutlers-Store
21 — Guardhouse
22 — Magazine
23 — Fo't of Timbered Ravine to West

cussion only inflamed the excited minds of the warriors.

While it was decided ostensibly to hasten to Redwood for con-sultation and advice, the war flame was fanned at every turn. There were constant accessions to the party as it wildly and excitedly rode to the agency, and each accession was fuel to the flame. Every *tepee* and wicky-up along the way contributed to the hellish legion that poured out naked, with hair streaming to join the wild cavalcade and catch and echo the war-cry. The hills of the Minnesota rang with yells as through the blinding dust rushed the ever-growing stream of frenzied warriors. Explanations by the way were unnecessary.

The war-cry was sufficient, and it is not probable human eyes ever witnessed a wilder scene than was this flight of demons along the trail that resounded with the throbbing footfalls of beasts inspired to their utmost endeavours by their frenzied riders, who fast and faster came as the murderous resolution of their hearts spurred them madly on and blinded them to all thought of right or reason. The earth trembled as the thundering cavalcade pressed on in its wild flight, the hideous war-cry echoing savagely along the broad valley of the Minnesota, rousing Sioux braves from their slumbers and thrilling their hearts with emotions transforming them at once into maddened demons.

It was small wonder Little Crow was swept from his poise by this frenzied horde and hurried into the bloody torrent that bore him to his ruin. But the blood of Acton had fired the hearts of this crazed legion, that fell upon the Redwood Agency like a pitiless storm, awakening the whole frontier in one horrifying shriek from its confiding stupor.

Little Crow lived in a brick house about two miles above the agency. He was still in bed when the head of the column of warriors reached his place, and was shocked to hear the familiar war-whoop that roused him from his slumbers. He sat up with his blanket about him and heard the startling story of the spokesman of the party. Soon his house was packed to the limit of its capacity, with scores unable to gain admission, and the excitement was intense. The wild ride had dispelled every thought of a peaceful solution of troubles real and fancied. Every voice was for war, and the demand that the famous chieftain should lead the savage hosts was unanimous and emphatic.

Beads of perspiration gathered upon the forehead of Little Crow, who no doubt dreaded the ordeal, wisely understanding the great hazard that attended a war upon the whites. But he had lost popularity with his people of late years, and now was offered an opportunity to reinstate himself. There was, too, a dream of long-cherished and far-

TWO VIEWS OF FORT RIDGELY, IN 1862.

reaching results. He yielded to the demands of the frenzied and impatient horde, and without breakfast joined in the plans for the massacre of the traders and others at the agency, upon which the warriors had already fully determined, and hastened away at the head of the wild horde like a flying demon.

First News of the Outbreak at Redwood

A garrison was never more tranquil than was that of Fort Ridgely on the morning of August 18th, Midsummer quietude was all-pervading. Lieutenant Sheehan and his fifty men had just departed homeward after a month and a half of service and companionship with Company B. The Renville Rangers, a party of some fifty men, who had spent a day or so at the fort, had just gone on their journey to Fort Snelling, where they were to be mustered into the service for active duty in the south. Accompanying them were a number of members of Company B.

The Indian payment incident at the Yellow Medicine Agency, which had furnished the only diversion of the season, was apparently closed, and with the absence of so many who had helped to infuse animation into the routine duties of frontier garrison life, a Sabbath-like stillness had settled down upon the post. There was nothing to suggest activity. There was nothing upon which to found the hope that there was anything in store for Company B but humdrum garrison duty. The youthful officers and men who in the main made up the company, were impatient for an order to go south, and could they have ordered their destiny in this matter by ballot, there would have been a unanimous vote, with cheers and a throwing of caps in the air, to move within an hour.

But this could not be, and with patience and fortitude the soldiers, whose companions had just left them, and whose only diversion of the summer had terminated with the Yellow Medicine event, relaxed into enforced quietude, without the remotest suspicion that before night more than one-fourth of their number would be called upon to meet death in one of the fiercest and most merciless combats recorded.

At about 10 o'clock in the forenoon, August 18, 1862, came, like the lightning's flash from a clear sky, the startling news of the horrible massacre begun three hours previously at the Redwood Agency. Down from the northwest, nearing the fort, was seen the approach of people in great haste. The attention of the garrison was generally attracted to the unusual spectacle, but without once suspecting the cause of it. J. C. Dickinson was in the advance and was the first to enter the fort. He had scarcely told in a few words of the uprising when a team immediately following him entered under the lash, with a load of refugees, among them a wounded man, who had made his escape after being shot at the agency.

That savage wrath had burst like a flame was at first inconceivable, but the testimony that the scalping-knife had flashed from its sheath to follow the deadly work of the gun was all too evident to be questioned. The soldiers gathered around the refugees whose tales were told in shocking, dramatic detail. Captain Marsh did not deliberate, but ordered the assembling of the company at once. Charles M. Culver, the drummer boy, for the first time sounded with meaning emphasis the long-roll. Thrilled with the story of the massacre and the clamour of the drum, men were quickly in line to receive orders.

With a haste that seemed imperative a detail of forty-six men was made at once to proceed to the scene of carnage, under the belief that the situation was yet controllable, and in any event demanded the presence of soldiery at the agency. It was simply a matter of moments between the receipt of the news of the outbreak and the departure of Captain Marsh and his detail for the scene of the bloody work thirteen miles away.

These were the men to whose lot it fell to go on this expedition:

Captain—
John S. Marsh
Interpreter—
Peter Quinn
Sergeants—
R. H. Findley
S. A. Trescott
J. F. Bishop
Corporals—
J. S. Besse
W. E. Winslow
T. D. Huntley
C. H. Hawley
Privates—
Charles Beecher
Charles R. Bell
W. H. Blodgett
John Brennan
Leyi Carr
E. F. Cole

Privates (cont'd)—
W. B. Hutchinson
Chris Joerger
Durs Kanzig
James H. Kerr
Wenzel Kusda
Henry McAllister
John McGowan
James M. Munday
James Murray
Wenzel Norton
J. W. Parks
M. P. Parks
John Parsley
Thomas Parsley
H. A. Phillips
N. Pitcher
A. Rebenski
Ezekiel Rose
J. Serfling

James Dunn	H. A. Shepherd
J. W. Foster	C. W. Smith
C. E. French	N. Steward
A. Gardner	S. Steward
J. Gardner	W. A. Sutherland
J. A. Gehring	O. Svendson
John Holmes	S. VanBuren

At the command, "Forward," the men moved out with elastic step, the very embodiment of splendid soldiery. Teams were hastily hitched up, and carrying light supplies of ammunition and provision, followed and soon overtook the command. Captain Marsh and Interpreter Quinn were on mule-back, and the men now climbed into the wagons that more haste might be made in reaching the agency.

Fort Ridgely was now practically deserted, Lieutenant T. P. Gere remaining in command of the post with fewer than thirty men. The situation had suddenly become one of the keenest anxiety, and this was increased by the constant accessions of refugees, whose tales of horrible deeds gave evidence of the rapid spread of the frightful work of carnage started at the agency in the morning, but now sweeping over the adjacent settlements.

Fugitives who came in over the agency road, and who had met Captain Marsh and his men, pronounced the expedition to the ferry one destined to end in the greatest disaster. This was neither reassuring nor comforting to the remnant of the company left in command of the fort, and was rendered less so because the convictions expressed were those of men of keen discernment, who were well informed on the deplorable situation. In fact, these fugitives, when meeting Captain Marsh, cautioned him of his danger, and advised him, if he would not turn back, at least not to enter the valley of the Minnesota River, which he must do three miles from the agency if he persisted in reaching the ferry.

Before Captain Marsh had covered half the distance to the agency his command had witnessed buildings aflame and corpses by the wayside to warn him of the danger that threatened him, and the whole frontier as well. There was no time to deliberate. To march into the jaws of death, as seemed imminent, might make the fall of Fort Ridgely a certainty, and thus expose the frontier settlements to annihilation. On the other hand, if a brave and almost superhuman effort could yet stay the savage hand dripping with blood, incalculable loss of life could be prevented. Captain Marsh knew his men. He had no doubt of their splendid courage. The fleeing refugees warned them that to enter the valley was almost certain death, but all this was met with a stoical determination to do faithfully and bravely the duty pointed out to them by their commander, who believed the great good possible to be accomplished was worth the hazard the undertaking involved.

While this march was being made on that quiet summer day, hearts were beating anxiously at the fort. As the men passed out to the north-westward in the forenoon, they were watched for a mile or so, and disappeared, with a *bon voyage*, below the intervening prairie-ridge, entering, as it proved, on the threshold of eternity. Refugees came in in increasing numbers, and pointed to the distant columns of smoke as those of burning homes. Some of these people were wounded, and all were fatigued and terror-stricken. There were increasing evidences of the approach of the savage horde throughout the western and north-western settlements.

There were none so dull as not to realise that the situation was profoundly critical. Marsh and his little detail were well within the environment of the savages. That they would stay the bloody hand, or even extricate themselves from their perilous predicament, became hourly more doubtful. There was no reserve force to go to their assistance. The fort itself and all in it must fall if vigorously attacked. This was self-evident. Its hope was not in its ability to resist an onslaught, but in the great good fortune that should delay an attack until better preparation should obtain.

When within six or seven miles of the agency, Captain Marsh, seeing evidences of danger on every hand, ordered his men to abandon the wagons and resume their former order of march. The pace of the men was quickened, and believing the Lower Agency the centre of disturbance, and that once there cool and wise heads could be conferred with and a stop put to the hellish work, the command hurried with a zeal worthy of a better fate than awaited the brave detachment. Reaching the top of Faribault Hill, three miles from the agency, a view of the Minnesota valley presented itself. Sickening scenes had been witnessed by the wayside, and there was little else than desolation to be seen from the hill-top. Only men of the rarest courage and of the most perfect discipline would have entered that valley of death in the face of all that was known.

At the fort the horrible condition at the agency had now been fully detailed, striking terror to every heart and sealing the doom of Marsh and his men. Among the refugees who arrived in the afternoon from the agency was Rev. J. D. Hinman, an Episcopal missionary, stationed at Redwood. Having arisen early to start on a journey to Faribault, he was out in the tranquil morning that gave no suspicion that the curtain was about to rise on one of the most appalling massacres, at his own door, ever known to American history. He was ready for his departure between six and seven o'clock, when unusual signs for the hour among the Indians attracted his attention.

The Indians were almost naked, and carried their guns. Their numbers increased, and people began to wonder at their unusual appearance, which some interpreted to mean that a raid was to be made on some Chippewa band known to have invaded the neighbourhood. The Indians squatted nonchalantly on the steps of the various buildings, their demeanour betraying no sign of hostility.

Now a signal gun broke the silence in the upper part of town. Even this was doubted to be a sign of hostility until other shooting up the street and the hasty fleeing of people towards the bluff overlooking the river began to be alarming. White Dog ran past Mr. Hinman at this juncture, and to an inquiring word replied that "awful work had been started." He was no doubt himself taken by surprise, though later in the day his cunning and his treachery played an important part in the betrayal of Marsh. Little Crow also passed Mr. Hinman about this time, but with a scowl declined to answer an inquiry of the missionary, though they knew each other well, and the chief, now sullen, had always been polite and friendly.

The firing had now become a fusillade, and people were being shot down on every hand. The traders were the first objects of hatred to fall, riddled with bullets. As the bloody work progressed the savages grew wild and furious, their hideous yells, the crash of their guns, work of the torch, the shrieks of their helpless victims, begging vainly for mercy, creating a scene horrifying in the extreme. Rev. Hinman fled before the spreading tide of death had reached him, and gaining the river, fortunately found a skiff with which he hastily crossed, making good his escape to the fort.

With this additional information from so high an authority, what could the fate of Captain Marsh and his detail be? Every heart-throb echoed this inquiry; every glance betrayed the awful misgivings that tongues hesitated to utter.

Night began to gather its unwelcome folds around the distraught garrison. Refugees, principly women and children, had swarmed in with sickening tales, to increase the burdens now illy proportioned to the garrison's defenders. Lieutenant Gere, who now commanded the fort, though but twenty years of age, had combined within him soldierly ability, courage of the highest order, and discretion beyond his years. His bearing was an inspiration, and he possessed the perfect confidence of what remained of Company B under his command. The gloom of night had added its dangers to the situation, with no tidings from the brave men who were last reported as they were descending into the valley near the agency.

The men under Lieutenant Gere maintained a courage and loyalty equal to any sacrifice. Whatever fate willed, they would resolutely meet. Dispositions were made for the night to guard as far as possible against a night surprise, and with the few men widely dispersed, the garrison settled down to a death-like stillness, when the first tidings came of the fate of Marsh and his men. Privates James Dunn and William B. Hutchinson were the first to arrive with the story of the frightful disaster at the ferry, they having been dispatched by Sergeant John F. Bishop, who was in command of the only known remnant of Company B to escape the merciless slaughter at the ferry. The little party were carrying a badly wounded comrade, while Bishop himself was wounded. Their progress being thus impeded, Bishop dispatched Dunn and Hutchinson to apprise the garrison of the disaster, himself and party reaching the fort at ten o'clock at night.

Now the thrilling story was told in detail. Marsh's slender detachment descended into the Minnesota valley at Faribault Hill at about midday, and marched across a bottom for three miles over a road not unfavourable to a treacherous foe, grass of a rank growth affording shelter on either hand. When within a mile or so of the ferry the captain halted his men for a moment's needed rest. Resuming his march the men were moved in open order by single file to minimise the danger from exposure, and in this order continued to the ferry-house, situated on the east side of the road, ten or twelve rods north of the ferry.

Just two weeks previously to a day most of these men were actors in the dramatic incident at Yellow Medicine, when, on the 4th of August, they were surrounded by nearly a thousand armed warriors, when the government warehouse was attacked. Coolness and courage won the day for these same soldiers on that occasion. May they not now overmatch the red-handed savage and yet bring order out of chaos? There must have been this lingering hope, though conditions were so changed as to make the hope chimerical.

Along the river at the ferry were clumps of willows and other brush, together with a rank growth of weeds and grass, with here and there a sandbar deposited by the river in flood-time. Knowing the stealthy nature of the Sioux, and that war had been inaugurated, the surroundings were such as any American soldier, willing to meet his foe in the open, would feel ill-at-ease in.

On the high bluff just across the river was the Redwood Agency, the objective point of Captain Marsh, and where he had hoped to meet prominent Sioux chiefs, and through their co-operation restore order. He apparently could not realise that the agency had been blotted out, and that every soul who had made up its white citizenship lay prostrate where he fell, shot to death and mutilated beyond recognition. The slope leading from the river to the brow of the agency hill was studded with a thick growth of brushy timber. The disembowelled and acephalous body of the ferryman had already been found, with the ferryboat on the north side of the river, ready for the soldiers to enter upon, as the Indians had no doubt carefully planned, divining that Marsh would seek to cross to the agency side.

Indians there were in plenty, but they kept themselves well concealed. A few warriors on horseback revealed themselves indifferently on the prairie south of the agency, and at considerable distance from the ferry, their evident purpose being to attract attention from the forces masked in the region of the ferry. Near the ferry landing on the opposite or agency side of the river, was a lone Indian, chosen for a conspicuous part in the tragedy to be enacted when the plans of the cunning Indians were matured. This was recognised to be no less a personage than White Dog, who himself was clearly taken by surprise by the outbreak as his demeanour to Rev. Hinman revealed in the early morning.

White Dog was a prominent Indian at the agency, having been president of the Indian Farmers' Organisation, and his selection as a man likely to inspire confidence in Captain Marsh was neither spontaneous nor accidental. Through Interpreter Quinn Captain Marsh addressed White Dog, who, in reply, suavely invited Marsh to cross, assuring him that the Indians did not wish to fight the soldiers, and that if Marsh would cross to the agency a council would be called to meet and confer with him. Two soldiers who went to the river's brink to obtain water as this conversation was being carried on, discovered in concealment on the opposite side, near White Dog, many Indians.

However, Captain Marsh ordered his men forward from the ferry-house to the ferry-landing, purposing to cross, his men halting at a front along the river. Sergeant Bishop having stepped to the water's edge for a drink as the ferry ropes were being adjusted, saw evidences in the roily condition of the water that the Indians were crossing upstream with a view to a rear attack. This conviction expressed to Captain Marsh, was intuitively grasped by White Dog, who knew the moment was critical, and now doubted that Marsh would enter upon the ferry. He therefore fired the signal gun, as was his part in the tragedy, to which Quinn, the white-haired interpreter, sensing its meaning instantly, in his last breath, cried, "Look out!"

A deadly volley came from the ambuscade on the opposite side of the river, killing many a brave soldier who had had no opportunity to defend himself. Quinn was among those to fall at the first volley, riddled with no less than a dozen bullets. The volley was high and mainly passed over the heads of the soldiers. Marsh and Quinn stood nearly side by side when the volley was fired, but the captain was unscathed, and instantly ordered his men to fall back to the ferry house.

Now came the awful realisation of Bishop's prediction, for with deafening yells there rose from ambush in the rear, and within short range, a legion of naked, frantic devils who poured a merciless volley into the already staggered ranks of Marsh. The effect was deadly. Now the men fought for their lives, and to extricate themselves from their perilous predicament.

The losses were already so great that to attempt a stand would be simply to blindly challenge fate. (As stated by Chaska in 1863, when referring to this bloody incident, White Dog gave the death-signal prematurely, for which he was bitterly assailed by Little Crow and other prominent leaders in the massacre. The signal was not to have been given until the savage cordon had been so extended as to prevent the escape of a single man of Marsh's command, in event the soldiers could not be gotten upon the ferry and there annihilated.)

The Indians had secured possession of the ferry-house by this time. The fighting now was of the most desperate character, being hand to hand or at the range of a few paces. The soldiers made deadly work in the ranks of the savages, who were no match for the trained infantrymen in open combat; but realising they could not withstand the already overwhelming and constantly increasing numbers. Marsh gave the order to gain at all hazards the thicket along the river, of which the savages had not yet secured possession. This was accomplished under a furious fire, fifteen out of the original number, after fighting like demons, reaching the sheltering copse.

To reach the fort over an unknown country, pathless, and beset with a desperate enemy, was the only hope of the brave commander and his shattered force. The thicket was raked with the guns of the savages, but the men were now fighting from cover with a deliberateness of aim that kept the enemy well at bay. Covering their retreat carefully, the men fought their way down through the brush until they apparently must soon expose themselves to Indians seen out on the fort road, who were believed to be moving eastward to intercept the retreating detachment. Captain Marsh believed safety lay alone in crossing to the south bank of the river, and led in an effort to accomplish this end. This was at about 4 o'clock p. m.

The Minnesota River at this point was fifty yards or more in width. Lifting his sword and revolver above his head the captain waded successfully two-thirds of the way across. Getting beyond his depth he could no longer retain his weapons of defence, and dropping them, attempted to swim. In this he was unsuccessful, and called to his men for assistance. Brennan, Dunn and VanBuren, all men of heroic mould, hastened to the rescue of their commander, but he was doomed by the treacherous waters, and though seized by Brennan's strong arm, as he was sinking the second time, and brought to the surface, and although the captain grasped the shoulder of the athletic hero daring all to save him, the hold of the officer and that of the soldier were broken in the struggle, and Captain Marsh disappeared beneath the merciless waters to rise no more.

Now the command devolved upon Sergeant John F. Bishop, than whom there was no better or braver soldier. Beset with calamity, dogged with disaster and wounded besides, with one of his men, Private Svendson, so seriously wounded that he must be carried by his comrades, Bishop was put to a test summoning all his tact, courage and endurance. He at once decided to keep the north side of the river, instead of crossing it as Captain Marsh had designed, and this decision no doubt saved the lives of Bishop and his fourteen men, as the Indians, believing the soldiers to have crossed the stream, themselves crossed to ambush the men on the south side.

While the Indians were lying in concealment, awaiting the approach of the would-be victims, the little command, under cover of a favouring hill on the south bank of the river, passed successfully to safer and better protected ground downstream. Stealthily, cautiously, vigilantly the wearied and persecuted men pressed onward, not unmindful that their enemy's plan of warfare always embraced the deadly ambush.

Night was fast approaching. Whether its protection in an unknown and pathless country was preferable to daylight and exposure, was difficult to determine. With nothing to eat and bearing a wounded soldier in need of surgical treatment, there could be no thought of halting, not with the certainty that Fort Ridgely could be but a few miles distant at most. But did the fort exist? Had not the desperate enemy, flushed with success and drunk with frenzy, pressed on to overpower and annihilate the well-nigh defenceless garrison? Surely it was within his power to accomplish this result.

When, after nightfall, Sergeant Bishop sent the sturdy soldiers, Dunn and Hutchinson, forward, there was ample reason to feel the fort might have fallen, though no cannonading had reverberated through the valley to indicate an attack; still, known conditions were such that a fierce and sudden attack on the garrison might be successfully made in a manner to preclude the use of artillery. Sergeant Bishop felt, as he was justified in doing, that Dunn and Hutchinson were men to be relied upon to successfully learn and apprise him if the fort had fallen. But the two soldiers found the garrison in the hands of Lieutenant Gere, and made a successful entry, as did Bishop and the remainder of his men an hour later, twelve hours from the time of their departure under Captain Marsh in the forenoon. The garrison was well prepared in mind from what had filtered to it, for the news of the disaster; yet it was stunned to speechlessness when the list of casualties was announced.

The Killed.

Captain John S. Marsh (drowned)
Interpreter Peter Quinn
Sergeant Russell H. Findley
    "   Solon A. Trescott
Corporal Joseph S. Besse

Privates		
Charles R. Bell	Edwin F. Cole
Charles E. French	John Gardner
Jacob A. Gehring	John Holmes
Christian Joerger	Durs Kanzig
James H. Kerr	Wenzel Kusda
Henry McAllister	Wenzel Norton
John Parsley	Moses P. Parks
John W. Parks	Nathaniel Pitcher
Harrison A. Phillips	Charles W. Smith
Henry. A. Shepherd	Nathan Stewart

The Wounded.

Sergeant John F. Bishop

Privates	
William H. Blodgett	Ezekiel Rose
Wm. A. Sutherland	Ole Svendson

37

Early on the morning of the 20th, William A. Sutherland and William H. Blodgett arrived at the fort, after experiences and endurance almost unbelievable. These men were shot down in the engagement at the ferry. Their escape, their sufferings and their heroic struggle for life can scarcely be matched in history. Sutherland was shot in the breast, the ball passing through the right lung, and out near the point of the right shoulder-blade, at his back.

The wound rendered him unconscious for a time, and while in this condition the Indians took from him his gun, cartridge-belt and box, his cap, coat and shoes, leaving him destitute of clothing, save his shirt (saturated with blood from his wound), and his trousers. The mystery is that he was not scalped, but his escape was no doubt due to a distracted state among the savages who were rent with dissension over the personal effects of their victims. Sutherland fell near the river, where he lay for several hours. Returning to consciousness, he found himself crazed with pain and thirst. Lifting his head cautiously, he looked about him, half stupefied, yet curious to learn whether his comrades, who were in action when he fell, had been annihilated.

While the savages had completed their hellish work, they were still in the vicinity, and he could hear their voices not far away, and the firing of guns far and near warned him of the havoc being wrought upon the settlements of the vicinity. He determined to crawl to the river and slake his burning thirst, even though to do so should cost him his life. He tested his strength in an effort to turn over, having fallen on his face when shot. He found he could move his body, and down through the high grass and weeds he dragged himself to the water's edge, leaving a trail stained with blood to betray him should an Indian cross his path. He was much refreshed with copious draughts of water, and crawled back into the weeds, where he meditated, and wondered if escape was a physical possibility.

He reasoned that no attempt at escape should be made before nightfall. Thirst compelled him to make several visits to the river. Near his drinking place was a skiff, lodged against the river's bank, and partially filled with water. The water-logged boat suggested a possible means of escape, and he resolved that if not discovered and slain before dark he would make a superhuman effort to save his life. At about ten o'clock at night, after all the savages had joined in the hideous orgies of the scalp-dance on the agency side of the river, he felt that now if ever he must carry out his resolution. He crept cautiously to the water's edge, removed as much water from the boat as possible with his hands while the craft lay on its edge, and pushing it into the stream, got in.

There was no seat in the boat, no oars, no paddle, and nothing with which to bail out the water, of which there was a considerable quantity at the outset. He sat down in this in the bottom of the boat, hatless and without clothing to protect his shattered body from the penetrating chill of night, with no nourishment of any kind. Thus, he began his solemn journey, dependent wholly upon his boat and the current of the sluggish river.

As he drifted silently away under the south-western hills, the hideous din of the scalp-dance, conducted but a matter of rods away from where he had lain for hours, became less and less distinct, until croaking frogs or an occasional bittern alone broke the silence of night. In this hapless plight, this country boy of twenty summers, who had left all the comforts of a happy home, tenanted with loved ones, to enter the army and serve his country, began a voyage under conditions seeming to challenge fate and which fiction, in all its reckless extravagance, would scarce attempt a parallel.

All that night, all the next day, and all the following night until nearly dawn, this ghostly figure drifted silently along, now backwards, now sidewise and now for an hour or so whirled helplessly in an eddy. The nights were gloomy and solemn, but not more so than the light of day, that revealed the pall of death on every hand. Sutherland was seized with a delusion that haunted him against reason, from the outset of his journey. He felt that he was helplessly being carried in the wrong direction—that he should go up stream instead of down, and this fantasy gave him no end of trouble.

He was shot on Monday afternoon. He entered his boat Monday night, and there remained until the break of day Wednesday morning. He knew his progress had been very slow, but he felt that if the boat had carried him in the proper direction, he must be in the vicinity of the fort. At all events he found that he must abandon the waterlogged boat, for he had become so stiffened he could scarcely move. Against his better judgement, the bewildering delusion that had been his pursuing nemesis, impelled him to land, by paddling with his hands, on the wrong side of the river, or on the side opposite the fort. Benumbed and weakened, but stimulated with the hope that he would soon reach the garrison, he picked his way through a jungle of underbrush, and out of the valley and up the wooded hills until he reached the open prairie on the highlands.

He saw Indian cabins that were strange to him, but no trace of the garrison or of any familiar object. His heart sickened, and despair overwhelmed him, and he sank to the earth. But his great will-power triumphed, and he rose to his feet again. The sun had now risen to flood the earth with its exhilarating light. Sutherland realised that he must return to the shelter of the river valley, as he was in great danger of being discovered; and as he turned his face to the north-eastward, to his amazement and joy he beheld Fort Ridgely in the favouring light of the morning sun, on the hills beyond the river, the colours flying at full-mast, assuring him that without doubt the fort had not fallen.

He now knew he had abandoned his boat not far above the road crossing the river by a ferry, and leading to the fort. He set out to reach the river at the ferry-crossing, but on his arrival at the stream a new disappointment awaited him. The rope spanning the river had been cut and the ferry was gone. There was but one alternative: he must swim the river or perish in the attempt to do so. He lost no time, but got down into the water, which was soon beyond his depth, compelling him, while suffering excruciating pain in the effort, to exert himself to keep from sinking. By the assistance of the current he landed on the opposite side, where, having been carried several rods downstream, he experienced great difficulty in pulling himself up the abrupt and brush-grown river bank.

He accomplished all this, however, and walked a mile, most of the way uphill, and reached the fort, a gaunt, bent, blood-stained, half-naked spectre, as if risen from the dead to affright his surviving comrades. He arrived at the garrison between 8 and 9 o'clock of Wednesday morning, August 20th, and an hour later the Indians came in swarms over the road by which he had barely made his escape.

But Blodgett's escape was even more miraculous. It would not be rash to say that it has no recorded parallel. He was shot through the abdomen, the bullet penetrating the intestines. He lay concealed from 2 o'clock in the afternoon until between 9 and 10 o'clock at night, without aid, comfort, water, nourishment or the knowledge that a soul of the command beside himself had survived the battle. For an hour after the engagement the savages were busy all about him, scalping his fallen comrades, whose cries for mercy he heard, as the cruel knife was applied, or as the deadly war-club fell upon their heads.

The savages were once within ten feet of him, but a distracting quarrel between the Indians who were conducting a search a few feet away, and which ended in a physical encounter for the possession of a gun, diverting their attention from his concealment, no doubt made his escape possible. When the wild orgies of the savages were at their height at nightfall on the agency side of the river, and when he felt sure the Indian guards had been tempted to the exciting scenes in celebration of their awful deeds of blood, Blodgett arose, and although in agony scarcely endurable, started downstream along the river's bank, first having refreshed himself with a drink of water, to make the fort if possible.

Man's endurance was never put to a severer test. With no food since breakfast, without water for hours and crazed with thirst, and the sufferer from a wound almost invariably mortal— these were the conditions under which this young soldier, determined to reach his comrades, set out in darkness, without path, guide or a knowledge of the country, at times feeling that consuming pain would, in spite of his endeavours, thwart his strong will. After struggling along for a few hours, during which he had made about three miles, he found he could go no farther in the darkness through the vines and brushwood which at every step seemed to be tearing his wound open anew, and he lay down and rested as best he could until morning, tortured unmercifully throughout the night by swarms of mosquitoes.

When daylight came, he carefully picked his way, at all times keeping himself under cover of the trees near the river, so as not to expose himself to the Indians, in which manner he advanced about six miles before nightfall. After the darkness came on, he realised that he must abandon all hope of saving himself, unless he could reach the highway on the prairie uplands to the north of the river, as his strength was too rapidly failing him to stem the jungle of brush, brambles and tangled grass. He therefore resolved to cross the bottom, climb the hill, and gain the highway if possible, though he would thus be much more liable to discovery by the savages.

Having pushed along over the pathless ground in the darkness of night for an hour, he reached the fort road, and started slowly on his way to the garrison. When he arrived at the Three-Mile House (three miles from the fort), he entered it, and finding a match, lit it, and was in the act of searching for something to eat or drink, when he was startled by a man's voice on the outside, saying) "If there are any whites in there, let them come out and go to the fort, for I just passed an Indian camp in the valley, only a short distance away."

Blodgett suspected this to be the ruse of an unfriendly half-breed, who was simply attempting to betray him into the hands of the savages; but he could lose nothing by making himself known, and stepping out, called in the darkness to the unknown spokesman, who proved to be John Fanska, a German of New Ulm, who had gone to the agency on business just before the massacre, who was frightfully wounded by an arrow which had been fired into his back during the outbreak at Redwood on the 18th, and who had thrown a blanket over his head and escaped to the timber near the river in the excitement.

The arrow-head had completely buried itself in his back, and reaching shelter, writhing in agony, he attempted to withdraw the arrow, but only made matters worse by breaking the shaft off where it was attached to the cruel barb. But one thing could be worse than this torture, and that would be to fall into the hands of the savages. This greater dread made the sufferings of the wounded man endurable, though the point of the arrow-head had penetrated his right lung. Like Blodgett, he had thus far eluded the Indians, and was endeavouring to reach the garrison.

Blodgett, with his new-found companion, reached Fort Ridgely at 2 o'clock on the morning of Wednesday, August 20th, thirty-six hours after receiving his frightful wound still undressed, and with nothing to eat since breakfast of Monday morning, covering a distance the way he came, of fully eighteen or twenty miles. (Blodgett survived his frightful experience, and resides, as at 1909, in San Jose, California. Sutherland recovered and served with his company in the South until the close of the Civil War.)

Ezekiel Rose made his escape, wounded, from the ferry disaster by night, and fearing the fort had fallen, made his way through the country to Henderson.

In the terrible conflict at the ferry, the fighting assuming an almost hand-to-hand stage, the ranks of the soldiers became shattered, and when Captain Marsh gave the order to seek shelter in the brush below the ferry road, a number of men were so far detached to the northward from their comrades, and were so engaged in the fierce struggle, with their ranks being decimated to the bounds of extermination, that they fought their way out along the road upon which they had entered the death-trap, and their guns becoming too hot for service, fell in the combat, or took to shelter individually, wherever they could find it. Six, beside the two wounded men, Blodgett and Sutherland, thus miraculously escaped with their lives, and returned to the Fort under the cover of night. Those who escaped with Captain Marsh, and were taken into the fort by Sergeant Bishop, after the drowning of Captain Marsh, were:

John F. Bishop	William E. Winslow
Truman D. Huntley	Charles H. Hawley
John Brennan	Levi Carr
James Dunn	William B. Hutchinson
John McGowan	Antonie Rebenski
John Serfling	Samuel Stewart
Ole Svendson	Stephen VanBuren

James Murray.

Those who became detached and for lack of ammunition or on account of the non-serviceable condition of their guns were forced to seek individual shelter, and who thus escaped to the fort in the night, were:

James W. Foster	Thomas Parsley
James M. Munday	Ambrose Gardner
Charles Beecher	Ezekiel Rose

(Beecher did not reach the fort until Wednesday forenoon, just in time for the first day's fight Rose escaped to Henderson.)

★★★★★★

Note—After the preparation of these manuscripts, learning that Blodgett was believed to be living, I instituted a search for him, covering a period of nearly a year. Through the western pension agencies, I persisted in my search, and was finally rewarded through the San Francisco Agency. Though I had never met Blodgett since the close of the war, I wrote the account of his experience as in the foregoing as he related it to me at the time of its occurrence. Locating him, I asked for a statement for this volume, and received from him under date of January 4, 1908, the following account, hitherto unpublished.—

O. G. W.

. . . .The company at once fell into line, and 46 men were detailed to go with Captain Marsh to the scene of disturbance, each man taking forty rounds of ammunition. . . . .I was one of the 46 men to go with Captain Marsh. Starting out, we were soon overtaken on the march by four mule teams. We got into the wagons and were hurried along. When out about eight miles from the fort we came to a house that had been fired by the savages. Here we saw a murdered man lying by the roadside. We saw several more dead bodies as we passed along. About two miles from the ferry (at the Lower Agency), before going down the hill to the bottom land, we could see mounted Indians pursuing parties on the other side of the river, and in many cases, they were overtaken and slain.

We descended to the river valley, which was covered with a rank growth of grass and weeds. On the left were some small thickets of wild plum and willow. On the right were some trees and stumps. The river was a few rods from and nearly parallel with the road we were on. As we approached the ferry the river made a sharp turn and ran nearly east for a short distance. Just at the turn a small creek came in, and the point of land between the creek and river was covered by a thick growth of willows. While going through this part of the road, it was thought best by some to throw out skirmishers to learn if there was likely to be any trouble; but Captain Marsh thought the Indians would not dare to molest the soldiers, and that probably the disturbance was caused by a few Indians who had by some means obtained liquor.

As we approached the ferry, which was on our side of the river at the time, we saw an Indian dressed very gorgeously in feathers and war-paint. He was standing on a log on the opposite side of the river. He at once began talking with Mr. Quinn, the interpreter, telling him to have the soldiers come over and smoke the pipe of peace. Mr. Quinn said to the captain that the Indian was a chief named White Dog, and did not belong there, and that he feared his band was also there, and that he feared the trouble was general. He also advised the captain not to venture on the boat.

While this conversation was going on, one of the men (John F. Bishop) went down to the river and dipped up water to past to the men in ranks. The water was roily, as though recently disturbed. He mentioned to the captain that he thought the Indians were crossing the river above, and that they would cut off our chance of retreat. I was standing second from the right of the company, in the front rank, and on looking to the right saw several Indians moving on the point of land between the creek and river. I at once told Orderly Sergeant Finley.

At that moment that terrible blood-curdling war-whoop of the Sioux, that no white man has ever succeeded in imitating, was sounded. At the same time White Dog discharged his gun and jumped back off the log. I felt a sharp pain in my side and back, and began to sink down. I first thought one of the boys had accidentally hit me with the butt of his gun. Then I heard a general discharge of guns and a chorus of yells, and saw two or three other boys fall.

I put my hand to my side and found a bullet-hole through me. I then tried to get up, but to do so was obliged to take my cartridge-belt off. While lying on the bank of the river many balls struck near me and threw sand in my face. I at last succeeded in getting up. I started back along the road we had just come in over. The grass seemed to be full of Indians as I ran back. I ran into the ferryman's house. While in there the balls pattered through the house and the window. The building was deserted, and I saw it would not do to stay there, so I ran out and across the road to the barn.

Here I found Comrade John Parks, lying badly wounded. I tried to help him up, but he could not stand. As I could do him no good, I ran on into the brush and tall grass. I saw three of our boys standing with their backs to a tree, each facing a different direction, and shooting as fast as they could load their guns. I ran toward them, intending to take the other quarter of the tree, thinking it possible that four of us might be able to make a stand, but just as I reached the tree the last one of them fell. I looked in the direction from which I thought the balls had come, and saw an Indian in the act of reloading his gun. I took a quick aim and fired, and had the satisfaction of seeing him fall. I then loaded my gun from the ammunition of Corporal Joseph Bette, and once more started for the brush.

As I ran, Comrade Edwin F. Cole came into the path in front of me. I told him to run faster. He said, "I cannot; I am wounded." I asked him where, and he held out his left hand, which appeared to be shattered. Lifting his left hand turned him into a path to the left I took the path to the right. Just then I heard a racket in front I dropped down and began crawling into the grass. My feet were still in the path, when Ezekiel Rose, our fifer, ran over my feet with two Indians in hot pursuit, but by some means Rose escaped. I then concluded to hide. I crawled under some wild morning-glory vines and reached back and straightened up the grass. Just then I heard Comrade Cole cry out as if in great pain, and heard two Indians laugh and call him a squaw. He continued to beg, so I concluded they were torturing him in some way.

At first, I thought to get up and try to help him. Then reason came to me, and I knew I could not save him, even if I gave my life for him. While these thoughts were running through my head, I heard the most sickening sound imaginable. It was a blow with a tomahawk, and poor Cole was no more. Had I made a move in his defence it would have only added one more to that awful slaughter. The Indians then lit their pipes and sat down to smoke. I could distinctly smell their "*kinikanic.*" They could not have been more than ten or twelve feet from me. They soon left, and all became quiet. . . . .

The battle at the ferry began at about 1:30 o'clock p. m., and lasted about 20 minutes. There were 22 killed outright, and 5 were wounded who escaped and reached Fort Ridgely between that time and 2 o'clock a. m. of the 20th. . . . .I lay concealed in the grass from near 2 o'clock p. m. until dark. It was a very warm day (August 18th) and I suffered from thirst. I could hear an Indian boy or squaw occasionally, not far away, and knew it was not safe to show myself. When it grew dark, I attempted to get up, but was so stiff and sore it was all I could do to rise, and I was obliged to leave my gun in the grass. I started toward a small lake to get a drink, but I was so sore and the ground was so uneven I moved with great effort. My feet would catch in some vine or root and cause me to stumble and almost fall, and every jar caused me great pain. I was obliged to go very slow, and feel my way carefully.

I at last succeeded in reaching the lake. After quenching my thirst, I concluded to lie down and wait for daylight before attempting to go farther. The mosquitoes were very troublesome all night. At times I think I must have lost my reason. I could not sleep much, and would rouse up and find myself talking to Jack Fauver of our company, who drove the ambulance, but who of course was miles away, if alive. I would thank him for coming after me, or ask him not to go and leave me. Then again, I would keep still and think I was hiding from the Indians.

Morning came at last, and as soon as it was light enough, I once more got up by the aid of a tree and started for Fort Ridgely. which was still twelve miles distant; I dared not go out into the open road, or show myself in the open grass land, but kept in the brush. It was very slow, and hard work to get along, so about the middle of the afternoon I ventured out into the wild meadow, there having been no signs of Indians, and was getting along better; but on looking around I saw four Indians. I was first attracted to them by the tinkling of little bells on their ponies. They were on the road on the hill, about a quarter of a mile away. They had just passed a thicket, and come in sight of the open space I had entered. I dropped into the grass, which was waist-high, and at once ran to the lake, which was only a few yards distant.

I jumped in and swam along the bank until I found some over-hanging brush and vines, I crawled up under them and waited, for I was almost sure they had seen me. After waiting some time and hearing nothing. I crawled up the bank, and this time I kept out of sight. Soon after I saw the Indians going up the hill about two miles away. Several times during the day I went into the river and bathed my wound, which had become very troublesome, as I was obliged to stoop and bend my body in order to get through the brush. I lay down once near noon and slept about an hour.

At about 5 p. m. there came up a thundershower, and it rained nearly an hour. It then turned colder, and I was very uncomfortable, with cold, hunger and a bad wound. I found a few bunches of wild grapes which I ate. At dusk that night I had covered but four miles, and now I was obliged to climb a high, hard bluff. It was a hard undertaking, and three times I lay down and said I could not make it, but after lying a while I got cold, and then would say "well, if I do not try again I will surely die here," so I sought another bush and pulled myself up once more, and gained a few yards. I could not get up on my feet without the aid of a bush, shrub, or something to take hold of, to pull myself up by my hands.

After a long and very discouraging effort I reached the top of the bluff. Here I saw a house which had been recently fired, and was still burning brightly. I stood by a tree for some time but could not see anyone moving, so concluded there were no Indians near. I passed the burning house a little to the left, and gained the road to the fort. It must have been nearly nine o'clock, and I had nearly eight miles to go. I was very hungry, as I had had nothing to eat since breakfast on Monday morning, and it was now Tuesday night, but once in the road, I was able to make better time. Once I heard the sound of hoofs approaching me. I left the road a short distance and lay down in the grass.

As the objects came up over a slight knoll, I could see against the sky they were cattle. I waited until they passed, and returning to the road continued on towards the fort. Near midnight, and when about three miles from the fort, I came to a house where we had often traded coffee and sugar for butter, eggs and milk. I went to the door and knocked, but no answer came. I then went to the back part of the house, got in through an open window and found some matches. I lit one, and found everything in the house upside-down and in confusion. I then, went into the pantry to get something to eat if possible, but could find nothing but a piece of ham bone, with very little meat on it, but what there was tasted good.

I was in the house only a few minutes when someone began pounding on the door. I dared not move or answer. Presently a man came to the window and asked if anyone was in the house. I knew by the voice that it was some German, so I answered. He said: "We had better hurry on to the fort, as the Indians are coming." I got out

As we went along, he told me he had been shot in the light shoulder with an arrow, on the morning of the first day of the outbreak at the agency. He had hidden himself in a haymow. He had pulled the shaft of the arrow loose, but had left the steel point imbedded in his flesh, and the point of it was penetrating his lung, and he spat blood. His name was John Fanska, and his home was in New Ulm. He was it the agency on business when the Indians began the slaughter. He was very weak, and we had to rest often. He could get up all right, and would stand and let me pull myself up by taking hold of his clothes.

When we reached the picket post about half a mile out from the fort, we were challenged by one of the men on guard who happened to be one of those who had escaped at the ferry on Monday. When I answered the challenge and gave him my name, he said: "My God, it can't be, for I saw Blodgett fall a second time." We were received, and taken immediately to the hospital, and although it was 2 o'clock in the morning of Wednesday, August 20th, Dr. Alfred Muller was still up, and dressed our wounds, after first satisfying our hunger, it having been forty hours since I had eaten.

We were put to bed and I fell asleep very soon. I was awakened by the sound of musketry, and therefore must have slept until about 1:30 in the afternoon. Now I heard those hideous yells again, and Little Crow had attacked the garrison with his warriors. . . . . When the firing began the doctor, hospital steward and patients made preparations to vacate the old log hospital back of the barracks, and go over to the stone quarters. As the others were leaving, I asked the hospital steward to help me dress, but he seemed to be in too much of a hurry to reach a place of safety to help anyone. I managed to get up and dress all but putting on a hat, and started across the street

It was more difficult for me to move after having lain down so long. I was obliged to go very slow. While crossing the street or passageway between the log building and the barracks, the bullets were flying past, and several times I could feel the wind fan my cheeks. When I reached the stone building, I passed along the west end, and reached the south, or front side of the building. Here one of our boys helped me up the steps, and said "I thought you would never get across that street."

Several of our men were wounded in this battle. . . . . . During the first 24 hours I was in the fort I was allowed to eat as the others did, but after that, and for two weeks, my diet was rice-water—nothing

48

more. Then I was allowed a morsel of more solid food the quantity being gradually increased. The second morning after reaching the fort, and while dressing my wound, the doctor removed some puss, and mixed with it were some grape seeds, and particles of food escaped from the wound in the side for fourteen days. The wound in the back, where the ball came out, was very painful, and had to be cauterised every morning. When I was shot, the ball entered between the two lower ribs on the left side, and passed out near the spinal column on the same side, making a wound about six inches long. This was said to be the first case of its kind on record, and Dr. Alfred Muller made a full report of the case, and it is on file in the Surgeon-General's office at Washington, D. C

W. H. Blodgett, San Jose. Cal.

★★★★★★

As an illustrative incident, the experience of Jas. W. Foster and Thomas Parsley, is related. Foster's gun becoming so hot a cartridge could no longer be forced home with the steel rammer, and finding himself quite alone, he dropped and crept to the sheltering screen of a vine that grew over a plum-tree. The ghastly work he had witnessed was burned into his brain, and he was so utterly defenceless, save the protection a clubbed-gun might afford him for a brief moment, that he hailed with delight the opportunity his concealment gave him for an instant's reflection. He had no belief that he would not be discovered and dispatched, but to reveal himself was certain death. He therefore coolly resolved to take the needed rest his shelter was affording him, allow his gun to become useful again if possible, and sell his life dearly if he must.

The last man having apparently fallen, the savages now nothing to fear, rushed in with their clubs, the crunching blows of which Foster could plainly hear on the heads of his helpless, pleading comrades. The savage demons were plainly seen by Foster in their fiendish contortions of exultation as they dispatched and mutilated the fallen men who had gone down in the open. Back and forth the ground was hunted over, but the running fight with Captain Marsh and the remnant of men in the thicket below the ferry road attracted many of the savages to that scene, though the ground where Foster and others had fought was guarded until darkness made it no longer possible to observe the movements of the savages.

By 10 o'clock at night fires were burning on the agency hill across the river and it was plain the awful work of the day was the occa-

49

sion of great joy in the camp of the savages. Night indeed was made hideous by the frightful revels of this scalp-dance, where the naked bodies of the savages, with jerking cadence, crouched and swayed, and writhed and leaped around the central fire, in the light of which could be seen as they bore them aloft, the bloody trophies of the awful slaughter, each fiend in his turn seeking to make more hideous the occasion by hisses, howls, groans and yells than his fellows had done.

Foster reasoned that this scene must have proven irresistible to the undisciplined Indian sentinels about him, and that this was his opportunity for escape. He arose with caution, and in silence moved with measured step north-easterly. He had gone but a dozen paces through the weeds and vines when he was startled by stepping upon a human form. No sound came from the body at his feet. Nothing could be heard in the deathly stillness except the beating of his own heart. Bending low, and in a whisper, he asked: "Is this one of the boys from the fort?" Feeling the body was not that of a dead man, he again whispered: "If this is one of the boys of Co. B, get up and let us go to the fort."

No answer came, but as he straightened up to proceed on his journey alone, the prostrate form moved, and there came from it in a low tone: "Is that you, Jim?"

"Yes," said Foster, "and let us get out of here at once."

The man whom Foster thus came upon proved to be Thomas Parsley, who, when his gun became useless, disarming him, fell, and like Foster, concealed himself and thus escaped. Indian pickets had been posted within a few yards of him until their whereabouts could no longer be determined in the darkness of night, but he feared to leave his concealment until a later hour, and as many half-breeds were on the war-path with the Indians, and as these were known to speak English well, and not suspecting a member of his company had survived. Parsley, though he believed he recognised Foster, even in a whisper, hesitated to disclose himself until assured in his own mind by this incident that he was not the sole survivor of Marsh's detachment.

In the midst of peace, repose and daydreams a demon had awakened from his slumber, to pile event upon event, tragedy upon tragedy, with startling swiftness in the making of North-western history. The day's tragedies were appalling indeed, and it is hoped that another such bloody page as that written upon this date will never again stain the annals of Minnesota.

The morning of August 19th dawned after a sleepless night at Fort Ridgely. Lieutenant Gere, grasping the wide scope of responsibility he had succeeded to as the ranking officer of the garrison, left nothing to luck or chance from the outset. One of the last official acts of Captain Marsh on the morning of the 18th, before starting for Redwood, was to write an order for the return of Lieutenant Sheehan and his fifty men who left on the 17th on their return to Fort Ripley, this order being placed in the hands of Corporal James C. McLean, fitted by courage, tact and endurance for such an assignment.

As the night of the 18th approached, with its rapidly-increasing number of refugees, and its harrowing tales from the settlements, and, finally, with the first tidings of the frightful disaster to Captain Marsh and his men, the garrison found itself in desperate straits. Lieutenant Gere dispatched a messenger in the person of Private William J. Sturgis, on the best horse at the post, with a message to the commandant at Fort Snelling and to Governor Ramsey at St. Paul, apprising them of the massacre and condition of affairs, and asking them to render promptly such assistance as the dangerous state demanded. Sturgis was also ordered to apprise Lieutenant Culver and Indian Agent Galbraith, then on their way to Fort Snelling with the Renville Rangers and urge their hasty return to Fort Ridgely.

With savages spreading over the country, the sending of messengers was attended with no little risk to those who were assigned to this duty, but Sturgis, like McLean, could be trusted to proceed alertly and execute faithfully.

With his twenty-odd men. Lieutenant Gere must make judicious dispositions. Nearly the entire effective force were posted as pickets, Gere personally placing the men at dark, with full instructions as to their duty. This was indeed a thin and slender line, for the defence of the garrison and the two to three hundred refugees, gathered in the buildings of the fort. The refugees realised this fact, and were in a constant state of nervous tension, needing but the sound of a gun to precipitate a panic, as was illustrated during the night when one of the outer pickets fired at some obscure object and ran in, shouting "Indians!" The scene that followed beggars description.

The alarm was accepted as the awful realisation of the expected, for conditions strengthened the feeling among these terror-stricken people that Nature's last penalty was to be inflicted, and, too, without any compensating qualifications, such as instant death, or death at the hands of a civilized foe, even.

These refugees were massed in the wooden buildings, forming the east and west sides of the square of the Fort. With a view to their greater safety Lieutenant Gere had ordered the removal of all these fugitives to the long stone barracks building at the north side of the square. The crouching, cringing, praying, grief-stricken mass was cowed into inactivity by the reign of terror that had swept the settlements and put them to flight, but the firing of the shot and the alarm accompanying it set the affrighted mass into a pell-mell scramble for such security as the stone building might afford. The value of discipline was never more forcibly illustrated than on this occasion

Among the fugitives were not a few men, and many of these lost their heads in the mad rush for the barracks, the windows of which they crushed to facilitate ingress, while numerous great double doors yawned to receive with ample facility the entire motley throng. But they were terror-stricken, and not the hindmost in the scurrying bedlam that made night hideous. On the other hand, the soldiers were self-reliant and the personification of composure, taking their assignments for a heroic defence of the garrison.

If Indians were responsible for the alarm, they were merely a reconnoitring party, for no attack was made on the fort, and the pickets were again posted, remaining without relief or sleep throughout the night, as did all the effectives of the garrison, watchful and in readiness for instant action. The night was one of constant vigil by the soldiers, and of supplication, moaning and ceaseless wailing in the barracks where the refugees were gathered, and daylight, whatever it might bring, was welcomed. The great, glorious morning sun, whose enveloping flood dispelled the gloom of night, had a mollifying effect. The mental and physical strain upon the soldiers, and the agonies of the fugitives were unchanged, but the sunlight of heaven, like a merciful anaesthetic, soothed the weary and consoled the distressed.

To the mad revelry at the Redwood Agency on the night of the 18th, in celebration of the horrible deeds of blood of the day, may be attributed the escape of Fort Ridgely from a night attack. What of the 19th, now unfolding, to be engraven with history?

The merciless carnage at the agency had furnished a scene for the Indians never before dreamed of, and by the side of which their combats with their hereditary foes, the Chippewas, were puerile and vapid. Wild with the excitement born of riot and bloodshed, the Indians were difficult of management by their chiefs, as they ever are, chieftainship never carrying with it the right or ability to discipline in matters of detail.

There was such pleasure in torturing, mutilating and murdering defenceless women and children, and this horrible pastime was attended with such slight risk to the young warriors, that they preferred to follow it up, rather than engage in the more serious tasks of meeting armed men in battle. Murder, plunder, rapine and outrage, were features new to the young savages, and, when Little Crow undertook to bend their energies against Fort Ridgely on the morning of the 19th, dissension resulted.

While in camp on the Sheyenne River on the 4th of July, 1863, on the Sibley Expedition northward, the writer, with John McCole as interpreter, visited the camp of the scouts of the Sibley command, and had a prolonged interview with Chaska, an intelligent scout well known to McCole, and who had rendered noble service in saving the missionaries and other whites, the previous year. Chaska only knew the story of the savages as he learned, it from them after the massacre, but related fluently and intelligently many things that were matters of but reasonable conjecture on the part of the garrison.

Asked how it happened that Little Crow did not attack Fort Ridgely on the 19th of August, Chaska replied that such an attack was Little Crow's plan, supported by nearly all the older Indians, but his forces became so weakened by dissension among the young men before he reached the garrison that he finally was obliged to give up the attack for that day, though he left the agency early on the morning of the 19th with a force of over three hundred warriors, bound for the fort. (The dissenting Indians spread over the settlements in the direction of New Ulm, which afforded a rich field for rapine and murder, and late in the day about one hundred made an attack on New Ulm.)

If Little Crow had not previously repented his hasty assumption of command, he now no doubt felt that his consent of leadership was a thankless task and a grave error. His plan of campaign was first to wipe out the Redwood Agency, and then forthwith to take Fort Ridgely at the time of its greatest weakness. This would give the savages freehand in all the settlements north of New Ulm and St. Peter, and the wily old chieftain felt deeply no doubt the insubordination that frustrated his plans. His judgment from the stand-point of the savage, having commenced the bloody work, was good, for had he attacked the fort immediately following the slaughter of Marsh's men at Redwood, the fort would inevitably have fallen, as the fewer than thirty men in the garrison could not have manned all the exposures, and with the fall of the Fort Sheehan and his men, with limited sustenance and ammunition, would, despite their valour, have been annihilated.

So also would the Renville Rangers, on their way back from St. Peter, have been blotted out. The obduracy of the young men among Little Crow's command no doubt saved all these remnants of soldiery and the lives of hundreds of settlers who were given time to make their way to places of safety, as Crow was averse to penetrating the more thickly settled country in the direction of St. Peter without first taking Fort Ridgely. While he was subjugating the recalcitrant warriors to his will, Sheehan reached the fort with his fifty men, and the Renville Rangers likewise came in safely, uniting elements of strength that could have been destroyed in detail, had he followed up with a prompt attack on the fort.

The night following the massacre at the Lower Agency, August 18th, as related by Chaska, it was determined in council, after the wild revelry and dancing over the slaughter with which their hands were still red, that Fort Ridgely should be attacked the next morning, August 19th, Little Crow mustering that evening over three hundred warriors for the onslaught. With no distracting conditions prevailing, this programme would have succeeded, but a disagreement on the way to the Fort on the policy of so soon turning from the defenceless settlements for so serious an undertaking as the facing of armed men, led to a division of forces, which reduced Little Crow's soldiery for the attack to about one hundred and twenty-five men.

Notwithstanding this diminution, the great war chief came to within a short distance of the fort, on the morning of Tuesday, August 19th, where, on a knoll to, the north-westward, in plain view, he held a council of war. The council circle was plainly visible from the garrison, and manifestly the deliberations were of a serious nature. Through a telescope which someone at the fort fortunately possessed, Little Crow was recognised as the chief orator of the occasion, standing in the centre of the council circle. Others than Little Crow also addressed the council, but the war chief, always conspicuous, was the only Indian to be recognised.

Serious as was the moment for the little garrison, there was something akin to amusement in the antics of an Indian who frequently rode around the council circle on a spotted pony at break-neck speed. What his spasmodic gyrations meant, no one could divine, or has ever learned.

These were moments of great peril for Fort Ridgely, whose fate hung by a thread. The garrison was on trial for its life in this council. A vote to defer attack meant that Sheehan and his men and Galbraith, Culver, McGrew and Gorman and the Renville Rangers might reach us in safety; a vote to attack at once meant death to all.

We watched the deliberations of the Indians with profound concern, knowing what an attack on the depleted garrison would mean. One-third of our company had been annihilated the previous day at the ferry, while other members of it were on their way to Fort Snelling with the Renville Rangers. These facts made the deliberations of Little Crow and his warriors of great importance to the garrison. Finally, there were signs that the stormy council was about to dissolve, and in a trice the savages rose and dispersed from view. Our suspense was even greater now than before. The holding of this council under our eyes was a bold piece of business, and the garrison had good reason to regard it with the suspicion that while our attention was visited upon the council a large force was stealthily approaching the fort under cover of ravines and woods from the opposite direction. But the Indians were having troubles we knew not of, as, naturally it was supposable Little Crow had his entire force well in hand.

He likewise, however, was ignorant of our condition. He had occasion to believe Sheehan and the Renville Rangers were still at the fort, His speech in the council is said to have been substantially as follows, eliminating the gall poured upon the heads of those who had failed him for the day:

> We know that for two months there have been from one hundred and twenty-five to one hundred and fifty men at the Fort (Marsh's company and fifty men of Company, C, called in June to attend the Indian payment.) We know we killed half of Marsh's company at the ferry yesterday. We counted them at the river before shooting. We know there must be over one hundred soldiers in the fort. We cannot take the fort with the braves we have today. We must take the fort. Our warriors must come tomorrow. We must get all our men together and we must attack the fort tomorrow noon.

These were, in substance, the conclusions of the council. It would be difficult to impress upon the mind of the reader the great importance to the frontier, of the failure, at a critical stage of the massacre, of Little Crow's warriors to obey and support unitedly their chieftain. The blood of over three hundred souls at the fort would have added to the sanguinary river that had already drenched the agency and the surrounding settlements, for bear in mind Fort Ridgely was only a fort in name. There were no protecting walls or breastworks, no trenches, no stockade. Desperately as the garrison might have defended itself, it would have inevitably gone down to death in one brief struggle; Sheehan's men would have been ambushed in the long, gloomy, wooded defile through which it must pass to reach the fort, if indeed spared to gain that point, and the Renville Rangers would have shared a like fate, and in addition several hundred settlers to the south-eastward would have been added to the long list whose lives had already gone out in unspeakable agony. It is not too much to say that the insubordination of Little Crow's warriors, on August 19th, saved the lives of a thousand people.

We have all experienced the soul's gratitude, when depressed with the gloom of prolonged darkness, at a rift in angry clouds, through which the sun poured forth a flood of golden light, as if bearing a joyous message from the land of eternal life, but a thousand times intensified in comparison was the thrill of joy that electrified every soul in the garrison when Sheehan and his fifty men, just as the Indians were dispersing from their council, filed rapidly into the Fort at the end of an all-night forced march of forty-two miles.

These men had been the guests and companions of Co. B for two months, and had left us but forty-eight hours before for Fort Ripley, receiving a soldier's goodbye and a God speed from Captain Marsh and the noble fellows who had, since their leaving only so short a time before, been slaughtered in the Battle of Redwood Ferry. The meeting of Sheehan and his men and the little remnant of Co. B in the garrison passes the bounds of description. There was no time for demonstration, but fraternal emotion never surpassed in heartiness and spirit the hail and welcome of this meeting, which, had Little Crow attacked the fort instead of holding a council, would never have taken place.

Courier Sturgis, after an all-night ride over a dreary road, reached St. Peter at dawn on the morning of August 19th, with his message announcing the dire straits of the fort and the upper frontier. Here he overtook Lieutenant Culver, Sergeant McGrew and five other men, all of Co. B, together with Indian Agent Galbraith and James Gorman, the latter in command of the Renville Rangers, all on their way to Fort Snelling. St. Peter was stirred to its foundations with excitement when the contents of the message of Lieutenant Gere and the verbal report of Sturgis spread with almost electric swiftness throughout the town, confirming what up to this time had been a rumour, but one that did not, in the public mind, portend a general uprising.

In this day no railroad had penetrated the valley of the Minnesota

River; nor was there any telegraphic communication between St. Paul and this upper country.

Men were never more prompt in responding to a call than were the brave fellows above named and the Renville Rangers, the latter newly-recruited, not even mustered into the service, and unarmed. Under the inspiration of this call to duty, great vigour attended every detail of preparation for the return to the fort. St. Peter was fired with excitement and activity as never before, and rendered promptly every requirement for the out-fitting of the men.

At 6 o'clock on the morning of the 19th the expedition set out, and without a break in the rhythmic step, the noble fellows covered in a forced march the distance of forty miles by evening, entering the fort amid wild shouts of joy and welcome, for at last the garrison considered itself on a "war footing," not only equal to self-defence, but strong enough to stay the bloody hand raised against the Minnesota valley.

Before leaving St, Peter a sufficient number of old Harper's Ferry muskets were secured to arm the Renville Ranchers, each man receiving a beggarly three rounds of ammunition; but what might have been frightful disaster was prevented by the favouring fortune that diverted the enemy from the fort road that day.

Thus, on the eve of battle, Fort Ridgely contained, at last, the following military strength:

COMPANY B, FIFTH MINNESOTA.

Norman K. Culver, First Lieutenant
Thomas P. Gere, Second Lieutenant

Sergeants.

James G. McGrew   John F. Bishop
Arlington C. Ellis

Corporals.

David W. Atkins   William Good
Charles H. Hawley   Truman D. Huntley
Michael Pfremer   William E. Winslow

Drummer—Charles M. Culver.

Privates

George M. Annis   John Brennan
Charles Beecher   Levi Carr
Charles H. Baker   William H. H. Chase
William H. Blodgett   James Dunn
Christopher Boyer   Caleb Elphee

Andrew J. Fauver	Antoine Rebenski
James W. Foster	Heber Robinson
Columbia French	Andrew Rufredge
Ambrose Gardner	Lorin Scripture
Elias Hoyt	John Serfling
William B. Hutchinson	Ole Svendson
Levi W. Ives	Allen Smith
John W, Lester	Samuel Stewart
Isaac Lindsey	Robert J. Spornitz
Henry Martin	William A. Sutherland
Arthur McAllister	Martin J. Tanner
John McGowan	Jonathan Taylor
James C. McLean	Joel A. Underwood
John L. Magill	Stephen Van Buren
James Murray	Eli Wait
Edward P. Nehrhood	Oscar G. Wall
Thomas Parsley	Andrew W. Williamson
William J. Perrington	Henry F. Pray
Martin H. Wilson	

In this list are all surviving members of Co. B who were in the fort at this time, including those who were so disabled as to be incapacitated for duty, the total number of private soldiers being forty-six.

COMPANY C, FIFTH MINNESOTA.

Timothy J. Sheehan, First Lieutenant.

Sergeants.

John P. Hicks	F. A. Blackmer
John C. Ross	

Corporals.

M. A. Chamberlain	Wm, Young
Z. C. Butler	Dennis Porter

Privates

S. P. Beighley	L. C. Jones
E. D. Brooks	N. I. Lowthian
J. M. Brown	A. J. Luther (w'd)
J. L. Bullock	John Malachy
Chas. E. Chapel	John McCall
Zachariah Chute	Orlando Mgall
L. H. Decker	F. M. McReynolds
Chas. Dills	J. H. Mead

Charles H. Dills
S. W. Dogan
L. A. Eggleston
Halvor Elefson
Martin Ellingson
C. J. Grandy
Mark M. Greer
J. P. Green
A. K. Grout
Andrew Gulbranson
Peter E. Harris
Philo Henry
James Honan
D. N. Hunt

J. B. Miller
Dennis Morean
Peter Nisson
Andrew Peterson
J. M. Rice
Charles A. Rose
B. F. Ross
Edward Roth
C. O. Russell
Isaac Shortlidge
Josiah Weakly
G. H. Wiggins
J. M. Ybright
James Young

RENVILLE RANGERS.

James Gorman, First Lieutenant, commanding.

Sergeants.

Theophylc Richer
Warren Carey

John McCole

Corporals

Louis Arner
Roufer Beurger

Dieudonne Sylvester

Privates.

Eurgel Amiot
Joseph Auge
George Bakerman
Rocque Berthiaume
Edward Bibeau
John Bourcier
Pierre Boyer
Samuel Brunelle
David Carpenter
John Campbell
Jaire Campbell
Antone Chose
George Dagenais
Frederic Denzer
Henry Denzer
Alexis Demerce

Richard L. Hoback
George A. LaBatte
Frederic Le Croix
Cyprian Le Claire
Joseph La Tour
Medard Laucier
Joseph Milard
Moses Mireau
Theophile Morin
Charles Mitchel
A. B. Murch
Joseph Osier
Henry Pflaume
Ernest Paul
Henry Pierce
Joseph Pereau

59

Francois Demerce	Thomas Quinn
Carlton Dickinson	Magloire Robidoux
James Delaney	Charles Robert
Louis Demeule	Joseph Robinette
Joseph Fourtier	Francois Stay
B. H. Goodell	John Wagner

In addition to the foregoing troops were: John Jones, ordnance sergeant, U. S. A.; Dr. Alfred Muller, post surgeon, and Benjamin H. Randall, suttler.

The organised forces, now, in the fort, including the disabled, to-talled one hundred and sixty officers and enlisted men.

The Renville Rangers were recruited for service in the civil war, but the Sioux Massacre diverted their organisation, and following the surrender of the captives at Camp Release, the company, after rendering three months of service for which no adequate reward was or ever can be made, became disintegrated, the men enlisting singly in other bodies or returning to civil life.

Out of the agitated mass of refugees there came to the surface some twenty-five men of sterling worth, to whom the garrison, in its day of need, was under unspeakable obligations, and whose valour and general usefulness contributed in no slight degree to the successful defence of the fort. Among these were a number of sturdy Germans from the surrounding settlements. These, with the one hundred and fifty-four officers and men enumerated above, raised the fort's defenders to about two hundred men. There was no possibility of increasing this strength. All the beleaguered garrison had dared to hope for had now been vouchsafed to it. If numbers were deficient, there must be the greater dependence on valour and tact.

Stationed at the fort was one lone representative of the regular army, in the person of Sergeant John Jones, whose official station was that of ordnance sergeant of the post. His years had hardened him to ripeness in the art of gunnery. He was over-exacting as a drill-master, accepting nothing as good enough that was not exactly right. During the quiet months of Co. B at Fort Ridgely, artillery, as well as infantry drill, was taken up, perhaps not so much to increase the efficiency of the men as to give them a respite from the manual-of-arms practice and infantry evolutions, in which they had become very proficient.

An unexpected emergency had now risen in the Indian uprising to put at its best the value of this artillery training under Jones, for there was no lack of gunners when the artillery of the post became a saving factor. Fortunately for the occasion also, was the fact that J. C. Whipple, who had successfully escaped to the fort from the Redwood Agency, was a trained artillerist, having served in a battery during the Mexican war.

No one can write of the stirring events at Fort Ridgely during the latter days of August, 1862, without painfully regretting that the names of many men who took refuge at the fort during the massacre, became lost to history, for many of these unknown men from unknown walks were lion-hearted, and willing to step into the breach and hazard their lives without a murmur, wherever duty called. Among these I recall a Mr. De Camp, (later killed at the Battle of Birch Coulie), whose Sharp's carbine became familiar music to the defenders of the fort. Then there were the Riekes, brave and brawny young fellows, and others, whose names should never have been lost to history.

An eventful day closed when the shadows of night on the 19th overwhelmed all in darkness. The garrison had known no sleep—no rest for thirty-six hours; but the strain was so great, the events that had rapidly succeeded each other so important, and the situation was so pregnant with grave possibilities, that sleep had not suggested itself as a necessity.

Fort Ridgely Viciously Attacked

ENGAGEMENTS OF AUGUST 20 AND 22,

(Figures in parenthesis in following pages refer to the earlier plan of the fort, page 25)

On the arrival of the detachment of Co. C, Tuesday morning, First Lieutenant T. J. Sheehan of that company, by seniority of rank, became commander of Fort Ridgely. If nothing could be gained in courage and efficiency in such a change, certainly nothing was lost. Brave and resourceful, vigilant and aggressive, the garrison, as results proved, was ably commanded. Pickets were posted for the night, and every precaution taken to guard against a night attack, as such an event was among the reasonable probabilities, but the long vigil was undisturbed, and the sun rose on the morning of the 20th in autumn splendour, with its message of good cheer. No news came from the outside world, and, there was no possible means of communication. An occasional refugee came in, the number of these distressed people in the garrison now reaching fully three hundred.

In the very nature of things, the fort could not long escape attack.

Its period of exemption had already exceeded the limit of expectation; but there was no occasion for disappointment or even for any impatience. Scattering bands of Indians disclosed themselves from time to time during the morning and until midday, in the country immediately surrounding, indicating that the savages were assembling in the shelter of the wooded valleys that headed near the fort on three sides. Plainly there was a general conversance of hostiles. Just when the attack would be launched and just what its plan would be, were conjectural matters, but Lieutenant Sheehan's preparedness, to the limit of his little force, was for any emergency, and wisely did he distribute his men and resources.

The reader will find the birds-eye plan of Fort Ridgely and surroundings presented in this connection, invaluable, in that it reveals at a glance what can be but imperfectly expressed at best in words. (See page 25.)

Having completed his plans and dispositions, Little Crow, the wily chieftain and fearless warrior, emerged from concealment at about 1 o'clock in the afternoon, and rode out into the open beyond the picket line to the westward of the fort, and likewise beyond musket range, yet near enough to be recognised. No doubt, understanding the importance of his capture, he believed a general rush would be made to seize him, since he was unattended and unsupported. He feigned a desire for a conference with the officers of the post, but declined with sullen indifference the invitation of Sergeant Bishop, sergeant of the guard at the time, to come down to the picket line. The ruse was shrewd, and the play of the foxy warrior dramatic, but Sheehan was not to be tricked by Indian cunning.

Seeing his plan had failed, the mask was thrown off, and the battle opened fiercely by the savages under cover of the wooded ravine at the northeast corner of the fort, which extended from Fort Creek to within a few rods of the wooden buildings north of the barracks. Little Crow had reasoned wisely when he planned to draw the attention of the garrison from the point at which he was to deliver his attack on the post, for he had massed the main strength of his force at the nearest point to the fort, and in the onrush which was a part of his attack, his warriors gained possession of the outer log buildings of the garrison.

When the first shot was fired the clarion voice of Lieutenant Sheehan rang out, in ever-memorable tones "Every man to his post!" The challenge of the enemy was daringly met, and the savages, having disclosed their hand, dispositions were quickly made that checked with around turn the dashing assault it was believed would prove irresistible. Lieutenant Gere was ordered to stay the attack with a detachment from Co. B, and posting a howitzer under J. C. Whipple, which he supported under a galling fire, opened with shrapnel at short and deadly range.

Sergeant McGrew, conspicuous for bravery and tact throughout the siege, supported by a detachment from Co. C, posted a howitzer at the northwest corner of the garrison, and opened vigorously on the enemy swarming from the wooded shelter to the northward; but impatient to reach the persistent force with which Gere and Whipple were hotly contending, and which, under shelter of the hill, was perilously near the fort, he ran his shotted gun into the open to the northwest of the buildings, and with an enfilading fire swept the slope to the grass-roots, calling forth a furious volley from the concealed enemy, but driving from the slope the desperate savages who were determined to force a breach in the defences at the point of original attack.

Nor would the savages abandon this point, though swept back by Whipple and McGrew and their supports, aided by a hot fire from the windows of the long barracks building. This, it had been well reasoned out, owing to the shelter afforded, and the short distance the protecting hill and its brushwood covering from the fort, was the vulnerable spot that alone held out hope to Little Crow's forces of from five to seven hundred men. The savages persisted in their attack on this point, but Whipple, with Gere's splendid detachment, and McGrew and his resolute supports, had, by dauntless courage and skilful tactics, become masters of the key, driving the Indians from the wooden buildings they had daringly gained, and making the continued near approach of the savages at this point too hazardous to be persisted in at short range.

The attack had gradually extended itself well around the garrison, seeking a point of vantage, but the defence was alert, and presented an unyielding front at every turn.

The hot musketry and cannonading were telling seriously on the supply of ammunition at hand, and it was found necessary during the fight to withdraw men from the defences to form a detail for the removal of all ammunition in the exposed magazines (22) to the stone barracks (1). To thwart this movement the savages must expose themselves to the raking fire of McGrew's howitzer, that officer having been ordered to cover the men engaged in the toilsome task of carrying by hand the heavy munitions a distance of two hundred yards, exposed to the missiles of the savages, happily at long range. The day was hot, and the men bending to their tasks in the din of battle and as conspicuous targets, found little opportunity to mop their dust-besmeared and perspiring faces during the hour or more required to complete the transfer of the precious fixed ammunition to more available quarters.

His men unable to withstand the withering fire that from the start had been poured into their ranks at the north, Little Crow executed a move that might have been successful with a larger force. Sheltering conditions favoured the concentration of a large force of the enemy at the south and southwest of the garrison. This move was executed under the personal direction of Little Crow, who sought by a bold stroke to so engage the forces of Lieutenant Sheehan as to loosen his hold on the northeast of the garrison, where the chieftain still hoped to enter the fort. The din of cannon and musket, and the wild shouts of the desperate and enraged savages, were incessant and at times deafening.

Sergeant Jones, supported by Lieutenants Culver and Gorman and the Renville Rangers, was in position at the southwest angle of the garrison, and was exposed to the raking fire of the enemy. Jones covered the ground over which the savages must make their way to an entrance, with a six-pound field-piece. Men were diverted as they could be spared to the protection of the scene of anticipated attack, and the fray was hot and furious, Jones' piece working havoc in the ranks of the savages, and holding the force in abeyance, while the Renville Rangers and other forces dealt effective volleys among the naked demons, making their repeated efforts at a sally and onrush too hazardous for Sioux courage.

The Indians had attacked the fort with full confidence in their ability to overpower and take it. Little Crow, in a towering rage, urged that the fort *must* be taken. It was the door which closed the Minnesota valley to his red-handed followers, and it *must* be taken. Nagged, brow-beaten and exhorted, his warriors returned time and again to the task set for them, eager for the flow of blood and the spoils of victory awaiting their triumphant breaking of the thin line of defence, but they could not stem the storm of musketry and the rain of shells that hurled them back, despite their frenzied efforts to force a hand-to-hand struggle, in which they felt sure of overpowering the fort's defenders, by their vast superiority of numbers.

By 4 o'clock in the afternoon it was evident they had put forth their supremest effort, and had failed to force a break at any point. Their disappointment and anger found vent in the most hideous yells ever uttered by savages. They fought in disorder at all points, and then would concentrate with an energy and ferocity entitling them to first place among Indian warriors. And so, the battle raged until nightfall, when the savages withdrew to the depths of the dark valleys, full of vengeance, as their defiant yells betokened, but worsted in the hot game of war for the day.

★★★★★★

A few errors regarding this engagement persist in repeating themselves. First, the engagement opened at not later than 1 p. m. of Wednesday, Angus 20th, 1862. Second, the garrison was in no sense surprised by the first or any other attack. Even to eminent and accurate an authority as Judge Flandrau, in his last and most interesting work, *The History of Minnesota and Tales of the Frontier*, repeats the error first given currency in Hurd's *History of the Sioux Massacre*, to the effect that the engagement began at 3 p. m and that the garrison was taken completely by surprise, "the first knowledge of the presence of Indians being the firing of a volley by the savages through an opening between the buildings." Pickets were posted well out from the garrison, rendering a surprise impossible. The first shots in defence of the fort were fired from the picket line. The precautions of the garrison were such that there could have been a surprise at no time, day or night, from the beginning to the end of the siege covering a period of nearly ten days. Third, there was no attack at any tune on the fort during Thursday, August 21st.

★★★★★★

But what of the night? This was the serious problem. The officers knew, and so did every soldier in the garrison, that the foe was not vanquished, and that he would return again to the attack.

With all its exposure, the true American soldier prefers to meet his enemy in the open, and in the light of day, and in this case, with his greatly inferior numerical strength, the fear of a night attack produced a deeper feeling of dread than was generally acknowledged. But the enemy retired poorly rewarded for his losses and his rough treatment generally, and silence profound reigned where for hours the din of battle had been almost deafening.

The silence and solitude of night witnessed no change in the garrison, save that in killed and wounded we had lost eleven good men. The men about the guns and the force that had manned the windows of the barracks and other buildings and openings, remained watch-

65

fully where they had fought. The artillery strength of the garrison was increased, Sergeant Bishop being placed in charge of a twelve-pounder field-piece, efficiently manned, for action. Every precaution having been taken by the alert Sheehan, with vigilance everywhere impressed, the men, weary and worn, settled down to a sleepless night.

Undeservedly brief has history dealt with the Renville Rangers, for no men during the massacre were put to so rigid a test as they. The company was very largely made up of French half-breeds, who were born among, had lived with and were related to, the very Indians who had risen to depopulate and make desolate the Minnesota frontier. With a single exception these men were loyal to every trust reposed in them, and no braver soldiers than they had proven themselves to be in the day's battle, ever went into action. It was one of these men, Joseph Osier, who fired the first shot from the garrison at the opening of the engagement.

Another, Geo. Dagenais, brave and athletic, dashed into the open and ran to one of the log buildings, of which, during the engagement, the Indians had taken possession, and firing through a crack between two logs, got his man, and running back to the barracks amid a shower of bullets, leaped into the building at an opening with the exultant: "I kill him one, I kill him one."

Little Crow was born on the banks of the upper Mississippi, and spent his childhood, and even early manhood, in the valley where Winona, Wabasha, Red Wing and other Minnesota towns and cities now flourish. For natural beauty the scenes of this noted Indian's early life stand almost unrivalled. The lofty, majestic hills, the beautiful valley itself, and the great river of unsurpassed Grandeur, had become a part of the very being of this haughty savage.

Driven from the valley that civilization might expand its borders, and knowing too, that the pristine beauty of the country (which was all to him) had been marred and desecrated by the white settler, still the heart of Little Crow never ceased to yearn for the land of his childhood, and the hope had ever lingered that someday, by some fortuitous stroke, this land might yet be restored to those who for ages held it by prowess and sacrifice. It was the land where his wild, roving nature had known all there was in youthful happiness— the land where the ashes of his ancestors were scattered.

Prof. A. W. Williamson, for more than a quarter of a century professor of mathematics of Augustana college. Rock Island, Ill., a member of Captain Marsh's company (B) stationed at Fort Ridgely at the time of the Sioux Massacre, who was a son of the noted Sioux Missionary, Rev. Dr. Thomas Williamson, and who was born at Lac Qui Parle in 1836, and therefore thus knew from contact, personally, intimately, more of Indian history and character than is given to many men to know, stated to the writer but recently that through Indian sources he was advised at Fort Ridgely that agents of the Southern Confederacy were at work among the Sioux about the time of and immediately preceding the outbreak, in an endeavour to impress upon the Indians the fact that the whole northern country was hard pressed in the civil war; that the men had all been impressed into the military service, leaving only a few soldiers to guard the frontier; that this was the supreme time for an uprising, and the driving of the whites back from the land of the savages.

Prof. Williamson, then a young private of Co. B, thought the report of so little importance that he did not recall that he ever discussed it with anyone; and while he never believed the rumour to have been well founded, its source was such, and it was so consistent with possibilities, withal, that the story had never ceased to impress him.

Whatever the truth, it is well known that Little Crow believed that Fort Ridgely swept from his path he would over-run and repossess the country to the mouth of the Minnesota River, if not beyond. What impressed him with this belief will never be definitely known, but that he possessed it, is beyond doubt. The dream of childhood days and of youthful haunts, and the promise of some mysterious influence held out to the war-chief that somehow, some day he would lead his people to the home of the olden time, were influential factors in determining his action when, roused from slumber on the morning of August 18th, he sat upon his couch, his blanket drawn about his shoulders, and heard the demand of his people that he should lead them in a war against the whites. Impelled alone by mental agitation, great beads of perspiration gathered on the forehead of Little Crow, and coursed down his face. He struggled with his decision, and relying on the hope of far-reaching results, gave his consent.

The die having been cast, the famous war-chief was from the outset determined upon a full realisation of his hopes, not to be enjoyed with Fort Ridgely in his path.

At midnight of the 20th, a dreary rain set in, adding not only gloom, but discomfort to the situation. The resulting darkness was utterly impenetrable for even the distance of a few feet, and amid these conditions there came a wailing sound from out on the prairie, startling in its possibilities, as some of the pickets had smelled the burning of *kin-nic-kinic* earlier in the night—a sure sign that Indians were near. If words were uttered, they were unintelligible to anyone who heard them.

The wail was repeated, and believing it the ruse of savages to attract attention from a movement against the garrison. Lieutenant Sheehan ordered Sergeant McGrew to fire a shot from his howitzer in the direction from which the sound came, so aiming his piece as to injure no distressed refugee, and yet to develop if possible, the meaning of the cry. Still the sound came as before. Sheehan now ordered a detachment of soldiers to proceed to the spot whence came the wailing, and the men soon found, groping in the gloomy darkness, a frenzied woman, lost, exhausted and crazed with grief and fear, and whose harrowing story and frightful experiences were sensational in the extreme.

No other incident disturbed the night. Lowering skies marked the morning of the 21st, but the day passed uneventfully. A large body of Indians came within plain view of the fort, and their presence was regarded ominously. They moved by and entered the Minnesota valley a mile below the fort, however, and passed down, as was later known, to attack New Ulm. Advantage was taken of the lull on the 21st to construct a protecting barricade for Jones, his gunners and supports.

ATTACK OF AUGUST 22

Friday morning, August 22nd, after the fourth night of sleepless vigil, the sun rose in splendour, its welcome rays dispelling the gloom of cloud and darkness, and cheering the souls of men who were under a strain severely testing their endurance, and who, though prone to cheerfulness, gave evidence of the mental and physical wear to which they were subjected, and from which lack of numbers forbade any relief. Except throughout the hours of darkness, there were few intervals during which the menacing presence of Indians, somewhere within the scope of vision, did not impress all with the necessity of preparedness.

As the morning hours advanced, portentious signs of attack manifested themselves, for the savages were clearly massing under cover of the surrounding wooded valleys. This movement went on throughout the forenoon, and it was evident Little Crow had vastly increased his numbers for this attack.

Shortly after noon the hellish legion left its cover and came quickly to its work, accompanying its approach with yells, such as only those who have heard them can appreciate or understand. The numbers were three times those of Wednesday's attack, and the plan was clearly to intimidate by boldness and fierceness of onslaught from all sides, with a hope of breaking the defences at some vulnerable point, then to complete the work with overwhelming force. For a time it seemed the tide, constantly augmented from the sheltering woods, and ravines, must prove irresistible, but the ringing blasts of Whipple's and McGrew's guns, and their supports, as in the first day's fight, staggered the savages, and swept them back in spite of their numbers, the men, posted identically as before, having made the defence of the ground with which they had become thoroughly familiar, a matter of scientific marksmanship.

Everywhere on the prairie were creeping savages whose heads were wreathed in turbans of grass and wild flowers of the prairie, the better to conceal their movements in seeking vantage ground from which to pour their terrible fire upon the garrison. Not only bullets, but the primitive arrow came in great numbers, and with furious impulse. With the latter it was sought to fire the buildings of the fort, burning punk being affixed to arrow points that were fired into many roofs, but the rains that had discomfited the garrison now proved to have been a blessing in disguise, for had the roofs been thoroughly dry, a condition would have resulted more dreadful than the bullets of the savages could create.

Great pressure was brought to bear on the south southwest of the garrison. The long government barn to the south (3) and the suttler store (20) to the southwest, fell into the hands of the enemy from, inability to extend a line for their protection. These buildings afforded shelter to the savages who were to change their plan of battle by making a furious attack, to be followed by an assault on the southwest angle of the fort. McGrew was ordered to throw a shell into the suttler store for the purpose of firing it, and in this was successful with his second shot.

The savages themselves about this time fired the barn. In furtherance of Little Crow's desperate attempt on the south-southwest of the garrison, the persistent force at the north-northeast which up to this time (about 4 o'clock p. m.,) waged an incessant fire, was largely withdrawn out across the open country, to the north, to the head of a wooded ravine (23) leading, from a point half a mile west of the northwest angle of the fort, in a southerly direction to the Minnesota river. Down this wooded ravine hundreds of warriors passed to join

ONLY LIVING MEMBERS OF COMPANY B, FIFTH MINNESO-
TA, WHO DEFENDED FORT RIDGELY.—1, Christopher Boyer; 2, O.
G. Wall; 3, Lieut. T. P. Gere; 4, E. F. Nehrhood; 5, M. H. Wilson; 6, C.
M. Culver.   On these two pages (4 and 5) are shown the only known living
members of Company B, Fifth Minnesota Infantry Volunteers, who were defenders of Fort Ridgely during the Sioux Massacre. Of the 12 survivors the six on this
page were of the party of Lieut. T. P. Gere, who commanded Fort Ridgely August 18, 1862. (Pictures shown in groups are numbered from left to right.)

forces with those massing, for a superhuman effort upon the south-west angle (12), which, though the savages must subject themselves to far greater exposure here than at the northeast, was itself the weak spot of the garrison for lack of needed shelter.

McGrew passing down to the position of Jones, at the southwest angle, Jones being in charge of the post ordnance, conferred with that officer with regard to the movement of the savages on the west, and asked permission to use the 24-pound field-piece then in park, for the purpose of dropping a shell into the wooded valley to the west, in the supposed region of the savages. The result was far more fruitful of benefit than was anticipated. A second shell fell into the camp of the savages where the squaws, *papooses*, dogs and ponies were in hiding, and at which place the deflecting savages had, in their passage, con-gregated for a brief halt.

The detonations of the exploding shell were alone terrifying (as light ordnance was used in the short-range engagement that had en-sued for hours), but the destructive effects of the shell were also seri-ous in the extreme, and produced surprise and consternation among the Indians. The experiment was repeated, with a sweeping range, to excellent advantage. Undaunted however, and bent upon his one de-termination to take the fort, Little Crow concentrated his principal force at the southwest.

Jones and his support, the Renville Rangers, were under a merci-less fire from the savages, who had pressed forward to so short a range as to literally perforate every foot of exposure of the barricade and headquarters building (3), but this fire was heroically returned, and with telling effect. The fusillade had become general about the gar-rison again, as the preliminary step to an assault at the southwest, and when the musketry of the savages had reached a furious stage, Little Crow ordered his men to club their guns and rush in. This order the half-breeds of the Renville Rangers plainly heard and communicated to their officers. This was the most critical moment the garrison had experienced. A charge of the overwhelming numbers would have been irresistible.

To stagger the enemy at this supreme juncture was the only hope of the garrison. Jones had double-shotted his gun with canister, and bravely hazarding his life in the act, dealt a withering blow to the massed foe at short range, at the crucial moment, mowing a swath down through their ranks that sent terror to their hearts as they were in the act of leaping, like wild beasts to the charge. The Renville

Rangers followed with a galling volley and a challenge in the Sioux language, hurled defiantly: "Come on; we are ready for you!"

Bishop had used his gun to good effect at the southeast, and the garrison now rose supremely to the occasion and dealt its telling blows fast and furious. The savages hesitated, wavered and recoiled, and though they fought on until night, could not again be nerved to the point of charging.

But the garrison had reached its last desperate extremity. It was on the brink of collapse through exhaustion of its supply of ammunition for the small arms of the men who had fought so gallantly. The guns in use were all muzzle-loading. There was powder available by opening spherical case shot, and fortunately caps for exploding it, but there were neither bullets nor lead of which to make them. Human resource was put to its test. The limited supply of small iron rods in the government blacksmith shop was resorted to, with which to prolong the struggle until all possible means of resistance should cease. These rods of iron were cut into slugs three-fourths of an inch in length, and a corps of nimble-fingered workers under the direction of Mrs. Dr. Muller set to manufacturing cartridges. With these (and their whistling challenge was terrifying,) the fight was continued until, as night closed in, the savages withdrew, with a howl of rage, but fairly vanquished.

But had the attack been prolonged, or had the foe returned to renew it, the garrison must inevitably have been lost.

No mind can justly conceive of, or pen faithfully describe, the mental and physical strain endured from this hour on by the garrison—a strain that burned as by a living fire, its burden into every soul. No sign of response had been made to the call of the 18th, for assistance from Fort Snelling and St. Paul. The world without was dead to the beleaguered fort. Surrounded, menaced and harassed by a desperate foe, all communication was extinct beyond the picket-lines. The officers and men had fought valiantly, and while their ranks were being gradually depleted, they would still bid haughty defiance to the hosts of the Dakota chieftain; but the exhaustion of their ammunition, except for ordnance, had reduced them to the last straits of desperation.

Under cover of night they could take the risk of fighting their way to safety down the Minnesota valley, but they could not abandon, neither could they take along, their burden of three hundred helpless refugees. If these must perish, then the soldiers must perish with them—must be the first to fall before the club and the knife, for the final struggle must be hand-to-hand. This was the firm resolution of the gallant men who had repelled heroically the savage foe whose hands were reeking with blood, and who placed the taking of Fort Ridgely above every other ambition.

The garrison could not know, unfortunately, that Little Crow's retreat into the dark valley as the sable mantle of night enveloped his vanquished host, signalised his departure from the fort forever. Unfortunately, it could not know this, I say, instead of relaxing, vigil must now, if possible, be greater than before, with the defence of the fort depending upon the cannon, the half-dozen rounds of slug-iron cartridges per man, and the bayonet.

And so, the strain, testing man's ability to retain his reason, continued for still four and a half days longer, or for a total of nine days.

At last, on the morning of August 27th, unheralded, Col. Samuel McPhail and William R. Marshall rode into the garrison at the head of one hundred and seventy-five mounted citizen-soldiers, and the long siege was raised, the reinforcements coming from St. Peter under cover of night, and thus escaping detection or attack. (I have searched unavailingly for the names of the men who raised the siege, for they are worthy of perpetuation in these pages.)

The defenders of the garrison, who had borne up for days from sheer force of will, and who were now relieved from the great and long-endured strain, had not realised their utterly jaded condition until their burdens were assumed by those who brought relief, and they soon gave way to the restful stupor that stole like a dream over their exhausted senses.

★★★★★★

Captain Gere, (a lieutenant during the siege, of Fort Ridgely) concluding an account of the long siege, has said: "It was a battle on the part of the garrison to *prevent a charge* by the savages, which, had it been made, could hardly have failed, as Little Crow seemed confident, to result in the destruction of the garrison and the consequent horrible massacre of its 300 refugees. It is but truth to add that no man in the garrison failed to do his duty, and that, worn by fatigue and suspense, and exhausted by lots of sleep, to the end every man was at his post, bravely meeting whatever danger confronted him. The conspicuous gallantry of the artillerists was the theme of general praise, and the great value of their services was conceded by all, while the active and intelligent support that rendered their work possible, is entitled to no less credit . . . . While the withdrawal of the

Indians on the 22nd terminated the fighting at Fort Ridgely, the weary garrison could not be aware that such would be the case, nor for a moment relax its vigilance; hence the forces continued to occupy the positions to which they had by this time become accustomed."

******

Fort Ridgely Never Surprised by the Sioux

Once for all, let it be forever known that Fort Ridgely was never surprised by the Sioux. Many writers, taking their cue from some sensationally-inclined word-painter of the early day, have pictured Little Crow's dashing demons in the act of taking the fort unawares. To the credit of the vigilance of the officers and men, there was never a moment from the day of the beginning of the massacre at the Redwood Agency up to the end of the exciting and perilous ten days' siege, when the savages could have surprised Fort Ridgely. Pickets were at all times posted and a close watch kept upon the movements of the enemy.

Little Crow at one time sought to draw the forces from the fort by a ruse shrewdly conceived, and in event of success there would have been a possible surprise from the opposite side of the garrison, but because of vigilance and of the well-known treachery of the Sioux, no opportunity for surprise was for a moment given. The attacks upon the fort were no doubt intended by the Indians as surprises, insofar as they could make them such from the sheltering woods and ravines surrounding the fort except on the northern exposure, but they were in no measure surprises in the sense of taking the fort unawares.

Daring Service of Messengers Sturgis and McLain

In all that has ever been written of Fort Ridgely's part in the Sioux Massacre, no account has heretofore been published of the wild ride of the man who bore the dispatches from Lieutenant Thomas P. Gere, commandant at Fort Ridgely on August 18, 1862, to Governor Alexander Ramsey at St. Paul, announcing the outbreak of the Sioux at the Redwood Agency, the disaster to Marsh and his detachment the afternoon of that day at Redwood Ferry, and the terrible deeds already being committed in the surrounding settlements. At the close of the civil war William J. Sturgis, the young soldier who made the ride for the life of the frontier, disappeared into the sea of civil life to work out the problems the future held for each soldier whose calling had been happily changed at Appomattox.

Sturgis' famous ride was a mere incident in that day of great deeds and great achievements, and was scarcely thought of, and he finally drifted to the region of the Rocky Mountains, where he rarely if ever met a comrade of his immediate service in the army. He was not given to writing for the press, and having taken up farming, lived a comparatively retired life. When the writer assumed the labour of gathering the scattered fragments of history that should be preserved ta Minnesota annals, he searched widely for each surviving member of the original Company B of the Fifth Regiment, then only a dozen or so in number.

This work covered a period of two years before the last man was found. Locating Sturgis, he was importuned for the story of his ride, but while he said the incidents of it were as fresh in his mind as at the time of his flight in the blackness of that August night, still he would have to await a period of leisure in which to take the matter up. Sturgis was now seventy-two years old, and as time was so rapidly depleting our ranks, and as much had already been lost by no effort having been made to preserve many incidents of value, a compliance with the request from Sturgis was insisted upon, and on the 4th day of January, 1908, he wrote a personal letter in which he told to me his story, and while he was in his accustomed health at this time, death called him a month later.

Greater stress of circumstances rarely falls to human lot than hovered over Fort Ridgely on the night of August 18. As darkness set in at the close of that day, Lieutenant Gere, a boy of twenty years, found himself charged with the gravest of responsibilities. He had but twenty-four effective men, all told. Capt. Marsh had depleted the garrison when he marched out in the forenoon with the forty-six men, destined to the Redwood Ferry. Helpless refugees had poured into the fort all day, many mangled and bleeding, others half-naked and distracted with fear and grief, while it was known the work of carnage was rapidly spreading in the surrounding settlements. Great hopes were buttressed upon Marsh's safe and speedy return with his precious detachment.

Darkness brought increased anxiety. Except in the quarters where the refugees were housed, a death-like stillness reigned throughout the garrison,—waiting, waiting in suspense. The crickets, on that summer night, were the only cheerful companions of the pickets, posted by

Lieutenant Gere in person to make assurance of proper dispositions doubly sure. The gathering pall of night had overwhelmed the anxious, expectant garrison, when an alarm came from the southwestern angle of the sparsely guarded picket line, and now came the staggering news that Marsh was dead, and that Interpreter Quinn and half the noble detachment of forty-six men had been ambushed and killed at the Redwood Ferry. Privates William B. Hutchinson and James Dunn, who were of the detachment and who, with Sergeant Bishop and eleven others under him, had escaped with their lives, and were on their way to the fort, were sent ahead by Bishop when within a few miles of the post to apprise the garrison of the disaster. Bishop's progress being impeded by the fact that his men were obliged to carry a badly wounded comrade, Ole Svendson.

The news was horrifying, and the bloody work had but just commenced. Unmoved by the terrible blow that came with the news of the day's disaster, or by the perilous predicament in which he found himself and those under him in pitiable numbers, the boy officer wrote dispatches to Governor Alexander Ramsey at St. Paul, the commandant at Fort Snelling, and incidentally to Lieutenant Culver, accompanied by Indian Agent Galbraith, Lieutenant Gorman and Sergeant McGrew, then at St. Peter, apprising all of the predicament, and calling for assistance.

Private William J. Sturgis was asked to impress for his use the best horse in the garrison, and to bear away these dispatches in all haste, with St. Paul as his destination. Responding like a true soldier, Sturgis received his dispatches, sprung into the saddle, and plunged away in the darkness at a wild pace. Down through the dark valley, and out on the highlands beyond Fort Creek, and away he sped. His horse was one driven into the fort during the day attached to the St. Peter stage (the stage that brought the 71,000 in gold to the fort.) The animal was thus familiar with the road, and headed homeward, but twelve miles of flight had completely exhausted him.

Overtaking a peddler flying for his life, Sturgis dismounted and joined him, the peddler having a good team. The tidings from the fort put new fear into the soul of the tradesman, and his efforts were redoubled. The peddler was making for Henderson, while owing to dispatches that must be delivered at that place, Sturgis must reach St. Peter on his journey. The men separated after an exciting ride of ten miles, each going his way. Sturgis remembered that there was a settler's house at this point, where our company, on its march to Fort Ridgely

SURVIVORS OF COMPANY B WHO WERE AT REDWOOD
FERRY AUG. 18, 1862.—1, Sergeant John F. Bishop; 2, W. H. Blodgett;
3, Levi Carr; 4, W. B. Hutchinson; 5, Ole Svendson; 6, Stephen Van Buren.

The six survivors shown above were with Capt. Marsh at the Redwood Ferry,
August 18, 1862, when 24 out of 47 of Marsh's men were killed. After the death
of Marsh, a remnant of his detachment was conducted skilfully under great diffi-
culties to Fort Ridgely by that efficient officer and always capable soldier, Sergeant
John F. Bishop, of above group.

several months previously, had halted to rest and lunch. He was thus enabled to easily find the house, and pounding upon the door soon brought forth from his bed a dazed settler, for the disturbance was at the dead of night. Sturgis assured the settler of the frightful conditions above, and demanded that he be taken to St. Peter with all possible haste. The thoroughly aroused and frightened man responded with energy, and soon the dispatch-bearer was being hurried pell-mell over roads none too good at best, and none too visible at night.

On, on, did the messenger urge the speeding of horses, restive under his grave responsibility that had to do with human life. Too well, knew he, that the breaking dawn would prove the signal to the crazed Sioux for extended scenes of carnage. Too well knew he, that unsuspecting settlers were dreaming, in ignorance of the butchery that would mark, their homes ere the drowse of slumber had released them. Every fibre of his body was tense. Every faculty of his nature was alert.

Aurora's first delicate shades were faintly gathering along the eastern horizon as Sturgis entered St. Peter, at a few minutes past 3 o'clock on the morning of Tuesday, August 19.

Unbelievable rumours had preceded him, and while they were traceable to no authentic source, they had been sufficiently sensational to keep St. Peter awake and in a state of frenzy all night: Among prominent citizens of the place, Sturgis found Lieut. Culver, Sergeant McGrew, Lieut. Gorman and Major Galbraith up and anxiously awaiting tidings from the north. Recognising the young dispatch-bearer, and knowing that his presence among them was of the gravest importance, he was quickly surrounded by an eager-faced, impatient throng. Sturgis gave St. Peter at this moment its first awful news of the Massacre. Despite the vague rumours that had filtered through from above, the town for the moment was stricken speechless by the frightful story and the impending dangers at which it hinted.

But the messenger's thoughts were upon the further discharge of his important duty, and he at once set about obtaining transportation for the continuance of his flight. Pandemonium now reigned in St. Peter, and he had the greatest difficulty in securing a horse. Personal safety was the thought uppermost in the minds of the inhabitants, and in the "to arms, to arms" tumult Sturgis was helpless. He sought Sheriff R. W. Tomlinson, appealed to him in the name of necessity, and not in vain, for the sheriff quickly hitched up his own team, and taking Sturgis aboard, drove to Le Sueur, making the twelve miles in just one hour. At Le Sueur, Sturgis obtained a livery horse, which he rode with all possible speed to Shakopee.

The exhausted animal was here discarded, and another obtained which bore him to the ferry, a well-known crossing of the Minnesota River in that day. The last horse obtained was a poor one, and at the Ferry was completely winded. Here, however, Sturgis found two men just leaving with a team for St. Paul. His horse having failed him, this was his only opportunity of proceeding. He stated his case and asked to be taken aboard. The men flatly refused to accede to him. He repeated his request in the nature of a demand, with the threat that he would take the team if further refused or delayed. He thus became an unwelcomed passenger. Recognising the justice of his intrusion however, the men soon yielded friendship to him, and exerted themselves in his behalf.

Arriving at Fort Snelling on the journey to St. Paul at 3 o'clock on the afternoon of Tuesday, after a ride of eighteen hours from Fort Ridgely, and one testing the metal of Sturgis, the dispatch bearer proceeded hastily to post headquarters, where, fortunately, in addition to the commandant, he found Governor Ramsey and Adjutant General Malmros in consultation with the military authorities regarding operations in the south and the rendezvous of recruits being assembled at Snelling. Sturgis delivered his dispatches with little ceremony. For the instant the governor and the commandant were stunned with the shocking intelligence of the massacre conveyed to them from Lieutenant Gere. They compared and reread the dispatches to make sure they had not interpreted more appalling disaster from them than they really contained.

The visible shock gave way quickly to a determination to act, and by 6 o'clock of that evening, a part of the Sixth Minnesota Vol. Infantry had embarked on a steamboat, bound up the Minnesota River, then regularly navigated. Sturgis accompanied the detachment as far as Shakopee, where he had left a horse. At the supper table in a Shakopee hotel he made the acquaintance of two men who had friends on the frontier, for whom they had the greatest concern. These men had horses, and it was agreed that the two should mount after supper and proceed toward the front. They rode to Henderson, where they found much excitement. They resolved to form a company of mounted men, and proceed to Fort Ridgely with all possible haste. They spent the night in perfecting their plans, and by morning had forty resolute men enlisted for a forward movement.

Ex-Indian Agent Joseph R. Brown was at Henderson, and dissuaded many of the volunteers at the last moment from venturing upon what he regarded as an impracticable undertaking. A number withdrew from the organisation under his influence. This discouraged others, and but six men finally remained true to the original determination—Sturgis, his two acquaintances from Shakopee and three determined Henderson men, Sturgis feeling the greatest concern for his comrades at Fort Ridgely. They proceeded, but out on the fort road, four or five miles from Henderson, the six resolute men met a half-breed just coming in from the Yellow Medicine country. He assured the horsemen they could never reach Fort Ridgely alive, and gave a graphic account of the horrible deeds he had witnessed for fifty miles, giving the latest information from the scenes of the massacre.

Reluctantly the men returned to Henderson, and Sturgis proceeded back to acquaint Gen. Sibley, in command of the reinforcements, with the information he had grained from the half-breed. Much to the disappointment of Sturgis, who had ridden without rest or sleep in the discharge of his duties to hasten the progress of assistance, he had to ride back to Belle Plaine, so slowly had the movement of troops dragged. Finding Gen. Sibley at the hotel in Belle Plaine, Sturgis acquainted him with all he had the morning of that day learned from the upper country. General Sibley asked Sturgis if he could, without rest, bear some dispatches to Gov. Ramsey, at St. Paul, and was assured by the efficient dispatch-bearer he would do his best.

This was at nightfall of Wednesday. Sturgis found difficulty in getting transportation for his new task, but was finally given an order by Gen. Sibley to take the sheriff's horse, that officer being then in town. The night was very dark and the roads strange, but Sturgis reached Shakopee at 4 o'clock on Thursday morning, August 21. Boats ran regularly as far up as Shakopee, and the boat for St. Paul would leave at 6 that morning. Leaving orders to be called promptly at 5:30, Sturgis threw himself upon a couch and had his first continuous hour-and-a-half of sleep since the previous Sunday night. He was called in time to eat his breakfast and catch the boat. He reached the governor's office at the state capitol in St. Paul at about 10 a. m., of that day.

Delivering this, his second dispatch, the governor asked in an impatient tone as to the procuress made by the troops, and rose from his seat and paced the floor when told Gen. Sibley was still at Belle Plaine the previous evening, where he had been since the evening of the first day out. There were no telephones in that day, and, asking Sturgis to remain in his office, the governor sent a messenger out after William R. Marshall, who came promptly. There was an animated discussion of the situation, in which Governor Ramsey expressed himself with much emphasis. Marshall seemed to fit the occasion uniquely, and the seeds were sown here that matured in his military advancement later.

It was the request of Governor Ramsey that Mr. Marshall go to the front as his, the governor's representative, and placing in Sturgis' hands dispatches for Gen. Sibley, Marshall and himself were shortly away for the front, arriving at Shakopee at night. They drove thence to Belle Plaine, over a rough and muddy road, in intense darkness, arriving at Gen. Sibley's headquarters early in the morning of Friday, August 22, Sturgis delivered his dispatches to Gen. Sibley, and left Sibley and Marshall in consultation.

The sequel of their conference was not long to be waited for. Marshall joined Sturgis, and they sat down at the breakfast table in a Belle Plaine hotel, and as they ate, the blare of trumpets was heard, and before they had finished, the advance guard was in motion, moving briskly through the principal street of the town. Marshall and Sturgis remained together until they arrived at St. Peter. Here Sturgis, for the first time since the night of Sunday, August 17, or nearly a week previously, removed his clothing and slept in a bed. He remained with the troops, and was with the first detachment to reach Fort Ridgely on the morning of Wednesday, August 27, where the beleaguered garrison, famished and worn, embattled and oppressed by a foe in whose heart mercy was an unknown element, received its long hoped for relief.

Ten days of fighting, vigil and suffering had reduced the garrison to a pitiable condition, and to be among the first to raise the siege was a matter of great satisfaction to the dispatch-bearer and to have participated in the joyous greetings of the besieged garrison and the men who had ridden all night to relieve our sufferings, a celebration no one has ever attempted to describe, was the privilege of a lifetime, and reward enough for all the hardships Sturgis had endured.

No less notable than the wild flight of Sturgis, was that of Corporal James C. McLain, the messenger who was sent on a no less perilous ride in pursuit of Lieutenant Sheehan, who left Fort Ridgely the previous day (Sunday) with his detachment of fifty men of Co. C, and who was long miles away on his return march to Fort Ripley, on the upper Mississippi. Bravely and dramatically McLain dashed away to perform one of the most gallant feats in the history of the massacre, but no account of the incidents of his long ride through a country overrun by the Sioux was ever preserved, and as he was years ago "gathered to his fathers," no account is now obtainable of the incidents of his valorous deeds.

The order detailing McLain for this service was one of the last official acts of Capt. Marsh before leaving Fort Ridgely on his fated mission to the Redwood Ferry on the morning of August 18. McLain's ride was by daylight, giving him some advantages, and yet increasing the dangers that beset him. He overtook Lieutenant Sheehan after a ride of forty-two miles, near Glencoe, and immediately started on the return to Fort Ridgely with Sheehan's detachment, marching all night and making his eighty-four mile journey without a moment's rest.

Noble Men and Women Among the Refugees

While the refugees who came into the fort from the surrounding settlements consisted mainly of women and children, not a few men were among their number, and among these men, as among the women, were those of true Spartan courage, and to their noble endeavours Minnesota owes a debt of everlasting gratitude. There were those who were cowed into a state of submissiveness that rendered them an impediment rather than a benefit to the distressed garrison. But the few of whom this may be written had been mentally dazed by the frightful experiences through which they had passed before escaping the bloodstained hands of the Sioux. Their peaceful and happy homes, in an hour of unexpected danger, had been fallen upon by savages who were merciless, and who found their greatest pleasure in their deeds of extremest cruelty.

It is needless to depict what many of these refugees had witnessed and experienced; and the wonder is not so much that they lost their virility and combativeness, as that they retained their reason. But there were noble specimens of manhood among the refugees, whose dogged courage and endurance contributed much to the successful defence of Fort Ridgely, these men, during the hours of conflict, without special or separate organisation, seeking the point where their services as individuals seemed most required, there to resist heroically and to share the dangers of a noble defence.

Many of these people or their descendants still live (1909) in the immediate vicinity of the old fort, and have proven their worth for sturdiness in civil life as they demonstrated it in the perilous days of the Sioux Massacre. The names of these people, men and women, will grow brighter as time advances and the world the better appreciates their heroic deeds for the State and humanity.

The artist's plate in the camera receives the beautiful image, imprinted upon it by the heavens' radiant gleam or the lightning's flash, but the image itself appears not until time shall have changed the conditions. So it is with the character and services of the refugees who helped to save Fort Ridgely, and for whom reverence increases as the years roll by; and while this book, in its treatment of the early stages of the massacre, has dealt largely with the achievements of companies B and C of the Fifth Minnesota and of the Renville Rangers, the splendid services of Sergeant John Jones of the regular army, and of gunner John C. Whipple, it is not unmindful of the glorious part the refugees had in the triumphant defence of the key to the Minnesota frontier, in an ordeal whose tests will never be fully told.

It is regrettable as a matter of history that the names of all who sought the protection of Fort Ridgely during the Sioux Massacre, were not preserved, but the making of such a record was of little moment at a time when the lives of all at the garrison hung tremblingly in the balance. To stay the savage tide that surged determinedly for the overthrow of Fort Ridgely, was a task of the gravest moment. Every hour was one of danger and expectancy. Every moment increased the tax laid upon human endurance. Those known to have reached the fort, and who nobly participated in its defence, are the following:

William Anderson	Dennis O'Shea
Robert Baker (killed)	Joseph Overbaugh
Werner Boesch	B. F. Pratt
Louis Brisbois	J. C. Ramsey
William Butler	B. H. Randall
Clement Cardinal	John Resoft
M. A. Dailey	Adam Rieke
J. W. DeCamp	Georgre Rieke
Frank Diepolder	Heinrich Rieke (died)
Henry Diepolder	Victor Rieke
Alfred Dufrene	Louis Robert
J. C. Fenske (w'd)	Louis Sharon
Jo. J. Frazer	Chris Schlumberger
T. J. Galbraith	Gustav Stafford
E. A. C. Hatch	Joshua Sweet
Patrick Heffron	Louis Thiele
George P. Hicks	Nikolas Thinnes

Keran Horan	Onesime Vannasse
John Hose	A. J. Van Voorhes
Joseph Koehler	John Walter
Louis La Croix	J. C. Whipple
James B. Magner	C. G. Wykoff
John Magner	Xavier Zolner
Pierre Martelle	*WOMEN.*
Oliver Martelle	Anna Boesch
John Meyer	Kenney Bradford
John Nairn	Elizabeth M. Dunn
Margaret King Hern	Mrs. E. Pereau
Mary A. Heffron	Wilhelmina Randall
Eliza Muller	Valencia J. Reynolds
Juliette McAllister	Mary Rieke
Mary D. Overbaugh	Mrs. R. Schmahl
Agnes Overbaugh	Mrs. Spencer
Julia Peterson	Julia Sweet
Mrs. E. Picard	Emily J. West

New Ulm

The siege raised, our first news came of what had transpired about us, particularly at our nearest neighbouring town, New Ulm, seventeen miles below. We had surmised an attack on New Ulm. We had witnessed during the siege, on different days, a movement of savages around the north and south of us, like the drift of a mighty river, floating as spectral figures over the great prairies for long intervals. Where could they be concentrating, except at New Ulm? But beyond this there was nothing upon which to base a suspicion. Now it was learned that Little Crow's forces who had held their council under the eyes of the fort on the morning after the outbreak at the agency, had fallen upon defenceless New Ulm on the afternoon of that day, August 19th, producing consternation, as the town was utterly unorganised and wholly unprepared for such a visitation.

Fortunately, Lieutenant Gere's message forwarded through Courier Sturgis, reached St. Peter before daylight of the 19th, requesting the immediate return of the Renville Rangers and confirming the gravest suspicions of a general Sioux uprising. Judge Charles B. Flandrau, one of Minnesota's ablest and best of the distinguished men who came into the Territory from 1845, to 1850, lived about a mile out of St. Peter. He was not only able and resourceful mentally, but had practical knowledge of Indian character. Learning of the uprising, he set out without a moment's delay to organise for relief and defence. Gathering a company about him, he started to intercept the enemy and give him battle as a check to his progress while defences were being more extensively organised.

When his command left St. Peter, there was no fixed destination, but both Fort Ridgeley and New Ulm were undoubtedly hard pressed, add to one or the other of these points it was expected the command would go. Fortunately, New Ulm being the nearer, that point was made, Judge Flandrau and his men reaching the town while it was defending itself at great disadvantage from an attack by the Indians, who were not strong in numbers in this attack, but who were numerous enough to threaten the taking of the town, a number of citizens having been killed and several houses fired by the savages.

Judge Flandrau had never received military training, but by the saving grace of good sound sense, he was admirably equipped for the great work that awaited him at New Ulm. An able lawyer, a keen student of human nature, a good organiser, and a man of dauntless courage, he met every demand of the emergency. Several companies of hastily organised citizen-soldiery centred at New Ulm on the urgent call sent out by Judge Flandrau, who plainly said the town could only be saved by accessions from the country south and east.

These organisations were headed by men well suited to the work before them, who ably seconded Judge Flandrau in putting the distressed town on a defensive footing. Little Crow's desperate attack on Fort Ridgely, on the 22nd, was most fortunate for New Ulm, as an indispensable day was gained by Flandrau, his lieutenants, and the inhabitants of the town to prepare for what must inevitably come—a second attack by the Indians.

The day also enabled Flandrau to send parties into the surrounding settlements, who gathered up scores of people whose lives were momentarily in danger, and who, had they been left in the settlements, would have fallen an easy prey on the following day, to the hundreds of marauding savages who raided the entire surrounding country. The inhabitants of New Ulm were almost exclusively Germans, who, characteristic of their race, were a quiet, industrious, peace-loving people, and the unheralded catastrophe that had burst upon them so suddenly, had overwhelmed them with dismay.

But every possible defensive precaution had been taken during the 22nd, so that on the following day the town was prepared to offer strong resistance to the furious attack of the savages, which began between the hours of 9 and 10, of the forenoon of Saturday, August 23rd. The defensive force under Judge Flandrau numbered about three hundred effective men, neither well nor uniformly armed, however. The non-combatants of the town numbered from 1,200 to 1,500 people, principally women and children of the village and of the country immediately surrounding. The attack of the savages was furious, and made with the confident belief that success was to reward their efforts.

The signs of the morning portending a fight, Judge Flandrau moved his forces well out, quite encircling the town. Speaking of the opening, Judge Flandrau has said:

> At nearly 10 o'clock in the morning, the body of Indians began to move toward us, first slowly, and then with considerable rapidity. Their advance upon the sloping prairie in the bright sunlight was a very fine spectacle, and to such inexperienced soldiers as we all were, intensely exciting. When within about one and a half miles of us the mass began to expand like a fan, and increase in the velocity of its approach, and continued this movement until within about double rifle-shot, when it had covered our entire front. Then the savages uttered a terrific yell and came down upon us like the wind. I awaited the first discharge with great anxiety, as it seemed to me to yield was certain destruction. The yell unsettled the men a little, and just as the rifles begun to crack, they fell back along the whole line.

★★★★★★

> Judge Flandrau modestly places the number of Indians in the attack at 650, basing his information on reports from unfriendly half-breeds subsequent to the engagements. This would mean two to one of Flandrau's force. A force of four to one would hardly have given Judge Flandrau and his brave men a harder fight than was the second Battle of New Ulm, lasting nine or ten hours; and this is a safer criterion by which to judge of the numbers of the enemy than would be the solicited estimates of half-breeds who were in the fight with the savages. An Indian invariably belies his strength and his casualties.

★★★★★

The most unfortunate part of this movement was, that in falling back from the open field, buildings were passed in the outskirts of town, of which the Indians were quick to take possession, and from the cover of which they became doubly troublesome and effective. Realising the danger rapidly threatening, Judge Flandrau and a number of brave fellows now charged up the hill, down which the forces had fallen back, and the movement was taken up with a shout that effectually checked the progress the Indians were making.

From this on the men fought aggressively and confidently, and the contest rasped hotly for several hours, with varying advantages. The Indians at length encircled the entire town, and pressed every advantage with great vigour. Their position on the bluff was a commanding one, and this they held persistently. Getting a footing in the lower part of town, the Indians began the firing of buildings at the foot of the main street of the village. This threatened to be the utter undoing of the noble defenders of New Ulm.

This offensive movement was one the defenders could not stay or stem. The wind proved an evil element in addition, as it blew so as to drive the smoke and flames up the main street. Under cover of the smoke the savages pushed their way up the street, and in combatting them the forces of Flandrau exposed themselves to a hot fire from the enemy on the bluff. The defenders now fought inch by inch and foot by foot to gain ground that would enable them to check the progress of the conflagration, and in this, by indomitable perseverance and hard fighting, succeeded.

After the conflict had raged for hours the defenders became hardened to battle, and grew to be in every way better soldiers. They had learned the tactics of the savages, and had become inured to their demonic yells, which at first were terrifying. Not only were the lives of hundreds of helpless women, children and aged and infirm, in the hands of these valiant men, but far-reaching consequences to the whole border were involved in the contest, and as the conflict lengthened, the defenders more and more forced the fighting, until at length, with nightfall, the savages withdrew, defeated, for they had failed of their purpose.

This battle was one of the most important events in the history of Minnesota, and will ever hold a distinctive place among the early-day frontier tragedies of the state; and New Ulm's distinction is unique, in that it is shared by no other Minnesota town.

After dark a new and less extended defensive line was formed and barricaded, and all buildings outside of this line, some forty in number, were burned. Thus the town, for the first time, was in good condition to resist attack, and the wisdom of this precautionary measure was apparent when the savages renewed the attack the following morning, only to abandon it definitely by noon.

Pestilence threatening, and ammunition and provisions becoming well exhausted, it was resolved to abandon New Ulm, and on Monday, August 25th, the venture of successfully reaching Mankato was made. In addition to the women and children, were eighty wounded men. To remove these a train of 153 wagons was made up, and the procession, which Judge Flandrau has described as the "most heartrending ever witnessed in America," set out on its sad and perilous mission, reaching its destination in safety. Though for a time abandoned, New Ulm was not again the scene of conflict or important molestation. The moral effect of a strong force of troops moving up the Minnesota valley to the scenes of the massacre, though the troops were not yet within striking distance of the enemy, exerted a salutary influence over the Indians, who had been roughly handled at Fort Ridgely and New Ulm, and who were beginning to sorrowfully abandon the hope of re-entering the Mississippi valley.

Birch Coulie

On Thursday morning, August 28th, Col. H. H. Sibley entered Fort Ridgely at the head of a column of about 1,200 men. These with Col. McPhail's men already at the fort, and accessions that followed rapidly, made up an army sufficiently largo to warrant offensive operations, though the equipment of these troops was grossly inefficient.

Preliminary to other operations, a detachment was sent out on Sunday, August 31st, with the Lower Agency as the objective point. This was still, as of old, the rendezvous of the Indians. Mainly, the expedition had for its purpose the interment of the men who fell at the ferry and the agency, and of others, and to discover, if possible, the body of Captain Marsh. The detachment for this purpose was composed of Co. A, Sixth Minnesota Volunteer Infantry, Captain Hiram P. Grant, and the Cullen Guards, mounted, Captain Joseph Anderson. The detachment was under the general command and Guidance of Major Joseph R. Brown, a noted Indian trader and frontiersman, and embraced about one hundred and fifty men, exclusive of seventeen teamsters, who had charge of as many wagons containing equipage.

In burying the scores of corpses that had been exposed for ten days in a summer's sun, the little expedition put in a day of trying experiences by the time of reaching the Redwood Ferry, and went into camp at night, (having seen no sign of Indians) in the Minnesota bottoms, just east of the agency.

Monday morning, September 1st, Captain Anderson crossed the Minnesota, and after burying the dead at the agency, proceeded up the west side of the river, while Captain Grant scouted about the country to the eastward, the two detachments rejoining each other at night at Birch Coulie, a location than which there could have been nothing more unfortunate from a military standpoint. The site had Major Brown's approval, and there being confidence in his judgment, he having lived for years among the Sioux, and knowing every rod of ground of the surrounding country, the men bivouacked, knowing they were in the enemy's country, but little suspecting the frightful catastrophe that awaited them.

The location of the camp, as stated, was unfavourable in the extreme, being in a depression where in event of an attack the men would be at the mercy of the enemy.

Company B of the Fifth, which for months had occupied Fort Ridgely, now that so large a body of troops had arrived, left the quarters and went into camp in tents northwest of the garrison. The writer remembers well, while lying on the ground about daylight on the morning of September 1st, of hearing the rattle of musketry. This was heard and commented on by many, and indicated plainly that Captains Grant and Anderson were hotly engaged by the enemy. It was not supposed the firing could be fifteen miles away, as it really was, Mother Earth being a better telephone than she was given credit for.

A relief, column was at once organised to go to the assistance of the Grant-Anderson detachment. This consisted of Col. Samuel McPhail, with fifty horsemen, Major Robert McLarren with one hundred infantrymen, and Captain Mark Hendrix with a mountain howitzer and the necessary gunners to man it. The whereabouts of Grant and Anderson could only be surmised, as no word had come from them since the day of their departure, but they could be located within reasonable bounds; so, the relief column need not, and did not, go far astray.

The movements of the relief column in fact had been detected by the savages, and a strong force of Little Crow's warriors was thrown against the McPhail-McLarren forces, to prevent their reaching Birch Coulie, which the Indians knew must soon fall into their hands if relief could be prevented. The relief detachment having a howitzer made excellent use of it in many ways besides pouring shot into the ranks of the Indians who had thrown themselves across the path of the soldiers.; The sound of the cannon gave heart to the desperately oppressed force at Birch Coulie, three miles distant, struck terror to the hosts of Little Crow, and admonished Col. Sibley that a hot fight was in progress.

Lieutenant Sheehan, the hero of Fort Ridgely, had accompanied the relief column, and as the commander of the expedition found the savage hosts too strong to make farther progress possible, dispatched Sheehan with a request to Col. Sibley for reinforcements. Sheehan, of all men in the relief expedition, was best fitted by tact, courage and experience for the hazardous mission, and while his horse was twice wounded by the savages, made the ride successfully.

Col. Sibley, in response, at once put his entire force on the march, leaving Fort Ridgely at sundown on Tuesday evening, September 2nd. He reinforced the relief column in the night, his own cannon, in charge of Sergeant Jones, and that of Captain Hendrix, being used for signal purposes in uniting the two bodies.

The exact location of the Grant-Anderson force not being known, and the night being very dark. Col. Sibley awaited daylight where he found McPhail and McLarren, moving his entire force forward at dawn. A march of three miles led to the horrifying death-trap that passed into history as Birch Coulie, a place that furnished one of the bloodiest pages of the Sioux Massacre, as well as one of the grandest exhibitions of courage and endurance, under the most adverse conditions, ever recorded.

At dawn on Tuesday morning, September 2nd, the camp of Captains Grant and Anderson was surprised and fiercely attacked at short range under cover of the brush and hills surrounding. The effect upon the little command was appalling. The rain of bullets dealt consternation and death to the unprotected camp, throwing officers and men into the wildest confusion. The storm increased as the savages warmed up to their work, and emboldened, forced their way to newer and nearer points of vantage, their yells and shouts and the beating of *tom-toms* adding to the terrifying din, amid which many men and horses went to earths It seemed that not a living creature could long survive the almost blinding cross-fire to which the men were subjected.

Horses, frightfully wounded, grave painful expression to their agonies. There were ninety of these noble beasts in the little camp, and nearly all were down, dead or groaning in death agonies, within thirty minutes after the firing of the first shot by the savages. One-fourth of the men had already fallen, dead or wounded, and yet the fire grew hotter.

The panorama surrounding the men was such as to daze their senses. The belching guns of the savages formed an encircling line of fire, while the exultant Indians, their writhing bodies swaying and leaping, made tame in comparison the *Inferno* of Dante. The men must return the fire to prevent a charge, which would have swept the little remnant of soldiery from existence in a twinkling.

If they would withstand the awful storm of bullets, they must dig, for without trenches there was no protection, and they *did* dig, using the three spades and one shovel available, and their swords, bayonets, pocket-knives and fingers, even. But hours passed before fairly adequate protection was secured, many a man's pit proving to be his grave. All day long the pitiless rain of shot fell upon the helpless men from all sides, imprisoning them in their little trenches from which they bravely fought beneath a scorching sun without food or drink or relief or the ability in any known way to communicate a knowledge of their distress beyond the cordon of savages, that, like the coils of a serpent, held them in its deadly folds.

On and on, hour by hour, the battle raged, until darkness relaxed in a degree only, the savage grasp. The roar of the howitzer of Captain Hendrix had been heard for hours, but its sounds had become a mystery rather than a hope. Night came none too soon, for the ammunition with which to resist longer was practically exhausted. The long vigil, surrounded by the dead and the moaning, helpless wounded, whose entreaties were almost beyond human endurance, ended at dawn when Col. Sibley and his men rode into the slaughter-pen as the savages fell back among the protecting hills and valleys of the Minnesota.

The scenes that met the gaze of the relieving column can only be truly known to those who witnessed them, for language, in its process of evolution, has not as yet arrived at a stage in its development for the faithful portrayal of the uncanny spectacle that Col. Sibley looked upon in dumb amazement when he entered the camp. Judge J. J. Egan, then a boy, a volunteer for the service and the occasion, says, in writing of the events in which he participated from first to last at Birch Coulie:

> The scene presented in our camp was a sickening one. Twenty-three men, black and discoloured by the sun's rays, lay stark and dead in a small space; forty-five others, severely wounded, and groaning and crying for water; the carcasses of ninety dead horses lying about, and a stench intolerable emanating from the whole ground.

BIRCH COULIE and GOOD INDIAN Monuments at Morton, Minnestoa.

The tents of the camp were literally cut to pieces, while the wagons, riddled and splintered, told of the awful ordeal through which the survivors had passed.

Wood Lake and Camp Release

Following Birch Coulie came a period of inactivity at the fort, painful to the restless men who felt that valuable time was being wasted; but while Col. Sibley would never have gained fame as a dashing Indian campaigner, it is due to say that at this time he was poorly equipped for an aggressive movement. His men were good, but his equipment was poor in the extreme, and his means of transportation no better. Having as far as possible overcome these defects, just one month from the day of the outbreak, or on September 18th, the march was taken up for an offensive campaign, the entire force moving down to and across the Minnesota River by ferry, a mile from Fort Ridgely.

The command proceeded with great caution up the west side of the Minnesota, camping below the Redwood Agency on the afternoon of the second day. The fifth day out, the 22nd of September, Wood Lake was reached, a shallow body of water about two miles from the Yellow Medicine Agency. The following morning, there being no signs of a forward movement, a party of the Third Minnesota started with teams on a foraging expedition, and had proceeded nearly a mile in the direction of Yellow Medicine when they were fiercely attacked by a large force of Indians. Major A. E. Welch, commanding the Third, hastened with his remnant of a regiment, about 270 men in all, to the rescue of the foraging party, and became hotly engaged.

The fighting Renville Rangers could not keep out, and were soon in the midst of the conflict. But all this was unauthorized, and instead of supporting Welch, he was ordered to fall back to camp. He persisted in dealing a hot fire into the ranks of the enemy, and instead of retreating, sent word back to Col. Sibley that he could hold his ground, and asked to be reinforced. Col. Sibley then sent a peremptory order to fall back to camp. Welch, reluctantly yielding under orders, was hotly pressed by the exultant savages, and sustained serious loss in the retrograde movement, himself receiving a broken leg.

In this enforced retreat, made amid bitter curses on the part of the soldiers, it was necessary to cross a small creek, which flowed through a narrow, deep ravine. Taking advantage of this confusing hindrance, the Indians poured in a merciless fire, and it was here Welch received his serious wound, and that many of his men were killed or wounded, but the men, assisted by the Renville Rangers, were able to save their wounded from falling into the hands of the savages.

At last the Sixth and Seventh Minnesota men, chafing under restraint while their comrades were suffering unjustly, as they believed, were put into action, with their fighting spirit at fever heat. Lieutenant Colonel William R. Marshall, with his five companies of the Seventh, joined the Third and Renville Rangers in a gallant charge that sent the enemy flying. The Sixth and the artillery rendered effective assistance at various points, once the order was given, and all combined, gallantly passed the Battle of Wood Lake over to history with victory complete.

The march from Wood Lake was resumed on the 25th, a day having been spent at the scene of the battle to bury the dead and study the movements of the enemy. On Friday, September 26th, the command reached the Indian camp nearly opposite the point at which the Chippewa enters the Minnesota River. The friendly Indians had secured possession of the white captives taken by Little Crow during the massacre, the warrior chief now finding his time taken up with the serious matter of self-preservation. Immediately prior to this date stormy times had characterized the life of the savages. A powerful and vicious element, steeped in crime and dripping with innocent blood, was determined the captives, about 250 in number, should be massacred.

Another strong element, though in the minority, bravely stood between the fiends incarnate and the helpless women and children who lived in mortal fear of annihilation. They had suffered agonies indescribable and indignities revolting and unspeakable, by the side of which death would have been merciful. The sound of cannon at Wood Lake, to them as sweet as aeolian strains, told of the near approach of their deliverers, and gave them a new interest in life; but they realised their increased dangers, now mingled with the first gleam of hope, and their suspense and mental anguish told frightfully on their endurance. Crushed in pride and spirit, exposed to the chill of rains and autumn winds, and compelled to live on food revolting to decent stomachs, there were no longer brave spirits among these unhappy people to encourage the weak, and the nearer deliverance came the greater became the danger that the whole captive mass would be butchered.

The red-handed assassins among the Indians were determined this should be done. The brave men among them, the "friendly Indians," who would hazard their own existence in the final struggle to save the captives, were favoured by the anxiety of those who had blotted out a thousand lives, to escape to places of personal safety. This was indeed a strong factor in saving from annihilation the helpless captives. The wish of the red-handed element was to accomplish the terrible execution of these people with gun and club, and then hastily escape into the great solitude to the north-westward, then known only to adventurous explorers. They were thwarted only by the courageous Paul (ma-za-ku-ta-ma-ne) who had the moral support of Standing Buffalo and other influential leaders, and who would have fought desperately had the final issue been forced.

Another point never historically developed, was the masterful skill by which, without internecine violence, the friendly Indians became the *de facto* possessors of the captives. This was not done openly or boastfully, but artfully and covertly, and while this might not save the lives of the captives, it would place them where they would not be the first to die. The loyal Indians interposed themselves by a concerted movement between the captives and their would-be assassins.

All plans matured, and the main body of Indians who had instigated and prosecuted the war on the whites, having pushed northward for personal safety, Col. Sibley rode into and took possession of the Indian camps and the captives, who were overwhelmed and prostrated when the hour of their deliverance finally came. That the power of their captors and tormentors had been broken, and that the forbidding incubus under which they had lived such wretched lives, had been swept away, was too much for their dulled comprehension, and they bowed down and wept, and then lifted their faces in thanksgiving to God, and as they rose and marched away into new life the actors in the theatre of war for the nonce disappeared from the stage.

Attack on Fort Abercrombie

Like Ridgely, Abercrombie was a fort in name only. The post consisted of three buildings—barracks, officers' quarters and commissary. When the news of the outbreak reached this distant frontier post, steps were taken to hastily put the garrison in a defensible condition by the construction of earthworks and other barricades. Abercrombie, situated on the west bank of the Red River, in what is now Richland County, North Dakota, did not learn of the outbreak until the 20th of August.

The post was garrisoned by Co. D, Capt. John Vander Horck, Fifth Minnesota Volunteer Infantry. The centre of attraction of the Indians was on the more southern frontier and during the period of quiet at Abercrombie Capt. Vander Horck put his post in the best possible condition for resisting the enemy, and wisely he planned, for the Indians desperately attacked the fort at 5 o'clock of the morning of September 3rd, which attack they continued until about noon, but they were repulsed by the gallant men of Co. D, and retired after sustaining severe loss in numbers.

The garrison was now confronted by several serious problems. Capt. Vander Horck, while on a round of the picket line before daylight of the morning of attack, was shot and seriously wounded by a guard who had seen Indians in the vicinity of his post, and who mistook the captain for a foe. First Lieutenant Cariveau was ill, and while Second Lieutenant Groetch had commanded with ability, it was discovered when this first engagement was over that but 350 rounds of ammunition for the old Harper's Ferry muskets, with which the men were armed, remained. By mistake, cartridges had been supplied to the post of a calibre not suited to the guns of the men. A force was at once organised to manufacture cartridges, the bullets for which were obtained by opening canister intended for the howitzers, of which there was an abundant supply. Sufficient ammunition was thus made for the infantry without seriously depleting the supply of the artillery.

On the morning of September 6th, just at the break of day, the Indians launched a furious attack upon the fort with greatly increased numbers, the attack lasting ten hours, during which time the fighting was at times hot and furious, but aided by the howitzers, which were splendidly manned, the garrison bade defiance to the enemy and drove him from the field with heavy loss. Though reinforcements did not arrive until September 23rd, over a month from the beginning of the outbreak, the fort was not again attacked in force, though the garrison was practically in a state of siege for weeks. Co. D lost five men, one killed and four wounded, in the two engagements.

The defence of Fort Abercrombie was heroically sustained. The mental and physical strain endured, severely taxed the officers and men, but they proved equal to every demand and every expectation.

Escape of the Missionaries

On the night of Friday, Aug. 22nd, after a hard day's fight with the savages, and while the enemy was yet reasonably supposed to occupy in large numbers the woods surrounding Fort Ridgely on three sides, Andrew Hunter, son-in-law of Rev. Dr. Thomas Williamson, the well-known Sioux missionary, crawled on his hands and knees into the fort to ascertain conditions and the advisability of attempting to pilot a party of forty souls into the garrison. He told in an undertone the startling story of the escape of the missionaries and their families from above the Yellow Medicine Agency—an escape thrilling and miraculous, made while the whole country was lying at the feet of the murderous Sioux.

The missionary party had reached a point not far distant from the fort on the afternoon of August 22nd, and plainly heard the storm of battle that raged for hours between the garrison and the hosts of Little Crow, and as silence succeeded the din of battle at dark the most intense anxiety was felt by the missionaries, as to what the result of , the fierce engagement had been. Had the fort fallen, and was the reigning silence the silence of death and desolation? Thus, queried all, and thus thought Andrew Hunter as he crept up to and into the garrison. The fort still survived, but it was so reduced in ammunition and supplies as to make it no longer a safe place of refuge.

The hearts of the mission band scarcely beat in the hour of anxiety during which Hunter had stealthily, his life in his hand, crept to the fort. Hunter was advised that it would be wiser for the missionaries to continue their flight, dangerous as it was, rather than to enter the fort in its exhausted condition, for it must fall for want of ammunition, if the battle were renewed, as was not improbable.

Thus, came to Fort Ridgely the first news received of the whereabouts and fortunes of the missionaries, the families and associates of the Rev. Dr. Williamson and the Rev. Stephen R. Riggs, whose mission homes were at Hazlewood, five or six miles northwest of the remote Yellow Medicine Agency. Great anxiety was felt for these well-known people, some of whom had been in missionary work among the Sioux of the Minnesota Valley since 1835, but no one had dared to hope they had escaped death at the hands of the savages, but one noble Indian, Chaska, had stood loyally by them; and with peculiar instinct had guided them, even through a country swarming with savages, by probably the only routes that would have made their escape possible.

Early in the evening of Monday, August 18th, Chaska and an Indian companion, Tankanxaceye, learning of the bloody work at the Lower Agency, hastened to the home of Dr. Williamson, warned him the lives of all the whites at the mission, as elsewhere, were in peril, and advised preparations for flight. Paul and Simon, also full-blood Indians, likewise acquainted Rev. Riggs of the conditions below as they had just learned them, urged flight for safety, and assisted in piloting the families of Riggs, Jonas Pettijohn, D. W. Moore and H. D. Cunningham to an island in the Minnesota River some distance away, where they remained until the following evening.

During this time Chaska and his Indian companion had conducted Dr. Williamson and family, and the family of his son-in-law, Andrew Hunter, to a place of safety and concealment farther down the river. Having accumulated the families at the sawmill, through the kindly efforts of the Renvilles, half-breeds, the Rigg's party set out on the north and east side of the Minnesota River on one of the most perilous journeys ever undertaken by man. To encounter Indians was death. To traverse their country and avoid them seemed impossible. Dr. Williamson was slow to believe the Indians had risen, *en masse*, for the slaughter of the whites, and lingered in the reckon of his mission-home hesitatingly; but the warnings of Chaska were so urgent that discretion admonished the aged missionary to seek safety for himself and friends without further delay, and well did he reach this conclusion.

The only available conveyance was an ox-cart. This was put to the best possible use, Chaska and Lorenzo concealing the occupants of the cart beneath robes and quilts, and starting on the perilous journey to Fort Ridgely, nearly sixty miles distant. The Riggs' party was overtaken the following day. Now, with the accession of three Germans who had escaped from the raided settlements through which the refugees must pass, the number of souls under the guidance and protection of the faithful friendly Indians numbered forty.

The trail of the missionaries had been taken up by the murderous Indians, but fortunately a severe thunderstorm intervened, and the torrents of rain obliterated the trail; it was given up, and the savages went into the defenceless settlements, to ply the work of destruction.

The movements of the missionaries were unavoidably slow, and attended with momentary danger. Dead bodies everywhere and charred ruins or burning homes made manifest the peril of the helpless refugees, but their Indian Guides were ever on the alert, watchful as eagles, and quick to detect the slightest signs of danger. Nor were they less alert in the matter of choosing the safer side of any dilemma. There was little rest for man or beast, and little upon which to subsist. So, day and night they trudged along, much of the time through coarse grass that lacerated their flesh, or jungles that hindered their progress.

Failing to enter the fort, the weary and worn party made its way heavy hearted still many miles distant, finally reaching Henderson, Sibley County.

It was with feelings of deep regret at the fort that these people were advised to continue their journey, beset with the greatest of dangers, but the garrison was in such peril that this was thought the wiser course to pursue.

An Incident Preceding the Outbreak

A few days before the outbreak a large party of Indians came to the fort, Cut-Nose among the number. The object of this visit can best be surmised by what followed. No outbreak had been planned in advance, though an uprising had been premeditated as the one course left open for redressing the wrongs the Indians had suffered.

CUT-NOSE

The visit of these Indians, as it was not uncommon, excited no suspicion on this occasion until the evening of the second day. The party, embracing fifty to one hundred people, had been unobtrusive and good-natured, but in the evening before they were to take their departure, they organised a war-dance west of the garrison thirty or forty rods, during which they worked themselves into a frenzied state. The writer was among a party of soldier spectators who sat on a pile of rails near the outer edge of the dancing circle. War-clubs and scalping-knives were in the hands of many of the dancers, and were flourished with unusual defiance.

In passing the rail-pile on which the soldiers were seated, one particularly offensive savage made a pass as if to grab the scalp-lock of a spectator, then flourished his wicked knife as if in the act of cutting a throat or lifting a scalp. The spectators, all soldiers of the garrison, were utterly unarmed. At this juncture Cut-Nose interposed himself between the circle and the pile of rails, and proposed the sale of his pipe to one of the soldiers, and while the deal was being consummated a general hegira of bluecoats was started in the direction of the garrison, so that the purchaser of the Cut-Nose pipe with surprise found himself deserted by his unarmed companions, but lost no time in imitating the discretion said to be the better part of valour.

The threatening demonstrations had by this time roused the whole post to the extent of causing the levelling of several pieces of artillery, full-shotted, upon the frenzied warriors. The wiser heads among the red men knew this was not the time and place for hostilities, and they were told through Interpreter Quinn their conduct was becoming displeasing, and likely to get them into trouble. They learned the guns were trained on them, and ceased their war-dance with a suddenness betokening acumen not always ascribed to the savage.

While the unusual conduct of the Indians in their dance was the talk of the garrison during the evening, no one believed it had serious portent, but rather thought it merely the result of excitement and indiscretion on the part of vagabond individuals. In less than a week after that time the whole frontier was strewn with death and distraction, and these same warriors who had visited us, possibly on a tour of inspection, were among the forces that desperately attempted to take the fort; and the hideous-faced Cut-Nose, whose name was derived from his having lost the outer part of his right nostril in a fight with Other Day in past years, distinguished himself in the massacre for some of the most fiendish deeds conceivable, and for which he paid the death penalty by hanging after the outbreak.

★★★★★★

Much was made of this incident by those sensationally inclined, and in a history published in 1863, dealing largely with the Sioux Massacre and the causes leading up to it, it was stated on the authority of a mysterious somebody, a Frenchman, whose name could not be used, that this visit was a part of a preconceived plan to precipitate a general massacre of the whites by taking the fort at this time. Interrogated as to this visit and its significance a year following the massacre, Chaska, Paul and other Indians who were conversant with matters pertaining to the massacre, expressed positiveness that there was no plan hatched in the "Soldier's Lodge," an Indian organisation, for an uprising, of which this visit was a part. The incident at Fort Ridgely was without any special significance, the indiscretion of the band being due to discontent rather than to premeditat-

100

ed design upon the fort, and as for the demonstration at Yellow Medicine on the 4th of August, it was the natural result of hunger and disappointment, as was well understood by the officers and men of our regiment who were at Yellow Medicine at the time to attend the payment, and who realising the seriousness of the situation and the sufferings to which the Indians were subjected, urged upon Agent Galbraith the importance of issuing at least food enough to prevent starvation, but without avail until the hungry savages, in their desperate straits, forced a crisis.

******

I recall that among the number on the above visit was old Betz, a squaw everywhere renowned for her great age, which was said to be at the time of their visit, 120 years. No trader's or pioneer's memory could recall when Betz was not old. She was not very tall of stature, but was quite fleshy. Her attire was not catchy, and her hair, in appearance, had not been combed for years. Betz was a child of the simple life. She lived close to nature, and was an economist. She knew that opulence only came to those who were willing to practice economy.

She had a hectoring suspicion that there were things in the swill-barrel outside the barracks kitchen that ought to be stimulating pancreatic activity, and not infrequently did she penetrate the mysteries of that receptacle to her elbows, in quest of specimens of vegetable

"OLD BETZ."
A frequent visitor of Fort Ridgely up to time of outbreak. Was said to be 120 years old.

matter or of discarded samples of the baker's handicraft, bearing them away in her short skirt, which she deftly gathered into the form of a basket for the purpose, and flinging a cold potato at the head of the blue-jacket who essayed to eye her pastime curiously, emphasising her effort with the one word Betz never got too old to hiss forth in scornful accents "*Se-chee!*" (bad.)

This venerable dame had never cultivated the art of "growing old gracefully," and was always cross and irritable, much to her disadvantage among the soldiers, who, though respecting her years, and always kindly disposed toward her, could not resist annoying her on her occasional visits to the fort.

Incidents of the Siege

Mark M. Greer, Co. C, was the first man killed in the fort, a bullet from the enemy's first volley causing his instant death, August 20th.

William Good, corporal of Co. B, was the first man wounded in the first day's fight. A bullet struck him squarely in the centre of the forehead, penetrating the skull. Good was supposed to have been instantly killed, and while he later gave signs of life, this manifestation was accepted as merely an evidence of the great vitality he was known to possess. The bullet could not be removed, but under surgical skill not less remarkable than his vitality, he recovered to live for several years, a greater mental than physical sufferer, however.

Among the severely wounded, Robert J. Spornitz, Co. B, was an early victim in the first day's battle, a shot entering one check and passing out at the other, tearing away the roof of his mouth. He, like Good, survived for many years.

Andrew Rufredge, Co. B, one of Lieutenant Gere's men at the northeast angle, and a supporter of Whipple's gun, was, like Spornitz, the victim of a frightful wound in the first day's engagement, the ball in the case of Rufredge cutting the lower jaw off well back towards the ears.

One of the most pathetic incidents of the siege occurred in connection with the wounding of Rufredge. One of the Rieke boys, a mere youth of sixteen or seventeen years, was assisting in carrying and passing ammunition for the Whipple cannon. While turned away from the gun in his work, Rufredge had received his wound, and had fallen upon his back, his lower jaw dropping upon his neck and breast. When the young German turned to pass to the gunners the ammunition he held, Rufredge lay at his feet, and the horrible spectacle so shocked and appalled the boy that he fell, and a few moments later died in his sister's arms, while Rufredge, under masterful surgical skill, survived.

Sergeant Frank A. Blackmer, Co. C, received what was supposed to be a mortal wound, but clinging tenaciously to life, recovered. (In later years he became a prominent physician at Albert Lea, Minnesota.)

One of the Renville Rangers, a three-quarters blood Indian, deserted to the enemy in the night, first succeeding in plugging the parked cannon with rags, to render them ineffective for quick service. The Renville Rangers, who were brave and loyal men, felt keenly the disgrace brought upon them by this traitor to the cause they were upholding.

When the siege was finally raised, the great mass of refugees for the first time fully realised their utterly destitute, helpless and bereft condition. The fear that had terrorised their hearts was removed. The protecting arm that had shielded them during the days and nights of danger at the fort could not follow them into the world; without homes to welcome them or friends to comfort them, they must turn away in utter destitution. Desperate as had been their condition, the crisis was not reached until now. The conditions were so exacting when these unfortunate people came into the fort, and during the siege, that no attempt could be made at keeping a record of their names, and when relief came, it was to a garrison so exhausted that this task was quite impossible. The mass of humanity finally became assimilated by the world at large, leaving no trace of individuality in history.

On the 18th, the day of the massacre at Redwood, the long-looked for funds for the Indian payment reached the fort. The fatal delay had only that morning borne its bitter fruit. The sum, $71,000, was in gold coin, and was in charge of C. G. Wykoff, clerk of the superintendent of Indian affairs, J. C. Ramsey, and E. A. C. Hatch. The funds were kept under strong guard until after the siege was raised. Had Little Crow known this treasure was in the garrison, he might, in view of the fact that he had already killed the hated traders, who always sat at the pay-table, have persisted in attempts to take the fort, which he could have done in the desperate straits to which the garrison was reduced.

Not only in the exhaustion of its supply of ammunition, was the garrison on the verge of collapse at the time of the last attack, but a really more serious crisis had been reached if possible, in the complete exhaustion of the water supply. On the day of the outbreak, August 18th, all available barrels, tanks, tubs and other vessels, were filled by hauling water from the spring, the accustomed source, half a mile distant from the fort, to meet a possible emergency. The supply had been consumed to the dregs, and a replenishment was only attempted when the unendurable necessities of the garrison, with its refugee mass, compelled it, and the obtaining of water was only accomplished finally at great hazard and under trying hardships.

About Losses

The story of the Sioux Massacre of 1862, cruel and revolting, has never been, fully told, and never will be. What was essentially descriptive of the appalling tragedy enacted along the Minnesota frontier, was given in brief narratives from individual view-points at the time of occurrence, and were reasonably accurate and faithful in narration, but limited in scope, especially as to the extent and consequences of the tragedy. One chronicler who went well into details, and practically the only one who attempted to write a "history," converts tragedy into farce-comedy when he sums up the results of the defenders of the frontier by stating seriously that the total number of Indians killed by troops and settlers during the massacre, from August 18th, exclusive of the Battle of Wood Lake, was just twenty-one. His enumeration of the savages slain is as follows:

> At the Battle of Redwood Ferry, 1; New Ulm, 5; Fort Ridgely, 2; Big Woods at or near Forest City, 1; Birch Coulie; 2; at Battle of Acton, with Strout, 1; Hutchinson, 1; Spirit Lake, 1; at Shetek, by Duly, 1; near Omahaw, 1; Abercrombie, 4; between Fort Ridgely and New Ulm, half-breed, 1. Total 21.

Serio-comically the historian assures his readers of the accuracy of his figures for two reasons; first, by asking the Indians to give him the number of their losses, and secondly, by verifying their report by hunting for dead Indians several days after the battles were fought.

The historian however rendered too much valuable service in compiling historical information to be taken seriously to task for his faulty conclusion in the matter of Indian losses, which no doubt exceeded his figures more than ten to one. During the two days' battle at Fort Ridgely a ton of ammunition was fired. At times the enemy was closely massed at short range. One double-shotted charge from Jones's gun at the southwest angle of the garrison on the afternoon of the second day's fight, when the Indians had moved up in close order, under Little Crow's command to club their guns and rush in, mowed down seventeen Indians, most of them killed.

This was but one shot out of scores made under conditions rendering it impossible that the enemy could have escaped without great loss. In fact, had not the fire of the garrison been deadly at every point of concentration of the foe, nothing would have prevented a charge, the one thing Little Crow realised would give him the prize he so earnestly coveted—Fort Ridgely. So ineffective a fire as the historian suggests would have merited the contempt of the savages, and the garrison would have been blotted out in short order.

On the afternoon of August 27th, the post having finally been relieved on the morning of that day, of its great strain and long vigil, John McCole, of the Renville Rangers, and the writer, entered the river valley from a quarter to a half mile southwest of the garrison, where we found a small abandoned cellar or "dug-out," in which were seven dead warriors, partially concealed by earth that had been dug from the overhanging embankment to cover them. Two other decomposing bodies were found in the underbrush near the cellar. It is the custom of Indians to completely bear their dead from the field of battle, and entirely beyond discovery, if not overtasked with the burden, or too hard pressed by their enemy. The nine bodies above noted were probably about one-tenth of the Indians killed during the siege of Fort Ridgely, and the casualties sustained by Indians in other engagements were proportionately large.

The battle at the Redwood Ferry was desperate and at very short range. In fact, it was almost hand-to-hand, and the few men who fought their way out of the ambuscade did so over the dead bodies of many of their foe. To say that but one Indian was killed in this engagement is to ridicule the brave fellows who cut their way through the savage cordon in the most desperate battle of the massacre.

Talks of Cruelty as Told by Refugees

When we touch the subject of Indian cruelty, as practiced on the helpless victims along the Minnesota frontier during the massacre of 1862, we enter upon a phase of the horrible uprising that rouses every feeling of resentment of which human nature is capable. How even savages in this age could perpetrate or approve such fiendish deeds as were committed, passes understanding. Even infants were tortured in a manner that would put to blush and shame the imps of the infernal reckons. The stories told by the refugees from the settlements, who straggled into Fort Ridgely the first two or three days of the massacre, no one has ever attempted to literally repeat.

Chapters have been written on the massacre at the agency and the ferry, and upon the attacks on Fort Ridgely and New Ulm, but no writer has ever given to the world an account of the awful scenes through which most of these refugees passed; and perhaps it is best that it is so. Wounded, persecuted, hunted, they were half crazed, their agonies of heart and body uncontrollable, while yet their tales of horror would dismay even the stoutest-hearted listener.

Some had by apparent miracle wrested themselves from the very jaws of death when the overpowering hand was raised to deal the fatal stroke, as was the case of one woman whose husband, after felled to rise no more, shot her assailant with the gun held in his death-clutch, perishing himself, but momentarily dumbfounding their assailants, during which the wife escaped, first into a cornfield near the house, and then by concealing herself in a clump of high weeds a few rods distant, where she was compelled to hear the heartrending cries of the man who had defended her to the last, and who, for his act in dispatching her assailant, was being tortured by every conceivable device to make his death one of prolonged agony.

When the shrieking and moaning of the helpless victim would die away, the cruel knife would be applied to again awaken the dying man into new suffering, until finally silence told the tale of death. The screams and shrieks of her two children, as if the heart of the poor woman had not suffered its full measure of torture, rang piercingly in the ears of the crouching, cringing mother, who could scarcely keep her hiding, though she knew that death by unspeakable means would be the only result of her attempt to rescue those being fiendishly tortured and mutilated and finally murdered.

To have been permitted to die a death worthy of a great cause, would have been tenfold more acceptable to this poor, wretched woman, than to save her own life while those near and dear to her were being cruelly put to death, but instinct admonished her of the worse than death she would suffer for revealing herself, without being able to render assistance. Death having stilled the cries of the unfortunate victims who had fallen into the hands of the fiends, the house was plundered and the torch applied, and having apparently satiated their thirst for blood, the savages, loaded with plunder, took the only family horse from the stable and made off, without farther search for the wife and mother, who had escaped with her clothing half torn from her body.

Distracted with grief and racked with fear, she lay in hiding until after sundown, when, with faltering step, first wildly scanning the surroundings in fear of a concealed savage, she ventured to the ruins of their smouldering home, where she found the bodies of her children, frightfully disfigured, and that of her husband, he having been scalped and otherwise mutilated almost beyond recognition, and his body partially charred.

Before the darkness closed about her, destitute, homeless and friendless, she turned her face toward the only known place of refuge. Fort Ridgely, which she reached on the morning of August 21st, more naked than clad, and frenzied with the mental and physical strain which had well-nigh unhinged her reason.

And so the historian might recount the tales of horror of one-half of the three hundred refugees who had made their way from the raided settlements to the fort, for such a mass of quivering humanity; such a collection of maimed, suffering people; such a gathering of odds and ends of blasted and obliterated homes and of half-crazed victims of the most diabolical crimes ever devised, was rarely ever before brought into one collection. The terror with which their souls were stricken had written its tale of horror on every face. The refugees had many of them come from remote settlements, over a trackless country, often without shoes to protect their bleeding feet, or raiment to hide their nakedness, every step of the way taken with fear and trembling, without sleep, rest or sustenance, and persecuted by the hideous scenes witnessed in the ravishing, slaying and maiming of dear ones of the home circle. It is best, I repeat, that the shocking details of the sufferings of these refugees were never handed down to history.

What befell their friends and what they narrowly escaped may readily be inferred from a few random instances of cruelty common to the massacre along the entire frontier devastated.

Below Yellow Medicine a few miles, on the east side of the Minnesota River, twenty-seven dead bodies were found in one group, the only living creature being a babe that had escaped the tomahawk to finally die of starvation at its dead mother's breast. In a building near the scene of this ghastly spectacle were found by Antoine Freniere, Government interpreter, seven small children, who were later burned alive by the Indians, together with the house the helpless little creatures occupied. Freniere was compelled to fly for his life, and could do nothing for the children.

August 20th, a party of Indians visited the home of a farmer named Anderson, with whom they were acquainted, and whose family had often befriended them, in what is now Kandiyohi (then Monongalia)

County. They asked for favours which were granted them, and without a sign of their evil purposes, while they were being waited upon, shot down the defenceless man who, without suspecting harm, was good-naturedly serving them. They had, among other things, asked for potatoes, and Anderson had sent his boy to dig them, and while the boy engaged in the task, they shot him dead, almost at the instant his father was murdered. Mrs. Anderson ran into the cellar with a small child, and having been unobserved, escaped, the Indians having failed to burn the house.

A daughter, Julia, fourteen years of age, seized a sister of ten years, and succeeded in hiding in the weeds near the house. These were prizes for which the Indians made diligent search, and whom they finally discovered. The girls were borne away on a pony, but night coming on they were taken but a short distance, where the savages camped. The girls passed a horrible night. The Indians, next morning, discovered their ponies had stampeded, and in the excitement incident, hurried in pursuit of them. The girls made their escape, and although hunted excitedly, succeeded in eluding their captors.

After two days and nights of excruciating hardships they reached Forest City, having covered a distance of some thirty miles. They emerged from the brush into a road in the neighbourhood of their home in their flight, where they stumbled upon the bodies of two neighbours—Backlund and Lorentson. The heads of both these men had been chopped off. Lorentson's scalp had been removed, and the skin, with the ears attached, had been torn from his face. The heads of the two men were set up side by side, with their hats on. Backlund evidently used snuff, for his snuff-box was placed near his face, while his severed right hand, lying by the side of his head, held between the thumb and finger, placed there derisively, a pinch of snuff.

The gratification of lustful passions led to some of the most fiendish abuses and cruelties ever recorded, and while the world should know the truth as a part of the history of this awful Massacre, crimes and cruelties of this nature are too forbidding to pass to the pages of a book.

Dr. Humphrey, the Government physician at the Lower Agency, a man who had done much for the Indians, was overtaken when endeavouring to make his escape from Redwood to the fort with his family, and was slain, as were his wife and two children, a third child, a boy, escaping by having been sent to a spring in a concealed spot for drinking water, he having heard the shooting a few yards away in time to hide. Dr. Humphrey was shockingly mutilated, his head being severed from his body. Emerging from his concealment when all was quiet, the boy who went to the spring, cautiously returned to where he had left the family, only to find his father dead and the bodies of his mother and little brother and sister burned in the house at which they had stopped to rest, and get a drink, that of Mayner, on the fort road.

From a murdered family near New Ulm, one little fellow, supposed to have been killed, had revived and was rescued. The bodies of all the family had been frightfully mutilated, and the ball of one of the eyes of the little boy who survived, had been dug out with a knife, and lay suspended upon his cheek, in a state of putrefaction.

Near New Ulm Wak-pa-doo-ta went to a house and looking through a window, saw a sick woman dying on a bed. He fired through the window and wounded her. At this an old man was seen to make his way upstairs. Fearing the old man was after a gun, and too cowardly to take any chances, the Indians fired the house and burned the occupants to death.

Mauley, the Redwood ferryman, was a mark of special vengeance, no doubt because of the fact of his having sacrificed every personal opportunity of escape to save those whom the Indians had hoped would be unable to pass the river barrier; but Mauley stood at his post until the last to reach the ferry in advance of the savages had been transferred to the side of possible safety. Highly incensed that he should have saved so many from their bloody clutches, he was shot down at his post, and before life was extinct, he was disembowelled, and his hands, feet and head were cut off and thrust within his bleeding body.

The Lake Shetek settlement, in Murray County, was attacked by Lean Bear, who first attained prominence at the council of *Traverse des Sioux* in 1852. Sleepy Eye and White Lodge joined him with their bands. The crimes and cruelties perpetrated in this settlement were shocking in the extreme, with but one compensating result—the death of Lean Bear—who fell at the hands of a settler, William J. Duly. The wife and two children of Duly were taken captives, as were a Mrs. Wight and child, and a daughter of a Mr. Everett. The prisoners were carried to the Missouri River, the tortuous journey covering a distance of seven or eight hundred miles. The children were mostly murdered in cold blood in the presence of the powerless mothers.

And so, might this chapter of horrors be lengthened into a hundred pages, with sickening details yet untold; but more than enough has already been recorded, except for the fact that the future has a right to know the price paid by the advance-guard of civilization for the heritage to be enjoyed by unending generations.

Execution of Thirty-Eight Indians

After the surrender at Camp Release a commission was appointed by Gen. H. H. Sibley, who had command of the forces on the Minnesota frontier, for the trial of Indians implicated in the massacre. The original commission was composed as follows: Colonel William Crooks, of the Sixth Minnesota Infantry Volunteers, Colonel William R. Marshall, of the Seventh, Captain Hiram P. Grant, Co. A. and Capt. Hiram S. Bailey, Co. C, both of the Sixth, and Lieutenant R. C. Olin, Co. B, third Minnesota. Of this commission Col. Crooks was president, and Lieutenant Olin judge advocate. The commission held its first session at Camp Release on the 30th of September, and its last one at Fort Snelling November 5th, 1862, sessions having been held at various other points mean time.

This commission tried 425 Indians and half-breeds on the charge of murderous participation in the massacre, and of these 321 were convicted, 303 being sentenced to death, while the remainder were sentenced to pay lighter penalties. The East set up the cry that these people were prisoners of war, and that it would be a crime against the nation to permit of this wholesale execution. As a result, an investigation was made by the general government out of which grew an order from President Lincoln that thirty-nine of the condemned Indians be hanged on the 26th day of December, 1862, at Mankato, and that the remainder of the condemned savages be held to await further orders. After thirty-nine of the most guilty had been selected, one was pardoned by President Lincoln, and the thirty-eight were executed as ordered, one large scaffold sufficing for the entire number.

Not an Indian was self-convicted. All swore positively to child-like innocence, and affected amazement that they had been accused. One negro, Godfrey, who lived among the Sioux, was among those executed. His plea of innocence availed him nothing, as he, like Cut Nose, was known to have committed some of the most monstrous crimes ever charged up to the account of a fiend.

The final death sentence was promulgated on the 6th of December, just twenty days prior to the date of execution.

Passing from crime to punishment, the scenes that followed the sentence were without a parallel in our national history.

The condemned in the main accepted their fate philosophically. They were treated with humane consideration by the officials in whose charge they were, pending the final act. They were privileged to select their spiritual advisers according to their individual preferences, and each made his choice. The condemned received much comfort from the Christian influences thus brought about them. As the day for the execution drew near the condemned were permitted to receive friends from among their fellow-prisoners who had escaped the death sentence. Through these, farewells were sent to family friends, and many little keepsakes were committed to the hands of those present to accompany the parting messages.

The condemned were never too deeply distressed to enjoy their pipes, and for the fatal scene upon the scaffold arranged their hair and painted their faces with painstaking effort. At the appointed moment the condemned arose from a sitting or reclining posture and walked with steady step to the death-trap, apparently glad the suspense was to be ended. There was no lagging. Every wretch was self-supporting and active, all chanting the death song. William J. Duly, of Lake Shetek, whose family had been murdered by the savages, and from whom he escaped after a desperate encounter in which he killed Lean Bear, was privileged to spring the trap that sent the thirty-eight murderers into eternity at one stroke.

Thousands of people witnessed the execution. The bodies were cut down after death was pronounced, and carted to a sand-bar in the Minnesota River, where they were buried in one trench. After a term of imprisonment, the convicted savages who had escaped the hangman's noose, were placed upon the reservation assigned to their people beyond the borders of Minnesota.

Dr. Alfred Muller

The great service rendered by Post Surgeon Dr. Alfred Muller during the siege of Fort Ridgely, has never been understood or publicly accredited. Dr Muller was a native of Switzerland, and had acquired his professional knowledge in the land of his nativity.

The outbreak filled the post hospital with many frightfully wounded men. Blodgett was shot through the abdomen, the intestines being penetrated; Sutherland was shot through the right lung, the ball passing entirely through his body; Good was shot squarely in the forehead, the bullet crashing irrecoverably into his skull; Spornitz was shot through the head; Rufredge had his lower jaw entirely severed on both sides;

111

DR. ALFRED MULLER.

Blackmer was shot in the head, and many wounded were brought in from the agency and the settlements, in addition to others wounded at the fort. The record made in these cases is unsurpassed, even in the world-famed Japanese army hospital service. Not a man, no matter how seriously wounded or mutilated, lost his life after reaching the care of Dr. Muller, nor was an arm or leg amputated.

In piling up work for Surgeon Muller, events followed each other swiftly under the rain of fire of the savages, but the perception of Muller was unerring, his execution rapid and thorough, and his devotion tireless. His surgical record is excelled by that of no other, in or out of the army. A few years after the close of the civil war, his estimable wife having died. Dr. Muller left his New Ulm home, in which he had located after his service, for his native land, where he died, at Berne. He came out of the unique Mountain Republic of Europe like a ray of light in a period of darkness, and having performed his mission, returned to pay the debt of Nature. Minnesota owes much to his memory.

******

Dr. Muller was born at Berne, Switzerland, in December, 1825, graduating from the Medical department of the University of Berne in 1851, immigrating to America a year later. Coming to Minnesota in 1856, he located at Stillwater, where he practiced his profession until 1861, when he was appointed Post Surgeon of Fort Ridgely, where he remained until 1867, when he removed to New Ulm, having retired from army service.

******

A Woman in Battle

The storm of battle is likely to strike terror to the heart of the true, normally-poised woman. Even strong men, whose profession is war, are often terror-stricken with the first shock of battle. The ordeal in this case was more than one of warfare. The surroundings were inconceivably trying. The hundreds of refugees added much to the nerve-racking trials of the hour. Almost without exception they were from homes made desolate by the gun, tomahawk and torch. The father, usually the object of first attack while endeavouring to defend his family, rarely made his escape, but under cover of his resistance occasionally some member would fly unobserved in the awful encounter to a place of concealment. If the home was not wholly taken by surprise, it would frequently happen that by concealment, several members of a family would escape; and of such remnants as these was the body of the refugees at the fort made up.

They came, often over long stretches of trackless prairie, being guided mainly by a general knowledge of the location of the fort, making their way with the greatest caution. Whether by day or under cover of darkness, every step was taken with fear and trembling. Reaching the fort at length, famished with hunger and thirst, and distracted with grief and sleepless vigil, they were just so much additional fuel to the flame, of pandemonium that reigned at the post—a condition in itself sufficient to unnerve any but the bravest and most resolute man. There was no assuaging the grief of these people, some half bereft of their reason, others sick and others wounded. Human conception is inadequate to grasp the mental and physical torture to which they had been subjected. They had witnessed scenes no pen can describe, and had suffered sorrows that break the heart; and added to all this in the fort was the startling realisation that to be defeated when attacked meant that the little garrison would become a veritable slaughter pen.

Amid scenes and conditions of this character within, and the din of battle without, accentuated by hideous yells, increasing in fury as the conflict grew fiercer, Mrs. Alfred Muller, wife of Post Surgeon Dr. Alfred Muller, was a notable figure. Mrs. Muller was in the prime of womanhood, and was well known to all the little garrison, where, with her husband, she had her home. In the days when danger was unsuspected, and military life at the post was of the commonplace kind, Mrs. Muller filled her wifely sphere with becoming womanliness. She was a native of Switzerland, and a good type of her race.

She was retiring rather than otherwise, but always at ease in her manner. In personal appearance she was of medium build, cheerful of disposition and comely in looks. When war was precipitated with all its horrors, she at once manifested a personality never to be forgotten, and for which she deserves to live forever in the love and esteem of the Northwest.

MRS ALFRED MULLER (ELIZA)

When the test of battle came there was no shrinking. No despairing thought revealed itself in her modest face. If fate had decreed the garrison must fall, she did not shrink from bearing her part bravely. Not many rifle shots had spoken in startling tones when Mrs. Muller had occupation at her husband's side. She helped to stanch the flow of blood and to bind ghastly wounds. She spoke words of comfort and cheer to the suffering, and her kind heart prompted many acts of gentleness unusual in the activity of battle. Wherever she was her demeanour was reassuring, and whatever she did her adaptability was an inspiration. "What can I do?" was not a question with her, but rather "What can I not do?"

After the engagement, of August 22nd, had continued for hours, it was found the supply of musket ammunition was exhausted. The depletion of the two days of fighting had precipitated a crisis. This necessitated the organisation of a corps of workers for the manufacture of such ammunition as could be extemporised. Of this work Mrs. Muller took charge, and through her gifted versatility she soon became an expert cartridge maker, and taught many other hands, now enlisted from among the useful women refugees, the art of dextrously turning out ammunition, for which there was the most pressing need.

I was detailed late in the day of August 22nd, to obtain a supply of this newly-made ammunition, and found Mrs. Muller and her workers busily engaged in a little room on the first floor of the barracks. The face of this truly heroic woman was intensely impressive to the glancing eye. There was a constant crash of musketry and the resounding of artillery all about the little garrison, the din being almost deafening. Amid this her mental poise was perfect, her hand steady, her eye alert, her voice gentle, and her face composed and natural. And so, this inestimable woman, from day to day during the siege, gave evidence of the most sterling qualities. Without price or the thought of reward she did well her part in the defence of Fort Ridgely.

It is said regretfully that she did not long survive the restoration of peace where the warlike tempests had raged that developed her great worth to the Northwest, and particularly to Minnesota, and it is fitting that she sleeps in the Fort Ridgely cemetery, where the State of Minnesota has equally fittingly erected a monument to her memory.

The Grand Old Ferryman

One of the noblest characters developed by the deluge of blood that made crimson the Minnesota frontier, was the ferryman, Mauley, at the crossing of the Minnesota River at the Redwood Agency. Self-preservation is the first law of nature, but there are times when some men become more than human, and rise superior to this selfish law. Mauley, the plodding, unlettered, unobtrusive old ferryman was such a man. History is adorned with no grander spectacle than was exhibited in this humble, unpolished frontiersman, and of all heroes who won renown in that conflict, his memory should have been the first to be recognised and honoured, as his was the first great service rendered when the tragedy that came like a fiery bolt from a clear sky, overwhelmed the agency in the early morning of August 18th.

Plain old Frenchman! He was but a grain of dust in the world of affairs. Men who regarded themselves as of superior mould, hardly had a word for him as they passed, his calling was so humble, his life so simple and his horizon so limited. But sterling manhood abounded within his noble breast, and when the terrible calamity befell the agency, he proved a hero without a peer. As was remarked of him, "This humble man whom nobody cared for, suddenly seemed to care for everybody but himself." Those who escaped the gun and warclub at the agency, sought safety in flight by way of the ferry, where all found the sturdy old Frenchman at his post.

He could have saved his own life with ease and certainty, having had ample time and warning, but he thought only of those who were in peril, and to the music of splashing lines and creaking pulleys he kept his boat plying back and forth until the overwhelming wave of savages reached the river bank.

He had just saved the last to come or at least had transferred across the sullen barrier, the last to reach the stream, when, in a towering rage for having snatched so many from the clutches of the swarming demons, he was shot down with fiendish glee.

Here was a man who deliberately gave his life that others might live,—the most noble sacrifice a mortal ever made, and France, the land that gave him birth, may well be proud of such sons; and may his memory ever be cherished and perpetuated in his adopted country as that of the hero of heroes in the fiery ordeal that tried men's souls at Redwood, for there does not exist in history a nobler instance of intrepidity or greatness of soul than this man exhibited. The rage of the savages knew no bounds when they discovered this faithful ferry-man had robbed them of many a victim, and they avenged themselves upon him with exultant shouts and fiendish cruelty, disembowelling him before life was extinct, and then cutting off his head, hands and feet and stuffing them into the bleeding trunk.

John McCole

It was my good fortune in point of satisfaction to have made the acquaintance of John McCole during the siege of Fort Ridgely, then second sergeant of the Renville Rangers, and a good soldier. Following the Massacre, the Renville Rangers having merged themselves into other organisations, we served a year together as bedfellows and messmates. This service, during 1863, was in the Indian country and in Indian campaigns. McCole had for some years been a clerk and an accountant in one of the stores at the Redwood Agency, and had, only a few days before the outbreak, enlisted in the Renville Rangers, with a view to going south, and thus escaped the terrible fate of his former employers and associates who were massacred on the morning of Aug. 18th.

McCole, long since gathered to the realms of the great majority, was of unusual intellectual burnish, and of a fortunate, gentle disposition, making him a favourite with all who knew him. His protracted service in the store of one of the leading traders had given him a wide acquaintance among the Indians, whose language he spoke with great fluency. On the Sibley Expedition of 1863, were seventy-five Sioux scouts, whom McCole knew familiarly, and with whom, at intervals, I was afforded through him an unusual opportunity to gather information regarding the massacre from a source not always available. These scouts were selected from the Indians who had proven themselves loyal to the whites during the massacre the previous year, but who had mingled more or less with their former friends and relatives after the surrender at Camp Release, were drawn into the maelstrom by Little Crow, to the extent of being participants, even if not voluntary ones, of the massacre, and thus the scouts had a double knowledge of what occurred during the outbreak.

The trouble at the Upper Agency, August 4th, 1862, when a massacre was narrowly averted, was told of with much earnestness, as were the sufferings and disappointments leading up to that event. Many deeds of cruelty were related, with a shrug, and with manifest disapproval; but of these there was the least disposition to talk, information being vouchsafed when asked for as applying to particular persons, as, for instance, to the old ferryman of the Lower Agency, the traders and residents of the agency, etc. One of the features of the massacre discussed without reserve, was Little Crow's failure to take Fort Ridgely when he had first planned to do so—the day following the massacre at the agency and the ferry. This failure was explained with the facial earnestness and artful gesticulations peculiar to Indian character,— traits that increase the force of language by half.

Only those who have vainly tried, know how difficult it is to extract information from an Indian; but McCole had the faculty of unlocking the secret springs of reticence of the red men, and securing a voluble flow of language when he chose to do so.

Standing Buffalo

One of the great injustices of the Sioux Massacre was sustained by Standing Buffalo. (Tatanka Nazin,) whom Captain McGrew, forty years after the outbreak, referred to as "the noblest red man of all." Standing Buffalo was the chief of a band of Sissetons whose village was on the, shores of Big Stone Lake, and was a self-reliant, level-headed man, whose friendship for the whites had breadth and depth. As the disappointment of the Indians increased, and their unrest became more manifest, Standing Buffalo, who dissented from proposed radical measures, was chided for his fealty to the whites; yet his sturdy character made him a factor of strength among the Indians, who had

117

great respect for him.

The trying ordeal through which the Indians passed at the Yellow Medicine Agency, while assembled to receive their annuities, elsewhere fully treated, produced widespread and justifiable discontent, and having grown desperate, a council of chiefs and warriors was called from among the six thousand savages in camp at Yellow Medicine, in August, 1862. This council was an extremely stormy one, and any man would have been very brave who would have dared to stand within the council circle and plead for moderation. Standing Buffalo stood in the breach as the foremost advocate of peace and patience. He did not believe in all white men, nor had he lost faith in all. He believed the white people in the main were friendly to the Indians, and wished to see justice done them.

Other speakers were in favour of violent retaliation for the wrongs inflicted on their race, and doubted that the white people were any of them honest or friendly, since the people chose their officers, and these officers were too often dishonest. Six weeks of indefensible dalliance on the part of representatives of the government had made the contention of Standing Buffalo unpopular, and his predicament not in all respects enviable. The council finally terminated with a vote in favour of resorting to arms as a means of righting wrongs inflicted upon the thousands who had been kept in camp for weeks, and who were finally at the point of starvation. This vote committed all the chiefs, without regard to their personal views or preferences.

The final decision of the council spread throughout the camp with great rapidity, awakening intense excitement. Standing Buffalo, realising that trouble was imminent, went at once to the headquarters of the troops near the warehouse where the stores were locked up, and under guard of the soldiers, and related what had taken place in the council of chiefs. He stated he had bitterly opposed the course adopted, but that he was out-voted; but in the final decision was tacitly bound by the council's action; but he said he had come to warn the soldiers to be prepared and on the alert.

Here was the Alexander Stephens of the Sioux nation. His judgment and sympathies impelled him to stand with the whites, and he had been resolute to the end of the council, but having taken part in the deliberations, he was, under the customs of his people, committed to abide by the result of the council. Nevertheless, there was no law or custom that could restrain him from at once warning the soldiers of their danger.

STANDING BUFFALO

This was characteristic of Standing Buffalo, and the same spirit animated him throughout the massacre. When, after the massacre, the Indians were making northward, pressed by the army, a demand was made upon Little Crow by General Sibley for the surrender of all the prisoners held by him. This demand produced great agitation, and the wonder is, that during the excitement and fierce contention that resulted, the prisoners were not all slain. A great council was held to determine what should be done— whether the prisoners should be massacred or surrendered unconditionally.

Standing Buffalo, whose people, so far as he was able to control them at least, had kept out of the massacre, was in this council, and urged the delivery of the white prisoners unharmed, and he took occasion in his speech to upbraid, in no uncertain terms, the Lower Indians, as those were termed south of the Yellow Medicine River, for bringing on the massacre, saying in this speech in part:

> I am a young man, but I have always felt friendly to the whites, because they were kind to my father. You have brought me into great danger without my knowing of it beforehand (the massacre.) By killing the whites is just as if you had waited for me in ambush and had shot me down. You Lower Indians feel very bad because we have all got into trouble, but I feel worse, because I know that neither I nor my people have killed any of

119

the whites, but that yet we have to suffer for the guilty.

But Standing Buffalo, notwithstanding his manliness and friendship for the white race, was ever kept in the false light of an enemy. The Sibley Expedition of 1863, made its long, toilsome incursion into the Devil's Lake and Missouri River regions, to either secure the surrender of all the Sioux east of the Missouri, or drive them by force of arms across that stream. On the 24th of July, 1863, as related fully in another chapter, the Sibley army overhauled a large body of Indians, who must have known a day or two in advance of the approach of the expedition, but who were evidently influenced not to fly the country, by a conviction that it would be best to peaceably surrender and throw themselves upon the mercy of the authorities.

But this plan, if such it was, was thwarted by a cowardly savage who shot Surgeon Weiser in the back, killing him instantly when he had ridden among the Indians unattended and unsupported. There was no sign of approval of this cold-blooded and treacherous deed, on the part of the savages, but it had so provoked the wrath of the soldiers that hostilities were opened at once, without an opportunity for explanations or redress. Standing Buffalo's band was supposed, though not positively known, to have been a part of this large group, but it is safe to say the offender neither belonged to nor was excused by this chief's people.

Here was Standing Buffalo probably again made the victim of bad company and untoward circumstances, and placed in a position where, for self-preservation and the existence of his family and his people, he was forced to fight those whom he had never broken faith with, and whom he had always befriended and defended in angry councils. That he was not made the prince of outlaws by adverse conditions, is a matter of wonder; but he was not, as no unprovoked cruelty has ever been charged to the name of Standing Buffalo, who, though never justly appreciated at his worth, was nevertheless much of a man among men, Indian that he was.

On June 5, 1871, Standing Buffalo met a tragic death. His lifelong friendship for the whites, even under adverse conditions, made him an object of derision among the lawless element of his race. It was near the Milk River Agency, in Montana, that Standing Buffalo was solicited by the Yanktons to join them in a raid on the Gros Ventres and Upper Assiniboines. Standing Buffalo urged that he had no occasion to join in such an attack; and further, that the whites would be displeased with such a wanton raid. This fired the Yanktons, who accused Standing Buffalo of a regard for the whites that made him unworthy of the respect of his own blood and bone, and unworthy of his chieftainship.

Tired of a life of perplexing conditions whose improvement, ever, circumstances seemed to forbid, Standing Buffalo silently resolved to end all. He announced his willingness at last to join the Yanktons and lead his warriors against their enemies; but his silent resolution was not one of conquest. He announced to his family that he would go on the war-path. He then made disposition of his horses and other personal effects, giving, with great deliberation, all his earthly possessions to his relatives and friends.

He counselled his brother and his son, and all his people, to keep faith with the whites, saying he was going into battle, and that he would never return. With a small party of his warriors he went forth and met the Gros Ventres and Assiniboines in large numbers. It was on an open plain, and Standing Buffalo led a wild charge into the midst of the superior forces, striking harmlessly with his "coo-stick," but never firing a shot. He fell from his horse in the midst of the enemy, his body pierced with upwards of thirty bullets.

Little Crow

Little Crow, in many respects, was the most remarkable man the Sioux nation ever developed. He was not merely an Indian chieftain of the hereditary type—a king by divine fiat, but was a man of peculiar intellectual force. In fact, endowed with education and purged of cruel instincts, he would have taken rank among able men.

Civilization was no enigma to him. He was a student of human-nature, and of all his race was the most masterful in diplomacy with the assents of the government. He was erratic and overbearing, and was not especially loved by his people, who regarded him as a tyrant. He did not sway them by reverence or admiration, but by his indomitable willpower. This dominated him, and through it he dominated them. Faithful and self-sacrificing missionaries who came into Minnesota early in the past century, developed some very excellent characters among the Sioux, who were tribesmen of Little Crow, and who had grown up with him from childhood.

These and many of the sub-chiefs would gladly have curtailed Little Crow's influence and authority, but the latter was far and away ahead of all his race, through craft and intellectual force, when it came

LITTLE CROW

to dealing with the government and its representatives, and he thus always held the whip hand; this collateral to his will-power making his authority supreme. Something of his nature may be judged and some of the reasons why his people had a dread of him may be appreciated when it is stated that he had fought with his brothers in earlier life, and had murdered two of them. In his violent encounters both of his arms were broken, and Indian surgery had not so reduced the fractures as to prevent deformity in the appearance of his arms when these members were exposed to view. It was this known fact that in part led to the identification of Little Crow after he was fortunately and almost miraculously killed by a farmer near Hutchinson, Minnesota.

Little Crow was a skilled warrior and a man of unquestioned courage. He had been impressed with civilization, and had adopted many customs of the whites; yet these were all put off in a twinkling when bloody hands were raised against the defenceless settlers.

Whatever Little Crow engaged in he excelled in. Indians are born gamblers. Gambling is the pastime of Indian life. Men, women and children, without exception, with one device or another, are inveterate gamblers. All are skilled gamblers, but Little Crow was an adept in the art. Card-playing, in fact, was a science with him. He knew the rules of all games, exacted an observance of them of all who sat in a game with him, would forecast the hands of his adversaries with unerring judgment, checkmate every device for his undoing, play with the greatest skill where his hands were the poorest, and quit—when his opponents had nothing more to put up.

After the Indians had received their annuities from the government, professional gamblers would flock in like buzzards at a feast, but Little Crow almost invariably pauperised them. Three of these professional gamblers, who went to the Redwood Agency in the early summer of 1862, taking money enough along with them to "start them in business," engaged in poker with Little Crow. They wore diamonds and fine raiment, and hired a liveryman at a good round sum to carry them from St. Peter to the agency, a distance of nearly sixty miles. Two or three days later they reached Fort Ridgely on foot, on their way back to civilization, destitute and dusty, but full of wisdom. They asked the acting post commissary, A. W. Williamson, to intercede in obtaining for them a ration of bread and coffee, telling him frankly what had happened.

Williamson detested gambling, but sympathised with the hungry. He asked the men if they met Little Crow on their trip, and they readily admitted he was the author of their sorrows. Williamson, from his infancy, had known Little Crow, and made the fact known with a smile, at which the travellers accorded the wily chieftain the distinction of being by all odds and in all respects the shrewdest gambler they had ever met.

Not only was the noted chieftain a man of superior mental mouldy but he was physically superior as well. A remembered feature of his development was, that his front teeth, above and below, were double.

Whatever may be truthfully written of Little Crow's vices and sins in general, it is to his honour that he protested with his warriors against the killing of women and children as wrong and cowardly; but his cut-throat followers were none the less cruel and merciless.

Little Crow met a tragic death as related in the succeeding chapter.

The Man who Killed Little Crow

AN ACCOUNT OF THE TRAGEDY

Of no other man who achieved notoriety during the period of the Sioux Massacre, is there so little known or has there been so little written as of Nathan Lampson, the aged farmer who, in company with his son, Chauncey, killed Little Crow. Feeling that, for the sake of history, something should be recorded of the man who was the principal actor in the culminating tragedy of the Indian war, I spent two years by correspondence and inquiry in an earnest endeavour, after over forty-five years had elapsed, to obtain a brief historical sketch of Nathan Lampson, and had about given up in despair when I located a daughter, Mrs. Francis B. Ide, of Bellingham, Washington, from whom and her husband I obtained a brief sketch of the life of her father, whose portrait appears in this book, and who was the hero of the berry patch near Hutchinson, Minnesota, on the evening: of July 3, 1863. In an interview I found both Mr. and Mrs. Ide, former residents of Minnesota, very familiar with the scenes where the tragedy was enacted, with the story in detail of the killing of the Sioux chief, and with the personal history of the victors in that conflict, and in possession of a photograph of the principal actor.

From them I learned that Nathan Lampson was born near Bennington, Vermont, September 6, 1800. At the age of twenty-one he went to Brattleboro, Vermont. From there he went to the State of New York, where he married Hannah Bugbee, who, with all their children with a single exception, died after a few years. He later married Roxana Chambers, and removed to Michigan. Seven children were the result of the second marriage.

After the death of the second wife Mr. Lampson married a Mrs. Bigelow, and shortly after removed to McLeod County, Minnesota, settling six miles north of Hutchinson. Mr. Lampson had always followed the occupation of a farmer, and while he had lived a retiring life, he was a devoted lover of his country, and a strong Union man, and gave to the Union Army during the Civil War, his sons Nathan, Marshall, James, Chauncey, J. B., his stepson, Albert, and his sons-in-

NATHAN LAMPSON.
The man who, with his son Chauncey, killed
Little Crow.

law. John French, Francis B. Ide and John Adams, his family thus contributing nine soldiers to the Union cause.

While for safety the Lampson family, like scores of others, lived within the Hutchinson stockade during the spring and summer of 1863, the father, Nathan, and son, Chauncey, spent most of their time looking after the farm, six miles north of town, though to do so they risked their lives. Provisions were scarce, and in the latter part of the afternoon of Friday, July 3, 1863, the father and son started out with the hope of being able to kill a deer. Having tramped to within an hour of sunset, they struck the Greenleaf and Waterville road, which they followed a short distance when they espied two Indians in a wooded dump nearby, picking wild raspberries.

Lampson and son had old-fashioned muzzle-loading rifles, and the stock of the gun of the father was broken and tied up with twine, but the barrel was serviceable, and both Lampsons were good marksmen. Half a dozen steps from where the Lampsons saw the Indians, grew a popple tree, about which was entwined a drooping grapevine, under the cover of which Nathan Lampson, levelling his gun on the larger Indian, who stood with his side toward him, fired, his bullet passing into the body of Little Crow just above the hips. The Indians were taken by surprise, and although Little Crow went down, he regained his feet, and both himself and son sent a volley of buckshot after Nathan Lampson, who had dropped upon his knees, and not knowing how many Indians there might be in the party, was attempting to make his way out of the berry patch.

One buckshot lowed through the surface flesh of his shoulder. Though mortally wounded. Little Crow made his way to the road, and seeing Chauncey, levelled his gun upon him, but Chauncey was equal to the emergency, and both he and Little Crow fired at the same instant, the bullet from Chauncey's gun killing the famous Sioux chief. Chauncey had a close call, but escaped without a mark. Nathan Lampson had the powder-horn, and as Chauncey supposed his father had been killed when the three shots were fired, and as he himself had no powder with which to reload his gun, he set out for the farm home, which he reached completely exhausted, a condition due to ill health, the presumption that his father had been killed, to the belief that many Indians made up the war party, and to the highly exciting experience he had just passed through. He prostrated himself upon the bed, and had lain there but a few moments, when there came a rap at the door. He believed the Indians had followed him, but he was exhausted, and his gun was empty. Resigned to his fate he responded, "Come in," and to his great relief a hunter entered, who prepared supper while Chauncey rested. Having been refreshed and recuperated, Chauncey and the hunter set out for Hutchinson, which they reached in safety.

Nathan Lampson supposing his son had been killed by the Indians, went directly from the scene of the tragedy to Hutchinson, reaching the stockade late in the night, as he did not expose himself until the darkness surrounded his movements with safety. There to his great surprise and joy he learned of Chauncey's escape; and the father, who for hours had been mourned as dead, was welcomed by his family as one returned from the grave.

On the morning of July 4th, a team was sent out, and the body of the dead Indian was taken to Hutchinson, where it was later recognised as that of the great war chief, Little Crow.

Nathan Lampson died at Wilmot, South Dakota, in November, 1896, over 96 years of age, and his son Chauncey died in Minnesota in February, 1865.

Death of Chaska

In my diary, under date of August 3, 1863, I find the following notation:

> Hearts were saddened this morning by the report that one of our faithful scouts, Chaska, a full-blood Sioux, but an ever-true friend of the whites, and one who was largely instrumental in saving the missionaries during the massacre, was taken, suddenly ill after reaching camp last evening, and died during the night.

This event was a mere incident in the army life of that day. Officers and men of the ranks had fallen on those wild, desolate plains, during our operations, to sleep the sleep of death in a land in which no mark of civilization had ever been raised, and we were compelled to desert their lifeless forms in their loneliness, to follow the stern mandates of war. When Chaska was seized with the illness that terminated his life, we had just completed, our second day's march, August 2, 1863, on our return from the Missouri River, from a point opposite where Fort Lincoln was in later years founded.

At no time on all the expedition were the spirits of the soldiers in so high a state of effervescence as now. After long and weary marching, fighting, scouting,—after days, weeks and months of suffering from the merciless sun of midsummer on scorching, treeless plains, famishing for water and worn with fatigue, our faces were at last turned homeward, or at least toward civilization, and the influence of the fact upon the spirits of the men is indescribable, and particularly was this true of the morning we filed out of our Missouri River camp; and none were more highly elated over the hopeful prospects than were the sixty Sioux scouts.

I saw the scouts that morning as they mounted their horses to take the advance, and having met and frequently talked with Chaska on the expedition, I could not help noticing the broad smile on his stoical face, as he lithely sprang into his saddle, recognising us with a nod, a smile and the usual "*Ho!*" The scouts were full of the infectious joy that swept over the vast camp, and gave expression to their feelings in a low, Indian chant as they rode away, beating time with their *moccasined* heels against the bellies of their horses. Chaska had left a wife and children in the valley of the Minnesota River, and his thoughts were of them, but the fates had unsuspectingly decreed that he should see and welcome the rising sun of but one more day.

My diary states that our first day's march from the Missouri covered a distance of eighteen miles, and that the second day's march covered fifteen miles. So, if the old trail, made by our expedition, is still traceable, the clay of Chaska, who saved the missionaries during the massacre, may be found near it, thirty-three miles east of the Missouri River, and no Indian more truly deserved a monument than he.

Gallant Sons of Fillmore-Freeborn Counties

CREDIT NEVER HERETOFORE HISTORICALLY GIVEN

As the processes of time the more deeply etch the story of the famous defence of Fort Ridgely, the salient facts will become the more prominent, the non-essentials dissolving and the essentials standing forth in relief. To students of history who pursue their investigations, the query will naturally propound itself: Whence came the men who bore the brunt of the fiery ordeal whose crucial forces were converged about the isolated military post, now merely a memory? In the analyzation will be found sons of foreign lands—men born under the proud standards of kings and emperors, England, France, Germany, Norway and Sweden, contributing stalwart defenders to the fort. Many brave civilians took refuge at the fort at the beginning of the outbreak, and rendered valiant service, but the burden of responsibility and brunt of battle fell upon the soldiers.

Fillmore County, peopled by a brave and hardy class of pioneers, who had come into Minnesota Territory and founded the first settlements within less than a decade previous to the Civil War, had the honour, and one of which its appreciation will grow as the years roll on, of contributing from her noble sons the principal force of soldiers for the defence of Fort Ridgely and incidentally to the Minnesota frontier in the incipiency of the outbreak. Company B of the Fifth Minnesota was almost exclusively a Fillmore County body in its original personnel, and no other company raised in the State of Minnesota during the Civil War, contributed so many lives in battle on the sacrificial altar of war as did this Fillmore County company of men and boys.

No company of even the famous First Minnesota, that was in blood from Bull Run to Gettysburg, sustained so heavy a loss in killed in action during its years of service as did Company B of the Fifth, and when Minnesota shall have grown grey in history, Fillmore County's name, earned at the sacrifice of lives in the defines of Fort Ridgely and the Minnesota frontier, will still live brilliantly and imperishably. Than those of Company B who sank to earth in the August tragedies along the Minnesota River in 1862, no braver or better men ever lived, and no grander tribute was ever paid a state or nation than that conferred by Fillmore County in the contribution of these heroic men. While all parts of Fillmore County contributed to the membership of Company B, the enlistments at Chatfield, so far as any single locality was concerned, predominated, with Preston second in the number of men furnished.

Next to Fillmore, Freeborn County stands enviably in the limelight of history, for Lieutenant Sheehan's fifty men of Company C of the Fifth Minnesota, earned a glorious name for themselves and their county in their heroic part in the defence of Fort Ridgely. In nothing were these men second to those of Company B, except in numbers and opportunity. Fortunately, they were on the march to Fort Ripley when the massacre began, else they would no doubt have been sacrificed at Redwood Ferry, for surely they would have been taken to that disastrous field had they been at Fort Ridgely when the outbreak occurred, instead of having started homeward the day before.

History records few more glorious deeds than that performed by these Company C men when they made a forced march by night of forty-two miles to relieve the distressed garrison of Fort Ridgely, after having marched all the previous day on their homeward journey.

Lieutenant Sheehan, in all his career, never did an act that redounded more to his honour than did this memorable feat of twenty-four hours of continual marching, but this accomplishment was merely an index to the character of the men as soldiers, who covered the name of Freeborn County with everlasting glory, by their deeds of heroism, wherever duty called.

The Renville Rangers, under Lieutenant James Gorman, were new recruits, enlisted at the Redwood Indian Agency less than a week before the outbreak. The men were seasoned, hardy frontiers men. They were brave and athletic. Their environment had familiarised them with Indian character, and had made them past-masters in the art of alertness. They had not enlisted to fight Indians, but their services in the defence of Fort Ridgely can never be overestimated. They knew the tricks of war at which the Sioux were adepts. They knew the Sioux language, which they overheard and repeated to the garrison. They were brave, daring and efficient men. They were organised and under good leadership.

These three military organisations, about one hundred and fifty strong, received and repelled the shock of battle, kept tireless vigil, inspired the weak, consoled the bereaved, and by the aid of brave souls from among the refugees, saved Fort Ridgely and hundreds of lives in and out of the garrison, dependent upon the valour of these men.

MIRACULOUS ESCAPE OF THE REYNOLDS FAMILY

The ordinary imagination is hardly elastic enough to grasp the condition of the surprised and panic-stricken settlers, when without warning they were swooped down upon by the cruel, red-handed Sioux, who took extreme delight in their tantalising, tormenting methods, to be followed by death itself.

Usually there was but one thing to do, and that was for the hapless, helpless settlers to fly for their lives. In these attempts hundreds were shot down as they ran, but occasionally a poor mortal would drop unobserved in the high weeds and grass, or in a patch of corn, and escape by hiding. In the excitement of clubbing, scalping and mutilating the fallen victims, and in plundering the buildings, and finally in the burning of them, some members of a family or party would be lost track of, and would make their way under cover of night, to some place of safety, usually to the fort, if not detected on the way and murdered. Frequently these escaping wretches would walk into the very jaws of death, and often, when not entrapped, were beset on every hand by dangers that were terrifying.

Joseph B. Reynolds and wife, Valencia Reynolds, were in the employ of the government as instructors at a school back some ten miles from the Redwood Agency, where there were no other whites employed or residing. On the morning of August 18th, Francis Patoile and a companion of Yellow Medicine drove up to the Reynolds' home and asked if they could have breakfast. Mrs. Reynolds replied affirmatively, and as the meal was about ready, she had the men sit down to the table. While they were eating Antonia La Blaugh, a half blood who resided with a neighbouring half-breed, John Moore, came to the house and asked to see Mr. Reynolds, to whom he stated that Moore had sent him to warn him of the outbreak at the agency that morning.

Mr. Reynolds sent La Blaugh after Moore, and as he departed, the news was broken to the men at breakfast, and Mr. Patoile asked to take the family to New Ulm, he having a team with him, while Mr. and Mrs. Reynolds had but a one-horse rig. In the Reynolds family were three girls, Mary Schwandt, Mattie Williams and Mary Anderson. These Mr. Patoile took into his wagon, together with a Mr. Davis and the companion who accompanied him from Yellow Medicine. Moore came hastily, and warned the people to fly for their lives in the direction of New Ulm, and pointed out the way least likely to be beset with Indians. Mr. and Mrs. Reynolds climbed into their buggy, but before they were out of the house a party of squaws had reached, entered and begun to plunder it.

Now began a wild chase for life. The parties became separated after a short distance from the house, and were not together again. Mr. and Mrs. Reynolds drove to within sight of the Redwood Agency, meeting a half-breed by the way whom they questioned as to the extent and seriousness of the outbreak. They were informed that matters could not well be worse, from reports received from the Indians themselves. They now met Shakopee, near whose village their home was, and asked him the meaning of the direful rumours. He said little to them, but told them to keep back on the open prairie. Indians were seen hastening toward the agency, giving new colour to the shocking stories that had spread like wildfire over the surrounding country. They dropped back to the south-westward so as to conceal themselves behind a ridge as much as possible.

When at the nearest point to the agency behind this ridge Mr. and Mrs. Reynolds abandoned their horse and buggy long enough to creep to the top of the ridge and peer over it, only to discover that a party of Indians were but a short distance away, gathering up cattle. They could see that the doors of the buildings at the agency were all open, and that the Indians were very numerous and in great confusion. They now felt confident the rumours of a general massacre at the agency were too true, and returning to their buggy hastily set out for New Ulm, as to reach the fort they must cross the Minnesota River, which was not fordable.

They took the open prairie instead of following the road, and saw many Indians to their left, hastening to the agency. They at length overtook the government carpenter of the agency, who with his family was hastening in a flight for life. His wagon was overloaded with his family and neighbours, so Mr. Reynolds took two of the carpenter's children in his rig. This was at a point very nearly opposite Fort Ridgely. They met two parties of Indians, and Mr. Reynolds attempted to enter into conversation with one of them, but could elicit no word of response. They also met two parties of squaws, one of which tried to persuade the fugitives to return to the agency.

Getting down to the settlement below the reservation, a large party of Indians was discovered on the side towards the river. This party was about a hundred rods away, and on foot. There were mounted Indians nearer, on either hand, and a naked Indian but a few rods to the front of the fugitives, who now felt that their doom was sealed. Reynolds called to the naked Indian, trusting for some friendly response, but the savage lifted his gun and snapped both barrels at Reynolds and his wife, without the piece being discharged. In despair Mrs. Reynolds turned her head, when she saw an Indian riding swiftly toward them. He called to them to turn back, and excitedly motioned to them to hurry.

This Indian got between the Reynolds rig and the Indian on foot who was trying to recharge his gun to get a shot at the fugitives. Now dangers thickened. The Indian who came to befriend and help the fugitives rode a white horse, so that he was easily distinguished from all others. He kept all pursuers at bay, and the race was a wild one, with little hope of escape. After a two-mile ride Reynolds and wife ran into a large party of squaws, accompanied by one man. That they would here be detained if not killed, they had little doubt. Reynolds, as he passed the Indian in the party of squaws, asked him if he intended to kill them, and he said "No; go on," and offered no resistance.

Reynolds and his wife now turned to the Minnesota River, and being opposite Fort Ridgely decided that their only hope, since they were still pursued, was to reach that place of refuge. Their horse being jaded unto exhaustion, they drove to the river at its nearest point, and hastily unhitching, Mr. Reynolds swam the stream with the horse, it having been agreed that Mrs. Reynolds should conceal herself and the two Nairn children and await the return of Reynolds, who was to go to the fort and obtain assistance and a boat if possible, with which to make a safe crossing. The Indians followed the trail to the river, but evidently concluded the Reynolds party had escaped safely to the opposite side of the stream or had been drowned.

Mrs. Reynolds wore *moccasins*, and shrewdly had the two children precede her, and she then covered their tracks with her own, toeing-in squaw fashion, along the soft earth of the river bottom. Owing to this forethought on her part the pursuing Indians did not follow her trail, and she went into hiding and remained in concealment until a party from the fort arrived, and calling to her to come to the water, she was taken over and herself and the two children safely conveyed to the fort, more than a mile away, and thus saved. Mrs. Reynolds was a very capable woman, and rendered great assistance, once at the fort, in caring for the wounded, making cartridges, etc.

The other party that left the Reynolds' home with Francis Patoile met a sad fate in their flight after being separated from Mr. and Mrs. Reynolds on the 18th. The Patoile party, after many frightful experiences, reached a point about eight miles above New Ulm, when they ran into a large party of Indians from which there was, from the first, little hope of escape. These Indians had been raiding the settlements, and with wagons loaded with plunder and their hands reeking with blood, were journeying toward the Redwood Agency. They had someplace obtained liquor, and many of them were under its influence. They surrounded the Patoile team and shot its owner, Francis Patoile, who fell out of the wagon, dead.

The other occupants of the wagon jumped out and ran for a neighbouring slough. All the men, however, were shot down before reaching the high grass of the marsh, and Mary Anderson, one of the girls, received a bullet which brought her to earth, the missile penetrating her abdomen. She was picked up however, and carried and put in a wagon, when the other two girls, Mattie Williams and Mary Schwandt, were followed into the slough and captured and borne away in the wagons. They all reached the agency at night, and went into camp near Little Crow's house, where they were kept for several days, subjected to nameless treatment. With a knife Mary Anderson cut the bullet from her body, after Waucouta, an Indian who had tried to assist her, had failed to extract the missile.

Poor Mary Anderson died from her wound and from exposure, but her girl companions remained with her to the last, and did all their kind hearts and generous hands could suggest to the last. She lay in a *tepee*, on the ground, and as it rained hard all night, death claimed her during the silent hours, while the little clothing she had on was saturated and her body cold and wet from the flooded earth, and thus her spirit left her. Joseph Campbell, a half-breed, directed a party of Indians who wrapped the form of Mary in a piece of canvas and buried it near where she died. Mattie Williams and Mary Schwandt remained in captivity, the victims of fiendish outrages, until rescued at Camp Release. These girls were told by the Indians that Mr. and Mrs. Reynolds were killed while trying to escape on the 18th, and it was believed among the Indians that this was true, as escape seemed impossible.

Mary Schwandt was released from her cruel captivity at the surrender of Camp Release, but only to learn that her father, mother, two brothers and her only sister had been murdered at their home on Beaver Creek at the beginning of the outbreak. (See *Captives*, the narratives of seven women, including Mary Schwant, taken prisoner by the Indians; Leonaur 2010.)

The Remarkable Experience of a Remarkable Woman

HOW FAMILIES WERE WIPED OUT

As far above Fort Ridgely as twenty-seven miles was a new, vigorous settlement, an extension of that known as the Beaver Creek settlement. All along this region the country was most promising,—the soil rich and responsive to cultivation, the natural pastures luxuriant, the water excellent and the region in all respects attractive. Hardly a day passed, up to the very hour of the massacre, that a new family was not added to this promising, happy community. Fort Ridgely was known well to this and all other surrounding settlements. While none dreamed of the hostility of Indians, still all appreciated they had cast their lot in an Indian country, or at least adjacent to an Indian reservation, and this fact made the military post seem a place of friendly refuge in case of any threatened danger, and it thus became associated with everyday life, and its location was well in mind as a result of prudent thought, though comparatively few of the settlers had ever visited the fort.

The settlements at and above Beaver Creek were so earnestly devoted to home-making that little note was taken of matters not immediately associated with patient industry, and hence the outbreak caught the people unawares, with no time for organisation or preparation when once the gleaming knife of the savage was unsheathed.

On Monday, August 18th, August Fross and Eckmel Groundman, of the settlement above Beaver Creek, started to the Redwood Agency, ignorant of the awful tragedy that had been enacted in the early part of that day at that point. When within a few miles of the agency these men were startled to find the lifeless forms of a women and her two children by the roadside, every indication pointing to the fact that a foul murder had been committed, and there were signs that Indians had committed the horrible deed. The men were so aroused that they resolved to report the discovery to the neighbours in the vicinity, and to their amazement they found that at the homes of the several settlers which they visited, were stark in death, entire families.

There could no longer be a particle of doubt as to the meaning of all this. The first house they visited was that of a Mr. Buss. Here they found the husband, wife and three children cruelly murdered. The next house was that of a settler named Monweiler, and here the family was slain. Hurrying to the home of John Rusby, they found the entire family, consisting of husband, wife and three children, dead, the latter, with their skulls split open. The men, filled with horror, now realised the danger that not only threatened their own lives and those of their defenceless families, but also of the entire settlement. They returned homeward in great haste, and informed the settlers of the impending danger. Hastily; word was passed from house to house, with a view to assembling all who could; be reached, for flight. The place selected for assembling the neighbourhood was the home of Paul Kitzman.

What followed here could not be better told than in the language of Mrs. Justina Kreiger, sister of Paul Kitzman, who related the facts to the Sioux Commission, appointed after the massacre. Mrs. Kreiger said:

"It was about 8 o'clock p. m., of Monday, August 18, 1862, when we all determined to flee to Ft. Ridgely. One of the neighbours, Mr. Schwandt, (Father of Mary Schwandt referred to in the preceding chapter) had not been informed of the raid and our intended flight, and on this account a delay took place to enable messengers to reach and inform him. When the messengers arrived at the house, they found Mr. Schwandt's oxen standing at the door eating flour. Feathers were seen lying around the yard, and the house seemed to have been plundered. John Waltz, son-in-law of Mr. Schwandt, was lying in the door, dead, shot through with three balls, causing, no doubt, instant death; It was now dark, and no other dead bodies were then discovered. The house had the smell of fire, as though something had been burning and had gone out. The daughter of Mr. Schwandt, *enceinte*, was cut open, as was learned afterward, the child taken alive from its mother, and nailed to a tree. The son of Mr. Schwandt, aged thirteen years, who had been beaten by the Indians until dead as was supposed, was present and saw the entire tragedy.

"He saw the child taken alive from the body of his sister, Mrs. Waltz, and nailed to a tree in the yard. It struggled sometime after the nails were driven through it! This occurred in the forenoon of the 18th. Mr. Schwandt was on the house, shingling, and was there shot, and rolled off, falling to the ground, dead. The mother of this boy was taken a few yards from the house, into newly-ploughed ground, and her head severed from her body. Mr. Fross, a labourer, was lying dead near Mrs. Schwandt. The boy remained in his retreat until after dark, when he came over to a settlement three or four miles distant, and stopped at a Mr. Suche's house, on the prairie.

"Here he found about thirty dead bodies, and a living child, two or three years old, near its mother, wounded and unable to walk. He took the child and travelled with it toward Fort Ridgely. After carrying his burden three or four miles, and being exhausted, he placed it in a house, promising to come after it the next day. He did this to get rid of the child, so that he might possibly make his own escape. The child was afterward found, a prisoner, at Camp Release, and brought to Fort Ridgely, and there died from the effects of wounds and the hardships endured among the Indians. The lad, August Schwandt, arrived at the fort, nearly thirty miles from his home, after traveling four nights and lying by of days.

"The messengers returning from the Schwandt home, thirteen families, with eleven teams, now started, and moved forward as fast as possible toward Fort Ridgely. We first made toward the Chippewa River, on the prairie, for safety. We journeyed until 2 or 3 o'clock of Tuesday morning, the 19th, and then inclined our course toward Beaver Creek, heading toward the fort. In this direction we went until the sun was some two hours high, and found we had made about fourteen miles. Eight Indians, on horseback—some naked and some with blankets on, all armed with guns—now came up with us.

"In our train were eleven men, armed with such guns as they had in the neighbourhood. Our teams, including the wagons and oxen, were so arranged as to afford the best protection. The men, at first, determined to fight the Indians, but, as they came within about one hundred yards, and our men were about to fire upon them, the Indians put down their guns and made signs not to fire, pretending that they were friendly Indians; and sad to relate, our men, believing them to be friends, did not fire.

"One Indian, with whom all were acquainted, who had frequently been at my brother's house, and spoke good English, came up to us. Paul Kitzman, my brother, stepped out from behind the wagons, and shook hands with this savage. The Indian kissed my brother, and showed great friendship. Judas-like he betrayed us with a kiss! This Indian inquired after our concerns, and where the teams were going. Paul Kitzman replied that 'We are in a flight to the fort, as all the people in the neighbourhood had been killed by the Indians'. The Indian answered that 'the Sioux did not kill anybody', that 'the people had been murdered by the Chippewas'; and that 'they were now on their way after the Chippewas, to kill them;' and wished our folks to return, as the Chippewas were down near Beaver Creek, or toward the fort, and that we would probably be killed if we went on.

"At the same time this pretendedly good Indian placed his hand on Kitzman's shoulder, saying, 'You are a good man; it is too bad to kill you'. Our folks were still determined to go on, and would not yet consent to return. This Indian then went around and shook hands with all of us, and said he would not hurt us, and that he was going to save us from harm. Paul Kitzman had great confidence in this man. He had frequently hunted with him, and thought him a good Indian.

"Seeing now his advantage over us, he beckoned to the others to come up. When they came, they were exceedingly friendly, shaking hands with the men and women, and telling the women to quiet the children, who were frightened at the sight of the savages. All of us were now fully assured that they were really friendly.

"Seeing their success, the Indians put up their guns into cases kept for that purpose, and the whites put up their guns in the wagons. All now joined in a friendly meal of bread and milk, and our folks, each of them, gave them some money; and as they had given such conclusive evidence of friendship, a return was agreed upon. All the teams were turned around, and we began to retrace our steps, the Indians traveling in company with us for some five or six miles. Our men now asked the Indians if they could unyoke the oxen and let them feed. The Indians made no objection and seemed pleased with the idea. Our pretended friends now wished something to eat. We gave them some bread and butter and watermelon. They retired about a quarter of a mile, and ate their meal alone.

"After dinner they motioned us to go on. Paul Kitzman, going toward them, was again requested to go on, the Indians saying they would follow directly. And again, assuring us they would not leave us, but would protect us from the Chippewas, and see us safe to our homes, we moved on. The Indians coming up, some took position alongside of the train, the others in front and rear. This new manner caused some suspicion, and the whites talked to each other in German, and thought it was best to fire on the Indians; but all the guns were in the wagons, and no one dared to touch them, lest the motion should be recognised by the savages as a commencement of hostilities.

"Notwithstanding the difficulty, all the men, at one time, except Paul Kitzman, were determined to fire upon the treacherous foe. He persuaded them not to do it, as he had all confidence in them. 'Besides, our guns are in the wagons, and each Indian has his in his hand, ready to fire in an instant, and every white man would be killed at the first shot, before a gun could be got out of the wagons.'

"We had now, by various stages, arrived at the place where Fross and Groundman had discovered the dead bodies on the afternoon of Monday, the 18th. Our hitherto friendly Indians now showed signs of anger, became impudent and frantic, and drew in line of battle behind our train, all having double-barrelled guns except one. Our enemy could make fifteen shots at one round, without reloading. They now came up and demanded our money. Our fears, in regard to their real and ultimate intentions, became a certainty in the minds of every one of our party. One savage came forward and received the money; the others all remained drawn up in battle-line.

"I had a pocket-book, and my husband came to me for the money. I gave him five dollars and kept the rest. He told me at this time he was going to be killed, and gave me a pocket-knife by which to remember him. After the Indians had received all the money, they started off to the settlements where the white people had been killed.

"We still went on with our train towards our homes, and within a mile and a half of our house we found two men dead, who had been recently killed. These men were not recognised by any of our folks, but had evidently been killed by the same Indians. We now all concluded our race was about ended. We were to die by these fiends. The men took the guns out of the wagons, and concluded if they could reach a house, they could protect themselves pretty well; but while going forward toward our house, thirteen or fourteen Indians came up behind us, when within one hundred yards of the house. The Indians immediately surrounded us and fired, all the men but three falling at the first fire. It was done so quickly I could not see whether our men fired at all; yet I believe some of them did. No Indians however, were killed by our party. Mr. Fross, a Mr. Gotlieb Zable, and my husband, were yet alive.

"The Indians then asked the women if they would go along with them, promising to save all that would go, and threatening all who refused with instant death. Some were willing to go, others refused. I told them I chose to die with my husband and my children. My husband urged me to go with them, telling me they would probably not kill me, and that I could perhaps get away in a short time. I still refused, preferring to die with him and the children. One of the women, who had started off with the Indians, turned around, hallooed to me to come with them, and, taking a few steps toward me, was shot dead.

"At the same time two of the men left alive and six of the women were killed, leaving, of all the men, only my husband alive. Some of the children were also killed at this last fire. A number of children yet remained around the wagons; these the savages beat with the butts of their guns until they supposed all were dead. Some soon after rose up from the ground, with the blood streaming down their faces, when they were beaten again and killed. This was the most horrible scene I had yet witnessed.

"I stood yet in the wagon, refusing to get out and go with the murderers, my own husband, meanwhile, begging me to go, as he saw they were about to kill him. He stood by the wagon, watching an Indian at his right, ready to shoot, while another was quite behind him, with his gun aimed at him. I saw them both shoot at the same time. Both shots took effect in the body of my husband, and one of the balls passed through his body and struck my dress below the knee. My husband fell between the oxen, and seemed not quite dead, when a third ball was shot into his head, and a fourth into his shoulder, which probably entered his heart.

"Now I determined to jump out of the wagon and die beside my husband; but as I was standing up to jump, I was shot, seventeen buckshot, as was afterward ascertained, entering my body. I then fell back into the wagon-box. I had eight children in the wagon-bed, and one in a shawl. All these were either my own children or else my stepchildren. What had now become of the children in the wagon I did not know, and what was the fate of the baby I could only surmise.

"All that I then knew was the fact that I was seized by an Indian and very roughly dragged from the wagon, and that the wagon was drawn over my body and ankles. I suppose the Indians then left me for a time, how long I do not know, as I was for a time almost if not quite insensible. When I was shot the sun was still shining, but when I came to it was dark. My baby, as my children afterward told me, was, when they found it, lying about five yards from me, crying. One of my stepchildren, a girl thirteen years of age, took the baby and ran off. The Indians took two with them. These were the two next to the youngest. One of them, a boy four years old, taken first by the Indians, had got out of the wagon, or in some other way, made his escape, and came back to the dead body of his father. He took his father by the hand, saying to him, 'papa, papa, don't sleep so long!'

"Two of the Indians afterward came back, and one of them, getting off his horse, took the child from the side of his father and handed it to the other on horseback, who rode off with it. This child was afterward recovered at Camp Release. The other one I never heard of. Two of the boys ran away on the first attack, and reached the woods, some eighty rods distant. One climbed a tree; the younger, aged seven, remaining below. This eldest boy, aged eight, witnessed the massacre of all who were killed at this place. He remained in the tree until I was killed, as he supposed. He then came down and told his brother what he had seen, and that their mother was dead. While they were crying over the loss of their parents, August Gest, a son of a neighbour, cautioned them to keep still, as the Indians might hear them, and come and kill them too.

"Here these boys remained for three days hiding as well as they could from the savages, who were passing and repassing. The boys went to neighbouring houses and turned out cattle and horses, and whatever live stock was shut up in stables, sheds or pens, and in this way occasionally found something to eat. On Wednesday morning, the 20th, they saw our house on fire. On the third night after the massacre, they concluded to go to the fort, twenty-seven miles distant, in reaching which they spent eight days and nights, traveling only at night, and hiding by day in the grass. They all reached the fort in safety,

139

but had some very narrow escapes. They often saw Indians, but were not themselves discovered.

"At one time these children, hungry and lonely, found a friendly cow, on whose rich milk they made a delicious meal. Another time on their journey, while lying hid in the prairie grass, they discovered a team coming on a road nearby. It carried, most likely, some white family to the fort. They were almost ready to jump up and shout for joy at the sight; and now, when about to run toward the team, what an awful shock these little children were doomed to experience! Behold, a company of painted savages arose from a clump of grass close by them, who ran and captured the team, and, turning it the other way, drove off, the screams of a woman in the wagon rending the air as long as her cries could be heard in the distance! Thus, disappointed they hid closer than ever in the grass, until night, and again took up their weary march to the fort. They knew not how many dangers unseen they had escaped. They saw on the route many dead bodies of men, women, children and animals. In one place seven dead Indians were all placed in a row. This was near Beaver Creek, as they supposed. There were also many white people dead at the latter place.

"I must now turn back a moment, to trace the fate of my baby. My stepdaughter, aged thirteen, as soon as the Indians had left the field, started off for the woods. In passing where I lay, and supposing me dead, and finding the baby near, crying, she hastily took it up, and bore it off the field of death in her arms. The other girl, my own child six years old, arose out of the grass, and two of the other children that had been beaten over the head and left for dead, now recovered and went off toward the woods, and soon rejoined each other there. These last two were also my stepchildren. I was still lying on the field.

"The three largest of the children who went to the woods returned to the place of massacre, leaving the boy in charge of the six-year-old girl. As they came to the field, they found seven children and one woman, (referred to in a previous chapter as found by Freniere,) evincing some signs of life, and who had to some extent recovered. These children were a son of Paul Kitzman, aged two and a half years; two sons of August Horning, one and three years old; a son and daughter of Mr. Groundman, the daughter aged four and the son one year, the girl having her hand shot off; two sons of Mr. Tille, one and two years old, and a son of Mr. Urban, aged thirteen.

"All these were covered with blood, had been beaten by the butt of the gun and hacked by the tomahawk, except the girl whose hand had

140

been severed by a gunshot. The woman found was Anna Zable. She had received two wounds—a cut in the shoulder and a stab in the side. These were all taken to the house of my husband by these three girls. It was now on the evening of Wednesday, August 20th. They remained in the house all night, doing all that could be done for each other. This was a terrible place!—a hospital of invalid children, with no one older than thirteen years to give directions for the dressing of wounds, nursing the infant children, and giving food to the hungry, in a house that had already been plundered of everything of value.

"The children cried piteously for their mothers, who were dead, or in a bondage worse than death. The poor child with its hand off moaned and sighed, saying to its suffering fellows 'Mother would always take care of me when I was hurt, but now she will not come to me.' Poor child! her mother was already among the dead.

"When daylight dawned, Mrs. Zable, thinking it unsafe to remain in this place, awoke the eldest girls and on consultation, concluded to leave the young children and go into the woods, or into the prairie. The girl of thirteen, and principal dependence of the little company, awoke my two stepchildren, and the one six years old who had taken charge of the baby in the woods the day previously, and August Urban, aged thirteen. These, taking with them the baby, quietly left the house, and went to the place of the massacre to look after me, as they knew I had been left on the field the previous day.

"As this little company were looking over the field, they saw a savage, as they supposed, coming on horseback, who turned out, fortunately, to be Antoine Freniere, the interpreter, who was riding for life to save if possible, his own family. These children and Mrs. Zable, after seeing Freniere, went about eighty rods from the field of the late massacre, and hid in the grass near a small creek. They were here but a very short time, when the savages from the river, with the ox-teams previously taken from the party now dead, came to the field, and stripping off the clothing from men and women, went toward the houses. They were soon seen at our house, gathering plunder; and when this was completed, they set fire to the house, and with its destruction perished the seven children left there a short time before!

"To this awful scene the escaping party were eye-witnesses! The Indians departed while the house was in flames, and the children came to Mrs. Tille's house near the woods, and being very hungry, diligently hunted the house over, and found flour and butter, and there cooked their dinner. Here, too, they fed the baby. They remained in the woods around the houses of the settlement for three days. The third day they saw a body of Indians go to the house of August Fros, plunder it of all valuables, and carry them away in a wagon. The baby had been left at Mr. Tille's house, asleep on the bed, where the party had last taken dinner;

"The little girls and Mrs. Zable, being frightened by the sight of these Indians, hid themselves in the woods until dark. They then started for the fort, and soon passed by our house, yet smouldering. They also passed the field of death, resting by day and traveling by night. In this way they journeyed eleven days.

"The incidents of this wonderful journey would be worthy of a loner description. They saw many dead bodies, both of white people and Indians. Indians, in small parties, were frequently seen prowling over the prairie and in the timber. The food of the children was principally corn, eaten raw, as they had no means of making a fire. They found a camp kettle, which they used in carrying water a part of the time. They left the baby at the house of Mr. Tille, and no further tidings has ever been heard of it.

"Our escaping party, when in sight of the fort, did not know the place. They feared it was an Indian camp. Before this, one had come near being left for dead. The child six years old, on the last day of their travel, had fallen down from exhaustion and hunger, and Mrs. Zable advised the eldest girl to leave her and go on, but the other children screamed and cried so piteously at the very idea, that the advice was not heeded. The little sufferer, too, showed signs of life. They all halted, and the advanced ones came back, and being near a creek the child was taken to it, and was soon revived by the free use of water on its head. Here they remained for some time, and, finding the rind of a melon in the road, gave it to the fainting child, and by rest and the tender care of the other children, it was again able to journey on with the others.

"They had ascended the hill, near the fort, and there sat down to deliberate what to do. Whether what they saw was an Indian encampment, or Fort Ridgely, they could not readily determine. The children believed the discovery to be Fort Ridgely, but Mrs. Zable thought it a camp of savages. Finally, the children declared they saw the troops plainly. This turned out to be true, as the troops soon came toward them, having discovered this little company on the prairie. The five children were soon in the wagon brought for their rescue, but the doubting Mrs. Zable, supposing the Indians coming, made off from the rescuers as fast as she could. The troops soon caught her, and all were brought into the fort. They were a forlorn-looking company—some wounded by hatchet-cuts, others beaten by the butts of guns, and others still bleeding from wounds made by gunshots, and all nearly famished by hunger and thirsty and scantily covered by a few rags yet hanging to their otherwise naked persons.

"As for myself, I remained on the field of the massacre, and in the place where I fell, when I was shot, until about midnight of Tuesday, August 19th. All this time or nearly so, unconscious of passing events I did not even hear the boy cry. All that part of the narrative covered by this period of time

"I relate upon the testimony of my children, who reported the same to me. At this time of night, I arose from the field of the dead, with a feeble ability to move at all. I soon heard the tread of savage men, speaking in the Sioux language. They came near, and proved to be two savages only. These two went over the field, examining the dead bodies, to rob them of what yet remained upon them. They soon came to me, kicked me, then felt my pulse, first on the right hand, then on the left, and, to be sure, felt for the pulsation of the heart. I remained silent, holding my breath. They probably supposed me dead. They conversed in Sioux for a moment. I shut my eyes, and awaited what else was to befall me with a shudder.

"The next moment a sharp-pointed knife was felt at my throat, then, passing downward, to the lower portion of the abdomen, cutting not only the clothing entirely from my body, but actually penetrating the fleshy making but a slight wound on the chest, but, at the pit of the stomach, entering the body to the intestines! My arms were then taken separately out of the clothing. I was seized rudely by the hair, and hurled headlong to the ground, entirely naked.

"How long I was unconscious I cannot imagine, yet I think it was not a great while. When I came to, I beheld one of the most horrible sights I had ever seen, in the person of myself! I saw, also, these two savages about eight rods off; a light from the north, probably the aurora, enabling me to see objects at some distance.

"At the same time I discovered my own condition, I saw one of these inhuman savages seize poor Wilhelmina Kitzman, who was my niece, and yet alive, hold her up by the foot, her head downward, her clothes falling over her head; while holding her there by one hand, in the other he grasped a knife, with which he hastily cut the flesh around one of the legs, close to the body, and then, by twisting and wrenching, broke the ligaments and bone, until the limb was entirely severed from the body, the child screaming frantically, 'O, God, O, God.' When the limb was off, the child, thus mutilated, was thrown down on the ground, stripped of her clothing, and left to die! The other children of Paul Kitzman were then taken along with the Indians, crying most piteously. I now lay down, and for some hours knew nothing more.

"Hearing nothing now, I tried to get up, and laboured a long time to do so. I finally succeeded in getting up on my left side and left arm, my right side being dead and useless. I now discovered, too, my clothing was all off. I tried to find some dead person, to get clothing to cover me. I could not get any, for when I found a dead person with clothes yet on, I saw Indian ponies close by, and fearing Indians were near, I made no further attempt. I then crawled off toward my own house, to hunt something to put on me, and, when near the house, I discovered something dark, close by, which turned out to be my own clothes, which had been torn from me. I bound them around me as well as I could, and, not daring to enter the house, which was not yet burned, I turned my course toward Fort Ridgely. It was yet night, but was light, from the aurora perhaps; at least I saw no moon.

"I made first to a creek, some five hundred yards from the house, and washed the blood from my person, bathed my wounds and drank some water. This night I made six miles, according to my estimate. I here came to a settlement in the timber, on some creek that put into the Minnesota River. I did not know the name of the settlement. It was now near daylight. Here I remained, weak, sick, wounded and faint from loss of blood, for three long days, drinking water, and this was my only nourishment all this time. At the end of these three days I heard Indians around, and being afraid of still other injuries, made my way to the left, through the prairie, and thought to find the Chippewa Indians, but I found none. I saw plenty of Sioux Indians.

"I think it was Saturday, the 23rd of August, I lay down and thought I should die of hunger. I then took to eating grass, and drank water from the sloughs. In this way I travelled at night, and lay by during the day. On Sunday night I came to a creek and found many dead persons. I turned over one of these to see whether he was a white man or an Indian, but he smelled so badly I turned him down again without ascertaining. He had on a white shirt and dark pants, and I suppose he was a white man. I saw great quantities of bedding, furniture and books scattered and torn in pieces, at a creek far out on the prairie. It was not Beaver Creek. The same night I crossed this creek. The water was up to my armpits, and the cane grass tall and thick. Here again I saw more dead persons. One woman was lying on her back, and a child nearby, pulled asunder by the legs. I then travelled around on the prairie, saw no roads, had nothing to eat. and no water for three days.

"During my wanderings, early in the morning, I gathered the dew from the grass in my hand, and drank it; and when my clothes became wet with dew, I sucked the water from them. This gave me great relief from the burning thirst I experienced. Finally, at the end of these three days of terrible suffering; I came to a road. This road I followed, and in a low place found some standing water in puddles in the mud, and tried to get it in my clothes, but the water was too shallow. I then got down and sucked up and eagerly drank the water from the mud. My tongue and lips were now cracked open from thirst. After this I went on and found two dead bodies on the road, and, a few steps farther, a number of men, women and children, all dead!

"On the thirteenth day I came to Beaver Creek, and, for the first time found out for certain where I was. Here I discovered a house in a field, went to it, and saw that everything had been destroyed. The dog was alive, and seemed to be barking at someone, but showed friendship for me. Being afraid that savages were around, I went again into the woods. After staying there for a short time, a shot was fired, and then I heard some person calling, I thought in German. I did not answer the call as I did not think it was for me. But, after all was still, I went on, and passed Beaver Creek, went up the hill, and then saw an Indian, with a gun pointed at some object. He soon went off in an opposite direction without discovering me. Fearing others were about, I went to the woods, and being wearied, lay down and slept. I do not know how long I slept, but when I awoke it was about noon.

"I was again lost, and did not know where to go. I wandered about in the woods, hunting for my wily, and finally, as the evening star appeared, I found my direction, taking an eastern course until I came to a creek again. I now saw I must be near the Minnesota River. I went into a house nearby, took a piece of buffalo-robe, went to the river bottom and lay down to rest. Here I found wild plums, and ate some of them. This night it rained long and hard. On the next morning I found that I was too weak and tired to travel, and so remained all that day and all the next night, wishing that the savages might come and put an end to my sufferings. It rained all this day.

"Here I felt sure I must die, and that I should never leave this place alive. The cold sweat was on my forehead. With great effort I raised up to take one more look around me, and to my surprise I saw two persons with guns, but could not tell whether they were white men or Indians. I rejoiced however, because I thought they would put an end to my sufferings. But, as they came near, I saw they had bayonets, and knew they were white soldiers, and made signs for them to come to me. The soldiers, fearing some trick, seemed afraid to come near me. After making sundry examinations they finally came up. One of my neighbours, Lewis Daily, first advanced, and seeing I was a white woman, called to his partner, who also came.

"They soon brought me some water, and gave me a drink, and wet my head, washed my face and carried me to a house nearby. Here they proposed to leave me until the other troops came up, but yielding; to my earnest entreaty they carried me along until the other portion of the soldiers arrived. One of them went into a house and found a dress, and put it on me, the clothes I had on being all torn to pieces, Dr. Daniels came along directly, examined my wounds, and gave me some water and wine, made a requisition for a wagon, fixed up a bed and had me placed upon it.

"Now the train followed along the river bottom some distance, then took to the open prairie. Here we found a woman cut into four pieces, and two children by her, cut in pieces also. They buried these bodies, and passed down from Henderson's house in the direction of the fort. All the soldiers seemed to take great care of me. The doctor dressed my wounds, and did all that could be done for me. The wagon I was in soon came into company with the burial party who were going into camp at Birch Coulie.

"The savages attacked this burial party on the same night after I was rescued by the soldiers, or rather on the following morning, Tuesday, September 2nd. In that disastrous affair (the battle of Birch Coulie) it was thought proper to overturn all the wagons, as a means of better security against the murderous fire of the Indians. When they came to the wagon in which I lay, someone said, 'do not overturn that wagon, for it contains a sick woman,' and they passed by. This was the only wagon left standing. Behind the wagons and dead horses, killed by the Indians, our men lay on the ground and fought the savages with determination seldom if ever equalled. It was victory or death. I was in a good position to see and hear all that went on during the battle.

"I was, too, in a most exposed position. The wagon was a fine mark. Standing up as it did above everything else on the open prairie, it afforded the best possible target for savage marksmen. The wagon was literally shot to pieces. Some of the spokes were shot off. The cover was completely riddled with ball-holes. The cup in which I attempted to take my medicine during the fight, was knocked away from my mouth by a passing rifle ball. I did not attempt to reclaim it. The smell of gunpowder almost took my breath away. Some five slight wounds was all the damage I sustained in this awful battle.

"I saw it all, from the commencement to the close. Sleep was impossible, and my hearing was wonderfully acute. The battle lasted all the day Tuesday, and all the night following, until about midnight, when the firing ceased for a white on both sides. Whether the weary white men or the savage Indians slept, I do not know, but I could not sleep. About daylight on Wednesday, September 3rd, the firing commenced again on both sides.; Some time in the forenoon I heard our soldiers crying aloud for joy. The shout went up: 'Reinforcements coming.'

"When the Indians left to go toward the reinforcements, the doctor and an officer came to look after me, supposing I could not have escaped so murderous a fire. They seemed perfectly astonished at finding me alive, and unhurt, except by the slight marks made by some five balls merely drawing blood from the skin. How I escaped must ever remain a mystery to myself and others. The blanket given me by a soldier, and in which I was wrapped up in the wagon during the Battle of Birch Coulie, was found, on examination, to have received over two hundred bullet-holes during the fight, and yet I was not hit except as stated. Who can imagine such an escape? Yet, I did escape, and am now (June, 1873,) alive to tell the story.

"When the troops had buried their dead we returned to Fort Ridgely. Here I was placed under charge of Dr. Muller, surgeon of the post. I hardly knew whether I was in the hospital or at the doctor's home, but I shall never forget the kind care taken of me by Mrs. Dr. Muller. The doctor extracted some nine buckshot from my shoulders, and the other eight are yet there, as they could not be taken out. My various wounds did not trouble me much, and were soon all healed.

"At the fort I found four of my children—all except one, children of my first husband. Two of my own boys, eight and nine years old, who had escaped with the thirteen-year-old August Urban, had reached the fort and been sent to St. Paul. At the fort I also found the five girls who came in with Mrs. Zable. Three of these were my first husband's children, and one of them my own by my first husband. My children had all been taken to my mother's, in Wisconsin, where I hastened, after a few days at the fort, to find them. I later recovered the child that had been taken prisoner by the Indians, which was delivered to Col. Sibley at Camp Release."

The heroine of this most remarkable experience was a native of Posen, Prussia, born July 13, 1835, and was the youngest daughter of Andrew Kitzman, who, with his family of fourteen children, immigrated to America and located near Green Lake, Marquette County, Wisconsin, in territorial days. Mrs. Kreiger and husband, with a large family of children, had taken up their new home in the beautiful Minnesota valley less than ninety days preceding the Sioux Massacre. History knows no more thrilling experience than that of this remarkable woman and her family friends on the Minnesota border.

Private WILLIAM J. STURGIS,
Who bore the first dispatch to Gov. Ramsey, announcing the massacre. Photo taken 43 years after close of Civil War.

W. H. BLODGETT,
Taken just before the outbreak.

Lieut. T. J. SHEEHAN, Commander of Fort Ridgely During Siege.

Lieut. T. P. GERE, Who Commanded at Fort Ridgely Aug. 18, 1862.

Sergeant JAMES G. McGREW,

Sergeant JOHN F. BISHOP.

Officers Who were Prominent in the Defense of Fort Ridgely.

Pictures were taken during Civil War, shortly after the Sioux Massacre.

Sibley Expedition of 1863

During the fall of 1862 and winter of 1863 an army was collected at the various posts and temporary stockades of the state, preparatory to a strong movement into the enemy's country north westward in the early summer of 1863. Only a few of the guilty Indians had been apprehended and punished in the autumn of 1862, hundreds of them having escaped to the plains lying between the Red River and the Missouri, with the upper boundary of their range extending to the Devils Lake country.

GEN. H. H. SIBLEY

The Sioux Reservation, at the time of the outbreak, extended from a point not far below Fort Ridgely, but on the opposite, or south and west side of the Minnesota River, to the head of Big Stone or Eahton-ka lake. This reservation was ten miles in width, and about one hundred and fifty miles in length, and was divided by the Yellow Medicine River, flowing into the Minnesota. That portion below the Yellow Medicine was known as the Lower Reservation, whose "capital" was the Redwood Agency, and was occupied by the M'daywakanton and Wakpakuta Indians, and that above the Yellow Medicine as the Upper Reservation, with headquarters at the Yellow Medicine Agency, occupied by the Sissetons and Wahpaytons.

MAP SHOWING ROUTE OF THE SIBLEY EXPEDITION OF 1863, AS ADJUSTED TO THE DAKOTAS OF TO-DAY, THE EXPEDITION PASSING PRIN-CIPALLY OVER WHAT IS NOW NORTH DAKOTA.

It was the lower Indians who precipitated the outbreak, and though many of the upper Indians were involved, there were, however, many who were kept out of it through the influence of Standing Buffalo and other northern chiefs. Driven from the scenes of their awful depredations, the lower Indians retreated into the land of the Sissetons and Wahpaytons, much to the displeasure of the latter, and particularly to that portion of the latter who had refused to stain their hands with the blood of the whites.

A civilized Indian, and one who did great service for the whites, when to do it imperilled his own life, gave it as his opinion that a very large number of the upper Indians resisted the temptations and entreaties of their lower brethren to join in the uprising. Some of the upper chiefs and many of the old and better disposed warriors were outspoken against the massacre, and these men, though unpopular with the less sturdy element, exerted a strong influence during the outbreak and later in the delivery to the authorities of the white captives.

It has always been regrettable that all the northern Indians were put upon practically the same basis by the government in the prosecution of the campaigns of 1863-4. The decades that have since flown permit of a rational analysis of that bloody chapter in Minnesota history known as the Sioux Massacre. The whole Dakota race was under distrust. The Indians who were true at heart, and who against strong pressure from the dominant element, opposed the heartless massacre, were Indians, and in the inflamed condition of the public mind fine distinctions were not drawn. The better element of Indians felt this indiscriminate censure, save in a very few notable instances. The lawless had brought the entire race under the ban.

The few loyal and faithful who were under the public eye received full credit for their good deeds, but not so those who were entirely beyond the horizon of the seat of carnage. The great mass whose hands were stained with innocent blood, and whose monstrous crimes had gone on lightning wings to appal humanity in the remotest limits of the globe, spread to the plains of the Northwest like a loathsome pestilence, after their defeat, to overwhelm with disgrace and contamination the bands who had stood aloof.

Those whose souls were the deepest dyed in crime pushed northward to near the British border, where they spent a winter of hardships (1862-3) that gave them ample opportunity to reflect upon the ways of the transgressor; but they dropped southward in the spring and merged themselves into all other elements of their race indiscriminately, so all were hunted alike and all put upon the same basis in whatever punishment was administered.

The campaign of 1863, was organised by Gen. John Pope, the plan being to completely subdue the Sioux hordes. Two expeditions were designed to execute the plans of the Department Commander, one under Gen. H. H. Sibley, organised in Minnesota, and the other under the command of Gen. Alfred Sully, the latter organised and outfitted at Sioux City, Iowa.

In the spring of 1863, the troops in Minnesota were shifted about from post to post to inure the men to hardships and exposure. The conditions were indeed trying, and may well be illustrated by the experience of one company of cavalry, as a sample of what all endured through this shifting process.

HARDSHIPS OF FRONTIER MILITARY SERVICE

On April 8, 1863, Co. F of the First Minnesota Cavalry (Mounted Rangers) left Fort Snelling for Sauk Centre to relieve a company ordered elsewhere. The weather was cold, the ground still full of frost, and lingering snow-drifts were visible. The sky was obscured by dull clouds throughout the 8th, the first day out, while a penetrating north wind blew a gale. This the men faced. At night, instead of turning into the dry bunks to which all had been accustomed for months, the soldiers lay upon frozen ground with one rubber and one woollen blanket beneath them, and a blanket over them, a tent sheltering them from the night wind. The next day's march was under partially clear skies, but in weather full of chill. The wind had sufficiently abated by night to make it possible to extract comfort from a camp fire, but sleeping with comfort was quite out of the question. In the latter part of the night a tempest sprang up from the northeast.

Breakfast was prepared in a blinding snowstorm and howling wind. There was no shelter for the fires, and nothing of which to make a successful shelter. Coffee could not be brought to the boiling point, and was "good" only in the degree of warmth to which it had attained. A pelting storm continued throughout the day's march, rain and snow alternating at intervals. There was not a dry thread in the company, and the men were benumbed with cold. St. Cloud, then an unpretentious village, was reached late in the afternoon, and the village of St. Joseph at night. Capt. Joseph R. Daniels requested the citizens of the latter place to open their houses to the men, but they absolutely refused to do so. The people were utterly dead to sympathy or feeling.

In fact, there appeared a general anti-Union spirit, heightened by the presence of soldiers. The request being met with a negative on all sides, Capt. Daniels ordered his men to take possession of all the barns in the village, if needs be turning out everything they contained. The people heard the order with a sullen scowl, and started for their stables in several instances to prevent the execution of the order; but they were swept aside by the wet and shivering men, who only needed a tip of authority from their commander, for a refusal of a reasonable request for their comfort under the circumstances had angered the men to the limit of endurance. The same all-day storm still raged at night, making it impossible to start or maintain fires. The men, drenched to the skin and benumbed, took care of their horses, and in the darkness that had gathered climbed into the haymows to lunch off the cold rations fished from their haversacks.

The skies were more auspicious on the morning of the fourth day, April 11, but the roads were bad in the extreme. The company, however, reached its destination and found warm and dry quarters awaiting it within the Sauk Centre stockade. Later it was ordered to Fort Ridgely over roads incomparably bad, by the way of Forest City, Hutchinson, etc. Much of this region, owing to heavy spring rains and lack of drainage and bridges, was a mere bog, in which mule-teams were utterly useless, and cavalry horses, even without their mounts, were gotten through with difficulty. The wonderful efficiency of man-power was well illustrated on this trip. When the soft spot to be crossed was more than two or three rods wide, the teams were unhitched and the animals separately gotten across in the most convenient way possible. A long line was attached to a wagon and sixty to eighty men would bend to the task of pulling it through.

At times the sloughs to be crossed were twenty to forty rods in width. Across these one heavily-loaded wagon was taken at a time, mired now and then to the hubs. The long line made it possible, however, for some of the men to be at all times on fairly decent footing, and human intelligence made it possible to take advantage of every favouring foothold.

The load men will thus move over otherwise impassable roads is scarcely believable; but the days devoted to this sort of service told heavily, for not only was the service itself arduous, but the men were in mud and water to their hips for hours at a time, for usually the sloughs were only separated by narrow ridges. Add to this marching, scouting and guard duty, and the reader has a basis for forming an idea what frontier military service consisted of.

ASSEMBLING AN ARMY FOR THE SIBLEY EXPEDITION

Early in June the process of assembling an army in the valley of the Minnesota, three or four miles above the mouth of the Redwood River, began. This place of rendezvous was designated Camp Pope, in honour of the major general commanding the department. From all the military posts of the state, including the many frontier villages where stockades had been erected, every available man was drawn, leaving only a force sufficient for garrison and patrol duty. The army thus assembled consisted of the following organisations. The Sixth Minnesota under Col. William Crooks; nine companies of the Seventh Minnesota under Lieutenant Colonel William R. Marshall; eight companies of the Tenth Minnesota under Col. James H. Baker; one company of Pioneers under Capt. Jonathan Chase; nine companies of the First Minnesota Cavalry, or Mounted Rangers, under Col. Samuel McPhail; eight pieces of artillery with one hundred and forty-eight men under Capt. John Jones; seventy-five Indian scouts under Maj. Joseph R. Brown, George McLeoud and Major Dooley, in all 4,075 men.

There was a train of 225 six-mule teams, as there was no point in the wild country to be penetrated during the all-summer campaign at which supplies could be replenished.

Camp Pope—Personnel of the Army.

Of this expedition Gen. H. H. Sibley was placed in command, with the following staff: Assistant Adjutant General, R. C. Olin; Brigade Commissary, William H. Forbes; Assistant Commissary and Ordnance Officer, Atchison; Commissary Clerk, Spencer; Quartermaster, Coming; Assistant Quartermaster, Kimball; *Aides-de-Camp*, Lieutenants Pope, F. J. H. Beever, A. St Claire, Flandrau and Hawthorn; Chaplain, Rev. S. R. Riggs.

The campaign to be entered upon would unavoidably be an arduous one, and men were selected very largely for their general fitness for the duties to be performed and the hardships to be encountered. Many of the men had for months done duty along the border that constantly brought under their observation the blackened ruins of homes destroyed the previous autumn, as a part of the work of the massacre, and were anxious to penetrate the enemy's country beyond these grim reminders of crimes and wickedness never to be atoned for.

The ruined and abandoned fields of the settlers, the bloated, blackened and mutilated corpses of men, women and children, the deserted farms along a frontier of two or three hundred miles in length, with their crops rotting where they had grown, were scenes that clung to the minds of all who had witnessed them the previous fall, like a repulsive nightmare.

Camp Pope was in the heart of the country occupied by those who had blighted with gun and torch as fair a land as the sun had ever kissed. Charred ruins were visible from its site, awful tragedies had been enacted within hearing of the spot, their agonies still echoing from fresh graves. There was, in fact, something sepulchral about this whole valley region, and the men longed for new fields of operation.

June 16, 1863, A Memorable Day—How Smallpox Restored Quiet.

On the morning of June 16, 1863, the "Sibley Expedition," as it was widely known, started on its long mission. On the previous night, after the heat of the day had subsided, a detachment of infantry moved out on the highlands to the westward to take the advance the following morning. The night of the 15th, was ideal. The gentle zephyrs were laden with the incense of wild flowers. Overhead the sky was serene and star-bedecked. The earth, warmed into new life, had sent into banishment many of the perplexities, incident to military life, in the open. The day had been warm, and along the southwestern horizon lightning flashes danced fitfully in a distant embankment of clouds, whose outlines were distinctly revealed by the quivering, shimmering electrical gymnastics, reflected by the glistening armour of the infantry detachment that filed up the western slopes of the valley in the dusk of evening to assume its place for the morrow.

Those who witnessed the beautiful spectacle have probably never forgotten it. Under benign conditions the camp was unusually merry on the night of the 15th, only, however, to receive a shock that produced a profound sensation. The surgeons had discovered a well-defined case of smallpox, and the news of the discovery swept over the vast camp like wildfire. Men had expected to be shot at—had enlisted, in fact, with the full understanding that they would be called upon to pose as targets for an unscrupulous and careless enemy, but both the parties of the first and second parts had utterly forgotten to mention smallpox in the original contract, and the omission led to serious reflection and eloquent silence. Fortunately, the disease did not spread.

Our First Day's March—The Mules and the Blues.

Gen. Sibley was a man of pronounced habits, and not the least among these habits was that of early rising. The rose tints of early dawn were never an unfamiliar sight to his men. The blare of trumpets woke the echoes of the Minnesota valley at 3 o'clock on that beautiful morning of June 16, 1863. At 4 o'clock, one of the grandest military pageants ever witnessed in Minnesota, before or since, filed out with the precision of clockwork, and wending its way for a time among the mammoth granite boulders of the valley, gradually ascended the hills to the westward.

The head of the column had reached a distance of nearly six miles on its journey ere the rear guard could move. Four thousand men do not constitute a very large army, but here were all the trappings and equipments of war, and not caparisoned for review, for there was not a soul in the desolate valley to witness the spectacle except the soldiers themselves. The artillery, ambulances and wagon train covered a distance of nearly four miles. A part of the column, and one the soldiers regarded with jealous interest, was George A. Brackett's large herd of beef cattle, taken along under contract to supply the army during the months it should campaign in the north western wilds.

We had now entered upon one of the most interesting phases of human experience. Savage hordes had made their last supreme effort to stay the advance of civilization. Minnesota was but partially peopled, and Dakota Territory (now North and South Dakota) was utterly uninhabited by the white race, save a settlement at Yankton; and one might journey, as our command did in 1863, for weeks and even months in the vast territory now covered with flourishing cities and thousands of rural houses without, beyond our own numbers, once seeing the face of a white man.

A hot June day tested the mettle of the infantry the first day out, and jaded the animals not a little. The weather was dry and the process of evaporation active, and as a result the column was enveloped in a cloud of dust, with no favouring wind to bear it away. While the long summer's campaign was one of unremitting hardships, this was perhaps the most trying day the expedition as a whole experienced during the season, and man and beast welcomed the opportunity to go into camp in the late afternoon, where a bountiful supply of excellent water and an abundance of good forage for the animals were found. A great white city sprang up on a beautiful plain ere the purple had succeeded the gold in the west, the vast camp covering more than a square mile in extent

Many grim ruins, the scenes of blasted hopes, cruelty and death, were witnessed during the day's march. Outside of the expedition itself not a sign of life was visible. The hardy pioneers east of the Minnesota had perished during the massacre, while on the reservation side the picture of desolation could not have been more complete had the whole region been transformed into a desert. Where a building had graced the wild wastes on the reservation, a deserted, blackened ruin, mute and forbidding, remained to tell of the hatred that had attached to every mark of civilization. The whites had everywhere been slain, and the murderers had gone, leaving desolation in their wake. Many men in the command had lost friends and relatives during the massacre, and they contemplated the prevalent signs morosely.

But the spell was broken at supper time, for then it was that several hundred mules, scattered throughout the vast camp, apparently discovered for the first time their strange environment, and the tale of the discovery was wafted back and forth until even the grave Gen. Sibley for an instant lost his grip on a facial composure always suited to the sanctuary on solemn occasions. The incident was not without its value, for it cut off all retreat to moodiness.

Camp on the Battlefield of Wood Lake.

Five o'clock on the morning of June 17th, found the head of the column in motion, although the rear guard did not move for three hours later. Nature was at its best. The fresh green that carpeted hill and dale had reached the prime of luxuriance. The bending blades of grass sparkled with their jewels of dew, while everywhere were new-born roses that, but for ourselves, were "born to blush unseen." A short march of eleven miles sufficed for the day. Gen. Sibley selecting the Wood Lake battle ground as the location of our camp. It took little stretch of the imagination to repeople with savages and soldiers the plains about, and Col. Marshall of the Seventh Minnesota pointed out the place of the charge and graphically described the action itself, which won the day at Wood Lake on the 23rd of the previous September, and where he received his baptism of fire as a soldier.

The Desolate Yellow Medicine Agency—Camp at Hazelwood.

On the morning of the 18th, after an hour's march, we reached the Yellow Medicine Agency, dismal and forlorn. The buildings that had been spared were abandoned to the elements. The windows had been smashed and the doors burst open, while unsightly weeds grew where active feet had borne proud and ambitious souls in better days. Nothing could disturb the reverie of the men who rode or walked over this historic spot that beautiful June morning, for here were the final seeds sown the previous year out of which grew the discontent that ripened into the massacre. Here it was the six thousand Sioux were assembled in July, 1862, and kept in waiting for weeks for their annuities, until starvation invaded their lodges.

The march was short again today, the expedition going into camp at "Hazlewood," the home and mission of Rev. Dr. Thomas Williamson, five miles northwest of the Yellow Medicine Agency. Here the general remained in camp during the 19th. To those with an inquiring turn of mind this was a spot absorbingly interesting. Dr. Williamson had come into the wilds of Minnesota before the majority of the men on this expedition were born—had come years before the founding even of a territorial form government, and out of his faithful labours had come, for an hour of calamity, such characters as Other Day, Chaska, Paul, etc.

The mission buildings were wrecked and desolate. Doors had broken from their hinges in the wind, windows had succumbed to gun and arrow practice, the premises were grown up to weeds, the garden fences were broken down, and general dilapidation ruled where order had reigned. This had been a social and spiritual oasis in a desert of savage life, but alas for the decrees of Fate, it had gone the ways of Tadmor, stricken to earth by those who owed it most. Rev. Dr. Williamson and his co-worker, Rev. Dr. S. R. Riggs, together with their families and friends, escaped with their lives by what seemed little less than a miracle.

Camp Release—A Cold June Day.

An early hour of June 20th, found the expedition in motion, still traversing historic ground, passing Camp Release among other points of interest. We indulged in an uncomfortable experience today. The sky was obscured by cold, leaden clouds, with a cold north wind blowing stiffly. The men, and particularly the cavalry and artillery, suffered from the benumbing cold, and all gladly sought the shelter of tents or the comforts of sheltered camp-fires after a march of fourteen miles. Fuel and water were plentiful here, and we remained in camp over the 21st, during which time the scouts thoroughly reconnoitred the surrounding country to make sure there were no Indians in these their old-time haunts to drop back after our passage to disturb the settlements to the southward.

The Beautiful Lac Qui Parle.

The 22nd, we crossed the Lac Qui Parle River, a stream that, from time immemorial, had been almost sacred to the hearts of the red race. Its brilliant waters and its stretches of woodland appealed tauntingly to Gen. Sibley to raise his portable city here, but the distance, after the previous day's rest, was not sufficiently great, and we pushed on to the "Big Mound" (now "Big Tom"), at which we camped for the day. This is a beautiful spot and is distinguished from all others in the region for its widely-seen promontory.

A Beautiful Country—Big Stone Lake.

The 24th, we traversed a beautiful country, camping in the evening on the highlands west of Big Stone Lake. We found a scarcity of good water on today's march, but the country was charmingly attractive. Our camp-ground this eve (Camp Marshall, in honour of Lieut. Col. William R. Marshall) is one which Little Crow's hosts had occupied the previous fall, a fact discovered by the finding of many pits in which the Indians had *cached* their cumbersome plunder from the settlements that had been raided during the massacre. In these we found great quantities of dishes, tinware, harness, chains, straps, pails and an occasional piece of furniture, and not a little corn, the latter being well preserved and useful. Teamsters found numerous "prizes" among the hidden harnesses, many of which were of excellent quality. The dishes were badly broken, due to lack of knowledge in their packing and handling, yet they seemed valuable in the estimation of the savages.

Celebrating a Birthday—First Buffalo Hunt

We were in the saddle at 4 o'clock on the morning of June 25th. The weather was propitious, buffalo were sighted off to the westward towards the *coteau*, and there was a troublesome spirit of adventure constantly preaching treason to discipline. Our battalion was on the flank. I communicated to a good-hearted and companionable officer riding near me that this was my nineteenth birthday, and that I would like to celebrate it on a buffalo hunt. I was agreeably surprised when he arranged that three of us should drop out, one at a time at intervals, and join each other when half a mile or so from the command and ride out at least in plain view of the first herd of buffalo we had discovered, several miles away. Following a ravine leading in the proper direction, we galloped away until sufficiently distant from the expedition, when we rode out on the highlands to get our bearings.

We could plainly discover three horsemen nearer the herd than ourselves, and quickened our pace, cautious lest we fall into the hands of an enemy, however. The other trio proved to consist of cavalrymen on nearer approach, and separating a huge bull from the herd we secured jointly, after many shots and much wild excitement, meeting every adventurous requirement, a prize worthy of all effort. The three cavalrymen fortunately proved to be members of our own company, who had fallen victims to the infection that tempted men on the left flank that day.

We filled our haversacks with choice cuts from the loins of the noble beast and hastened to join the command, now many miles away, but the location of which we could fix to a certainty by the great white cloud of dust that rose from and hung over the command like the token that guided the children of Israel. We had ridden but a few miles when the cloud ceased to exist—notice that camp had been established.

We must now ride to the trail and follow it in. Fortunately, one of the officers of our party possessed the countersign, and we were thus enabled to pass the lines on arriving at camp. Every man in our company had a ration of buffalo steak that evening, with enough on hand with which to cautiously bribe any powerful superior whose influence might be desired in case of trouble.

Finding of Human Skeletons.

This camp was near an old trading post. Here were found the bleaching skeletons of six men who had been killed by the Indians the previous year. Gen. Sibley caused the skeletons to be collected and buried. Nothing whatever could be found whereby the identity of these men could be determined. It is known, however, that of the few men at this place Henry Manderfeldt, George Loth, John Schmerch and two Frenchmen were killed here on the morning of Thursday, August 21st, 1862.

This was at or near the Myrick store. An Indian came and warned the men very early in the morning of their danger, and told them to fly for their lives, but they had heard nothing of the massacre below and paid little regard to what the Indian had counselled them to do. Only a brief space of time elapsed when a party of Indians were on the trading post in force. They opened on the helpless men and only two succeeded in escaping by plunging into the timber near at hand. One of these, Hilliar Manderfeldt, was pursued a short distance and killed, while the other, Anton Manderfeldt, made his way to the settlements after twelve days of almost unparalleled hardships.

This was Camp Jennison, named in honour of Lieut.-Col. S. P. Jennison of the Tenth Minnesota. On scaffolds supported by four crotches were many Indian dead found here, the Sioux method of "burial." These scaffolds were eight to ten feet high, the whole structure made of poles, and on top of each, wrapped in a blanket, lay a dead Indian, awaiting his or her turn to disappear into and become a part of the elements.

Not infrequently the boughs of trees were used to support the dead, and particularly the bodies of children, along the border of the lake. Big Stone Lake proved to be an attraction worthy of the compliments on every hand bestowed upon it, stretching away for a distance,

161

from end to end, of thirty-six miles.

Camp Between Lakes Big Stone and Traverse.

Breaking camp at 4 on the morning of the 26th, amid the usual blare of bugles, we were soon in motion on our journey northward. We were now entering a region that had suffered from prolonged drought. The earth was hot and parched, water scarce on the march, grass short and dry and the dust well-nigh suffocating. In the early afternoon we camped between Lakes Big Stone and Traverse, on the site of the Browns Valley of today. This became Camp McLaren, after Major Robert N. McLaren of the Sixth Minnesota. This beautiful spot was lavishly endowed with gifts suited to the comforts of an army. Despite the drought that had parched the highlands, the growth of red-top between the lakes was luxuriant, while there was an abundance of good water everywhere.

There was, to all, something unique about this camp. We were between two lakes, the waters of which flow in exactly opposite directions—those of Lake Traverse into the Red River of the North, and thence on into Hudson Bay, while those of Big Stone flow into the Minnesota on their way to the Gulf of Mexico. Traverse in that day was fed by numerous great springs in the lake bed, as was readily discovered by the men who bathed and swam in its waters. We remained in this camp the 27th, 28th, and 29th, during which time the cavalry thoroughly scouted the surrounding country. Indians had occupied the region during the winter and early spring, but had pushed off towards Devils Lake.

Adieu With Regrets to Camp McLaren

Regretfully did we turn our backs on Camp McLaren on the morning of June 30th, and set out north-westerly on our journey, the Indian guides leading the way into an unknown country. We now entered upon a boundless, treeless plain. The earth was dry and compact, great cracks an inch or two in width and a foot or more in depth scarring the surface of the ground and running uninterruptedly for rods. About the scattering shallow lakes there was a fairly good growth of coarse grass, but on the higher ground the grass was short and lifeless though "cured," so as to be relishable to the animals. Grasshoppers were numerous, and in some places during the marches of the summer had well-nigh robbed our animals of their needed forage. Finding good grazing, conditions considered, the expedition went into camp after a march of sixteen miles.

Here for the first time we became wholly dependent for fuel on "Buffalo chips," the excrement of the "cattle of the plains" that in that day roamed the prairies in countless thousands. Without these chips no expedition could have been maintained on the plains of Dakota. This fuel, in the form of thin discs, eight to ten inches in diameter, and scattered over the parched earth, was as dry and combustible as tinder. When it is stated that on a single camping ground enough buffalo chips could be gathered to cook the food of four thousand men for three meals or more, some idea may be had of the innumerable animals that made up the herds of buffalo that possessed the country in that day. The infantrymen used their bayonets and the cavalrymen their sabres in gathering this indispensable fuel, which served the expedition exclusively for months.

No camp was now established that was not thoroughly fortified with breastworks made of prairie sod. Henceforth every camp was thus protected, the first duty after terminating a day's march being the selection of details for work on the trenches and breastworks, the latter of which were about two feet high. Gen. Sibley never worried about what the enemy might do, but rather prepared himself well beforehand, and let the enemy do the worrying.

July 1st, we marched eighteen miles, the 2nd, sixteen, the 3rd, sixteen and the 4th, eighteen miles, going into camp at 1 o'clock p.m., after a march of nine hours under trying conditions, in the big bend of the Cheyenne River, on the south side of that stream, a few miles southeast of what of this day is the flourishing town of Lisbon, North Dakota. Gen. Sibley here established Camp Hayes, so named after Major Orrin T. Hayes of the cavalry.

July Fourth on the Cheyenne River.

This was indeed a strange Fourth of July. No man in the command had ever before seen one like it. No mark of civilization had ever been raised in this country. No surveys had been made. No white men had disturbed the solitude into which we had entered. Herds of buffalo were visible in almost any direction. Aside from these nothing was seen but arched skies and boundless plains. And the "best girl" and red lemonade, the "prominent citizens in carriages and on foot," the brass band, the shady grove, the "car of liberty," the orator, the reader of the Declaration of Independence—how painfully absent, and how eloquently silent! The best girl was probably the most missed of all, for during all the months of that campaign no member of the expedition ever saw the face of a white woman, nor could a letter or any other sort of message reach us.

Late in the day in celebration of the occasion McCole and myself visited the camp of the Indian scouts, and learned many things regarding the massacre of the previous year from the Indian point of view. The Indian narrator, once he bends to his work unrestrained by surroundings, is intensely interesting. My comrade and interpreter was intimately acquainted with many of the scouts, and knew the art of obtaining a voluble flow from the fountains usually concealed beneath a look of stoicism. A story once launched, its trend may easily be followed by carefully regarding the smiles, frowns, the intensity of gesture and the modulations of tone of the narrator, for an intelligent Indian is not an artful, but a natural raconteur.

Some of the more interesting information obtained at this interview is made use of in an earlier part of this book. One of the narratives, full of animation, fiery flashes of the eye and graceful movements of the hand, accompanied with intensity of expression, related to a battle fought on the ground partially occupied by our camp. We were principally in the valley, while the engagement was largely fought on the table-land in the south-eastern part of our camping ground.

STORY OF AN ANCIENT BATTLE—THE INDIAN AS A RACONTEUR.

The story was that while a large band of Cheyennes were camped on the spot where our tents were pitched, a war-party of Pottawattomie hunters who had invaded the country attacked the Cheyennes. The battle was graphically portrayed from beginning to end. The Pottawattomies came down on the Cheyennes like the wind, taking the camp by surprise and producing a reign of consternation and terror; but the Cheyennes flew to arms and checked the bloody work of their enemy. The Pottawattomies were driven to the table-land, and the party there practically exterminated in a fierce battle that lasted a whole afternoon. Asked how long since this battle was fought, Chaska counted back twenty-one years, which would make the year of the engagement 1842.

We remained in this camp from the 4th until the 11th day of July, awaiting the arrival of a detachment from Fort Abercrombie. The entire surrounding country was explored by the scouts and the cavalry, under various officers detailed for the purpose, and during these explorations many a choice buffalo and antelope steak found its way into camp, although hunting was among the things tabooed, theoretically, as dangerous both to hunters and military discipline.

Gymnastic Weather—Heat, Cold and Chill.

On the 9th, a hot wind swept up from the south and the earth being hot and dry the conditions were almost suffocating. Tents were like ovens, and as there was no other shelter and as the midsummer sun was torrid all suffered in the extreme. The following day the wind shifted to the northeast and brought down a volume of smoke from burning pine forests many leagues away in northern Minnesota, no doubt, that was almost insufferable. Tents were invisible at a distance of fifty yards. Then the weather had still another stunt in store for us, for on the morning of July 11th, the wind was squarely from the north and uncomfortably cold.

The smoke was less dense than on the 10th, but the cold was penetrating and drove all but the infantry into overcoats, for we took up the line of march again this morning, much to the gratification of all, since forage and fuel were becoming scarce at Camp Hayes, with no compensating attractions. Reveille was sounded at 2 o'clock this morning, and the command was in motion at 3. At the end of eighteen miles Gen. Sibley established Camp Wharton, where we remained during the 12th.

At 3 o'clock on the morning of July 13th, the expedition was again in motion, traversing a beautiful country and establishing camp after a march of twenty miles.

Beautiful Country—Taunt of the Mirage.

One of the attractions of the day has been the ever-recurring, ever-vanishing mirage, which has lured us on, day after day, with its beautiful setting just a few miles farther ahead—a beautiful apparition that justifies the assertion that there is something commendable in air castles. Day after day on the treeless plains, when the vertical rays of a summer sun revived memories of cooling shades and refreshing waters, the mirage would assert itself on the horizon and grow from a tiny first view to a vast landscape. Were we deluded by this apparition yesterday? Yes; but the one now before us is so realistic that we know those beautiful groves and that vast, placid lake are real, and that we shall camp tonight amid scenes such as we have dreamed of since the days of home life and civilization.

But like the end of the rainbow, the taunting landscape was not real, or it would fade away gradually, hour by hour, leaving the impression, despite the pranks of past delusions, that we had descended into a depressed area, and that presently we would mount the opposite rim to find ourselves in full view of an ideal camping ground. But today's lakes and groves were no more real than were yesterday's. A day would then pass with no taunting apparition—just the dull monotony of boundless plain and bending sky. Then gradually would come into view again visions of woodland and waters that kept men, wearied and worn with travel and hardships, in almost childish good humour, so true to nature would this beautiful picture rear itself within easy range of our vision.

Even the wary, who had been so often deluded, feeling there must be, somewhere, grove-girt lakes, were caught time and again with the conviction that at last we beheld the real things—wood-girt waters. The mirage will ever remain vigorous in the memory of the men who gazed upon and discussed it day after day, for it was always profuse in its promises, and not infrequently was the basis of a wager, involving a month's pay, and no less frequently it happened, on account of some rare new feature, more promising than ever, that the most sceptical were the losers. Today we witnessed the most unusual and remarkable of all mirage freaks. Whatever else the mirage spreads before its on-lookers on the plains, the grove and lake feature is never wanting. In this instance, beyond the lake, which itself was apparently distinct, was plainly visible a moving animal mass, raised quite above the horizon of the mirage.

Apparently, the mass was crossing a point of high ground, with the figures seemingly inverted. The mass came within the scope of vision out of nothing definable, and disappeared toward the westward at a vanishing point apparently above and beyond the mirage proper, but it was a part of the phenomenon, and made, for its variety and its myste-rious transition, a profound impression upon the many who witnessed it and speculated upon its cause, which was most generally believed to be traceable to the fact that a herd of buffalo were crossing a point of land embraced within the zone of the mirage. And so, I repeat, air cas-tles are not without benefits sufficient to justify their existence. These, at least, while they made promises they never redeemed, made many a man forget his pains for a day.

The weather has become normal again, and we enter camp at mid-day, located between three small lakes, all of which afford excellent water, much to the enjoyment of man and beast, as poor water is the rule, all being impregnated with alkali. We saw numerous herds of buf-falo today, and, as an every-day occurrence, many bands of antelope.

July 14th. Pretty early in the morning, but the bugles ring out brilliantly at 2 o'clock, the disturbance starting at Gen. Sibley's headquarters. The aim of the commander is to be well on our journey before the heat of a midsummer day becomes oppressive, and then to enter camp about midday. We make eighteen miles today and establish Camp Weiser, in honour of Dr. Weiser, surgeon of the Mounted Rangers.

July 15th. We made seventeen miles, camping on a beautiful lake in the shape of a horseshoe, with the opening to the westward. The land within the almost complete circle was sufficiently extensive to accommodate the entire command by compactly forming the camp. This lake was on the east side of the Cheyenne River and could not have been far from the site of Valley City. Tolac was the name by which the lake was known to the expedition. No maps to be found show its existence, and it has no doubt long since disappeared as a result of the cultivation of the country in which it was located, as its waters were shallow, though apparently permanent, for the season of our visit to it had already most severely tested its endurance. The waters of Tolac were so impregnated with alkali that they were almost unendurable to man or beast, despite the beauty of the lake.

Killing an Elk Within the Lines—Founding Camp Atchison.

The command was out at 2 on the morning of the 16th, and made good progress over the pathless plains, the early morning being delightfully cool and refreshing. At about 9 o'clock in the forenoon, the flankers on the west, who were riding along the banks of the Cheyenne, started an elk out of a clump of brush. The frightened beast turned from the flankers, who were near it, and ran towards the main column of the expedition. Half a dozen flankers charged in pursuit. When the animal was discovered, bearing down on the solid lines of infantry, discipline was severely tested, but not disgraced. Lieutenant Ara Barton of Co. F, Mounted Rangers, who had a distinguished part in later years as the sheriff of Rice County in capturing most of the James Younger bandits who escaped from Northfield, executed a flank movement on the charging elk and with a well-directed shot brought it to earth. (*See The James and Younger Brothers: the Story of One the Most Notorious and Legendary Outlaw Gangs of the American West* by J. A. Dacus; Leonaur 2017.)

We crossed the Cheyenne River today about fifteen miles north of where Valley City is located, going into camp after a march of eighteen miles. On the 17th, we made eighteen miles; on the 18th, seventeen miles, founding Camp Atchison, the most northerly point reached by the expedition as a body. From this point scouting parties were sent to Devils Lake and elsewhere to the northward. From 7 to 11 o'clock today, a drenching rain poured down, but the march was uninterrupted and the innovation rather enjoyed in fact, for it was most welcome, and especially as the sun came out later to dry the clothing and blankets of the men.

COWARDLY DEED OF LIEUT. FIELD—FUROR IN CAMP.

Lieutenant Albert R. Field of Co. G, Mounted Rangers, created a sensation in the newly-established camp by shooting a private soldier. The act was cowardly and malicious, and produced a furor of indignation throughout the command, which was only allayed by the assurance that Field should be dealt with promptly. The man was not seriously wounded, but that he was not killed was due more to poor markmanship than to good disposition.

Camp Atchison was named in honour of Ordnance Officer Atchison of the expedition, as was also the beautiful little lake on whose shores the camp was established. The location of this camp can be more definitely determined on the map of today than any other (save possibly Camp Hayes, at the first crossing of the Cheyenne) east of the James River. Gen. John C. Fremont had once visited this region on a tour of exploration and had named a beautiful little lake in honour of his wife, Jessie, and Camp Atchison was established on a lake two to four miles southwest of Lake Jessie. This would make its location in township 147, range 60.

GENERAL SIBLEY'S BUSY DAY—A DASH FOR THE MISSOURI.

The 19th of July, was Gen. Sibley's busy day. He had resolved to make Atchison a permanent camp, to the end that a vigorous campaign might be prosecuted in the direction of the Missouri River. The Indian scouts were satisfied the main body of Sioux were on the plains west of the James. These scouts had extended their observations well into the Devils Lake country, and had learned enough through their keen Indian discernment to forecast the movements and location of the body of which Gen. Sibley was in search.

The general called the commanders of his subdivisions together and upon their information selected 2,056 men for a forced march westerly, the expedition to consist of 1,436 infantry, 520 cavalry and 100 artillery and pioneers, with a sufficient number of the best teams to carry necessary ammunition and twenty-five days' rations. This left the post of Camp Atchison with about an equal number of men and at least two-thirds of the cumbersome train of wagons. All disabled men and animals were left in camp, which was fortified with breastworks and made thoroughly defensible. The men slated to remain at the new post were not pleased with the idea of being marooned thus, isolated from civilization by hundreds of miles of distance, in a treeless country entirely cut off from communication with the world. Those selected for the forced march were to enjoy no privileges not accorded their comrades, except that they were to be favoured with activity—a life always preferred by soldiers.

Reaching the James River—Indian Signs.

Gen. Sibley had little use for the sluggard. He believed every man should so time his habits as to be at his best for any duty at an early hour in the morning. He placed great value on the early part of the day for any mental or physical duty devolving on a man. There were other reasons why, on this expedition, excessively early rising was practiced, but they were simply in harmony with the habits of this sturdy and generally beloved man; so, there was no surprise when reveille broke over the plains at 2 o'clock on the morning of July 20th. A south-westerly course was taken up promptly at 3, and by noon a distance of twenty miles had been covered over the trackless country, when camp was established.

At evening a large party of Chippewa half-breeds, said to be three hundred in number, came into camp, producing something of a sensation for a time. Father Andre, a Catholic priest, was the spokesman of the party. When it was learned the visitors were of the Chippewa nation the soldiers viewed the innovation with a different, though not an indifferent, interest. The party was composed of a lot of hardy, swarthy, robust buffalo hunters, all mounted and well-armed. There was a generous sprinkling of full-bloods among them, but the former predominated. They were very friendly, and were especially so since, like ourselves, they were in the enemy's country.

They gave Gen. Sibley much valuable information, among other things stating that 4,000 to 5,000 Sioux were in camp some miles west of the James River, where they, too, were buffalo hunting. After a march of eight miles on the 21st, we went into camp on the James River, the location affording a good camping ground, and the general desiring to "feel" the country to the westward with scouting parties, but no Indians were discovered.

At the usual early hour on the morning of the 22nd, we were again in motion. The scouts discovered Indian signs today. The country is somewhat rough and rolling, but we nevertheless covered twenty miles before going into camp.

In the saddle at 3 on the morning of the 23rd, we made good progress, though traversing a hilly and somewhat difficult country for hasty military operations. At 2 p.m., we went into camp after a march of twenty miles. The Indian scouts manifest a feeling that we are in the immediate country of the enemy, though no Indians were seen during the day. Night finds our camp well intrenched and well picketed.

Running Fight of Fifteen Miles.

The command moved out of camp at 3 o'clock sharp on the morning of July 24th. About noon, having covered twenty miles or more, the command came upon a large body of Indians. The train was at once corralled and steps taken to intrench the camp.

Suddenly, from the right flank, we discovered great bodies of Indians gathering in groups on what Gen. Sibley named Big Mound, which, however, when we were on top of it proved to be an extensive hill, quite bluff-like on the north and west, with a considerable table-land on the summit, sweeping to the south and southeast.

The spot was one of the most charming we had thus far found in Dakota Territory. The beautiful grove that skirted the mound did not dissolve from view on our approach, as the taunting mirage had done so many times previously, but remained real and substantial. Trees we were unaccustomed to see, and to find on this vast, boundless plain like a jewel, this handsome setting, with a background of lakes, challenged the admiration of every lover of nature, even if we were not permitted to enjoy it in peace. Here, at this beauty spot, 5,000 Indians had their homes in the midst of great buffalo haunts.

Standing Buffalo's band constituted a part of this nomadic group, and no doubt there would have been a peaceful surrender of the Indians without the firing of a shot but for the act of a treacherous red in whose mental construction there had been no provision made for discretion. The Indians swarmed in great numbers on the hilltop to the eastward as the expedition approached on the plain below along the western base of the mound. Dr. J. S. Weiser, surgeon of the Mounted Rangers, and whose home was at Shakopee in the Minnesota valley, rode up the hill beyond the lines of the expedition, where he met and mingled with the Indians, shaking hands with many he had known in his home town, of which they had in early days been frequenters.

Here a cowardly Indian stepped behind Dr. Weiser and shot him in the back at short range, killing him instantly. The whole proceeding was witnessed by the entire army on the plain, as if it had been purposely staged for the occasion. The puff of blue smoke and Dr. Weiser's fall, stricken with death, was the signal for attack, and the Indians were put upon the defensive instantly, with a feeling of revenge so intent that even a flag of truce would have received scant courtesy for a time, though as an evidence that the shooting was not generally approved of, Dr. Weiser's body was protected from mutilation.

But this was a declaration of war admitting of no explanations, had explanations been offered. The cavalry was ordered to the scene posthaste, and for its availability was quickly engaged under Col. McPhail, though the whole body of troops was moved actively, save the Tenth under G. I. Baker, to whose lot it fell to protect the intrenched camp should it be attacked. The Sixth under Col. Crooks and Lieut. Col. Averill, the Seventh under Lieut. Col. Marshall and the cavalry under Col. McPhail moved up the hill in a battle-front of over a mile in length, while the artillery, under Capt. Jones and Lieutenant Whipple took positions to facilitate the movement of the troops up the slope. The engagement opened all along the line, and from the plain below was said to be imposing and dramatic—such as would appear a seven day wonder to the peaceful and enlightened North Dakota of this age.

The Indians made a determined stand, realising the advantage of their position, but the troops pressed them back steadily until the brow of the hill was gained, where the real crux came. The warriors numbered fully fifteen hundred, and their entire strength was summoned to stay the troops ere they gained the summit, knowing that once the hill was lost there was no longer hope of holding the expedition in check. While all the forces had not now gained the uplands, a sufficient number had done so to determine the battle, which had raged for two hours, in favour of Gen. Sibley.

The Indians fell back in great haste, crossing a plateau of a mile in extent and making a stand at the brow of the hill breaking to the south-westward. Once on the summit. Col. McPhail sensed the situation and seeing it was the purpose of the Indians to take shelter below the crest of the southwestern slope, ordered Lieutenant Barton of Co. F of the cavalry to charge the savages at the extreme left, and Captain Horace Austin, Co. B, to similarly charge a body taking shelter farther

171

to the right. The cavalry bounded off at full speed with sabres ablaze and the parched earth resounding like thunder beneath the hoofs of the flying column. The Indians quaked as the columns approached them, holding their fire, however, and delivering a furious volley before disappearing over the hill, down which they were found scampering in great confusion. The slope was too steep for the charging columns, but the men delivered a fire that brought down a number of the fleeing savages.

At the sound of the bugle these two companies galloped to the position taken by Col. McPhail to the right. Inactivity now pervaded the whole field for some unknown reason, but because of orders it was asserted, while immediately below us, half a mile away, at the foot of the long hill, the Indians, men, women, children, dogs, ponies and all personal effects, were compressed within narrow limits between two lakes in a state of panic, bent on escape. A column thrown around the westernmost of the two lakes would have completely checkmated this, resulting in the capture of the entire camp. The cavalry, occupying the most advanced position, and the only one in view of the retreating foe, were held very unwilling spectators while this movement was going on. Officers and men were almost uncontrollable as it became apparent the enemy was successfully eluding the grasp of the soldiery, but Col. McPhail, brave and aggressive, counselled obedience.

While thus lined up a furious thunderstorm broke over us, heaven and earth resounding with the echoing thunder. A blinding flash of lightning that made every horse crouch knocked Col. McPhail's sword from his hand and killed Private John Murphy and his horse, of Capt. Austin's company (B), on our immediate right. An orderly at this moment rode up and delivered a message which Col. McPhail eagerly glanced at. The bugle sounded the charge, and the two companies bounded away, A and L quickly joining.

Now began a spectacular movement without a rival even in fiction. The Indians had successfully escaped beyond their confinement between the lakes and were a mile on their way in the open, headed south-westerly. The progress of the cavalry was impeded at the restricting point between the lakes, but the force was quickly formed into fours and lost little time in making the passage, reassuming again a line of battle and sweeping over the plains in pursuit of the fleeing savages.

A supporting column, consisting of the Seventh and a portion of the Tenth, and a section of artillery under Lieutenant Whipple, was sent forward promptly, but to overtake and keep up with the cavalry and the flying enemy was a physical impossibility. The Indians, seeing they could not escape, put their entire fighting force at the rear to protect their retreat, and a running battle, covering a distance of fifteen miles, was fought at close range. No such spectacle was ever witnessed before in Indian warfare, the cavalry pressing hard to force a stand and the Indians fighting stubbornly to prevent it, and keep up the movement towards the Missouri. Several companies of cavalry (H, J and D) that had fought in the earlier engagement dismounted and were thus hindered in the chase, came up and joined in the running fight, though companies A, B, F and L had maintained, single-handedly, the running battle for ten miles before the reinforcements reached the scene of hostilities.

Two incidents of this running battle were shocking and should never have occurred even in the heat and passion of an engagement, though these cavalrymen had witnessed the unprovoked murder of their surgeon earlier in the day. One of these incidents was the appearance from the ranks of the enemy of a stalwart, muscular Indian, who had wrapped about him a beautiful American flag. He so displayed this that it could not be mistaken, evidently intending to meet and deliver himself up to his pursuers, possibly with a message asking for terms of surrender; but he became the target for a hundred shots, and realising as the column neared him that he must fall he began to shoot, bent upon selling his life dearly if he must.

Though hit many times, with the national emblem still about his shoulders, he loaded and fired his gun with great dexterity. His weapon was a double-barrelled shotgun. His mouth was filled with buckshot. He poured the powder into the muzzle of his piece for his last shot and without wadding spat a charge of bullets into the gun, apparently getting but one cap on. Raising his weapon, he swept it along, covering half a dozen men of the company before he was able to discharge it, finally exploding the cap and burying the charge of buckshot in an overcoat rolled up on the pommel of the saddle of Private Ezra W. Green. The charge was fired at so short a range, not exceeding ten feet, that the bullets did not scatter, but buried themselves deeply in the rolled coat, thus saving the life of Green.

The stalwart Indian now clubbed his gun, and with a desperate blow very nearly unhorsed Private Andrias Carlson, riding next to Green. The Indian had now more than a dozen bullet wounds in his body and still fought desperately, and was only finally finished by Private Archibald McNee, at Carlson's left, who rode out of the ranks and killed the savage. (All this occurred immediately in front of the set of fours in which I rode.)

The other incident was that in which an old grey-haired warrior gave emphasis to the law of the survival of the fittest. His years, probably four score in number, had made him a non-combatant. He had kept up with his people until his frail body had failed him, then dropping back helplessly through the lines he kept up his feeble trot, but to all appearances exhausted. He was as defenceless in the matter of arms as he was in the matter of age. A soldier rode out of the ranks of Co. B with drawn sabre. The old man heard his approach and glancing up and realising his fate pulled his blanket up over his head and trudged on until the cavalryman brought his sword down with such a blow as only stalwart youth can deliver across the back of the old man's neck, which must have well-nigh beheaded him. (These incidents were abhorrent to me, and have always seemed inhuman, if not criminal.)

Many warriors fell in the running fight, and their comrades were too hotly pursued to bear them from the field. These were ridden over by the cavalry and most of them scalped by those of the soldiers who had a penchant for bloody trophies.

The remarkable fight was continued into the night, and until the darkness was so intense the enemy on either side only knew the location of his adversary by the flash of the guns of pursued and pursuer. At about 10 o'clock at night, Lieutenant Beever of General Sibley's staff, guided by the sound of the running engagement, brought a verbal message from the commanding general ordering the return of all the forces to Big Mound. This order was displeasing to the officers and men, but was obeyed.

★★★★★★

It was insisted by Gen. Sibley this order was improperly delivered by Lieut. Beever. "Bivouac where night overtakes you if you can hold your ground; return to camp if you cannot," is said to have been the order.

★★★★★★

Five miles back we found the infantry and artillery, sensibly bivouacked. They fell in and were able with their hour of rest to keep pace with our reeling, jaded horses. But the night was densely cloudy and intensely dark, and with nothing whatever to guide us in this strange country we lost our way, running into annoying obstacles now and then to impede our progress and divert us into greater confusion of mind. The artillery was brought into use and several shots fired, but no response came. Our wanderings were continued until daylight, when, at about 4 o'clock, we got a response from a shot fired at that time by Lieut. Whipple. Thus guided, we reached camp at 7 o'clock in the morning. Rarely are soldiers put to a severer test than that endured by these men.

The cavalrymen had been constantly in the saddle for twenty-eight hours and a considerable portion of that time actively engaged in conflict, with nothing to eat and without water since in the forenoon of the previous day. The infantry had fared but little better, except that, so much, in the nature of things, was not expected from that arm of the service. The horses were in a pitiable condition, having been ridden excessively hard without food, drink or rest. Getting in, they were watered and picketed out. The camp had been broken and everything packed for the march when we entered it, so the exhausted men fell upon their faces on the plain, without waiting to prepare food, and with nothing to shelter them slept in the broiling sun until late in the day.

The chief bugler sounded the assembly, which was caught and repeated, rousing the men from their stupor to again take up the march. Making a distance of five miles, the command went into camp for the night, and here it was that many a soldier ate his first meal and drank his first cup of coffee in forty hours. Here the remains of Dr. Weiser and Private John Murphy were buried with military honours. Our day's rest and our square meal in the evening had fitted us for picket duty for the night, which was made anything but pleasant by a drizzling rain and a northeast wind full of chill.

★★★★★★

On the morning of the 24th, Lieutenant Ambrose Freeman of Co. D, cavalry, and George A. Brackett, beef contractor, dropped out of the lines for a buffalo hunt, not an uncommon thing for officers and men to do, though forbidden. They were five miles or more from the command, to the left and rear, on the day the Indians were encountered, but were cut off by savages while the Big Mound engagement was in progress, and Lieut. Freeman killed. Brackett had a most sensational experience, escaping and returning eastward on foot, his horse having been taken at the time Freeman was killed, reaching Camp Atchison after five days of wandering, more dead than alive and the hero of experiences and triumphs unparalleled. It was supposed that both men had been slain by the savages until meeting a party of

Chippewa hunters within a day's march of Camp Atchison on our return. The Chippewas had visited Camp Atchison and told of Brackett's safe arrival there.

★★★★★★

BATTLE OF DEAD BUFFALO LAKE.

July 26th. We moved out of camp at an early hour, following the trail over which the cavalry had fought the enemy on the 24th. As we reached Dead Buffalo Lake at 2 p.m., the Indians revealed themselves across the path of the expedition, well in advance. They were at long range and Lieut. Whipple's battery was turned upon them. They were observant rather than belligerent for a time, plotting deviltry as was suspected by those familiar with their tricks. Their purpose was later revealed when from the cover of a hill on the right a mounted force swept down like a hurricane on the hundreds of grazing horses and mules that had by this time been picketed out. The game was a bold one and would have proved a great triumph had it succeeded, but the mere presence of the enemy was enough to warn commanders of their danger.

This bold dash led to a hot fight between the savages on one side and the Indian scouts and the cavalry on the other. The Indians, as a counter move, attacked the left and front, but the Sixth Minnesota handled them roughly, with the assistance of the artillery. The battle lasted two hours, during which the Indians were worsted at every point of the field. The camp was well intrenched and strongly picketed for the night, but was undisturbed by the savages, and on the following day the command after a hard march of twenty miles over a rolling country, man and beast suffering greatly for want of water, reached Stony Lake. While on this expedition extremely early rising was the rule, early retirement was no less the practice. Camp was necessarily established with reference to grass and water, but these conditions were usually found at from 11 a. m. to 2. p. m.

BATTLE OF STONY LAKE—SPECTACULAR SCENE.

Stony Lake was a very small body of alkali water situated in camp, but immediately south of our line of march.

The morning of July 28th, was one of exceptional beauty. At the usual early hour, the command taking up its line of march from the lake, surrounding the train as was customary, was slowly wending its way up a long slope in a westerly course with the rear guard just ready to move, when, as if by magic, the plain swarmed with savages.

176

The atmosphere was tinted with smoke, as on an autumn morning, giving the flood of sunlight now enveloping the earth, a ruddiness that added spirit to one of the most picturesque military encounters ever witnessed. The Indians were naked, except as to the customary breechclout, and were all mounted. Their numbers had been largely augmented from along the Missouri, Sitting Bull being among the new accessions, and here for the first time "measuring swords" with the white race.

Fully two thousand warriors were in this spectacular engagement, dramatic beyond description. As if springing spontaneously out of the earth, these scurrying, painted demons, hair streaming and bending forward as if to accelerate the speed of their flying ponies, completely enveloped Gen. Sibley's little army, with yells calculated to make the soldiers "sit up and take notice." The Missouri was but thirty miles distant, and the expedition must be held in check until the families and personal effects of the Indians could be successfully transferred to the western shores of that river. Hence this was a battle of desperation on the part of the savages, who fought with a bravery admired even by their enemies. The engagement opened around the entire great circle, the object evidently being to find a vulnerable point into which it was plainly intended to pour a stream of savages at any sacrifice, but Gen. Sibley's forces were well disposed and fought gallantly, every soldier being engaged.

The ruddy sunlight gave the naked demons, in their desperate assaults, a weird appearance, smacking of romance rather than of real human endeavour, and the only hardship of which any man could complain was that of being required to perform duty while so tragic and graphic an exhibition was spread along the slope and over the plains in the depths of that wild, boundless solitude.

Mingled with hideous yells were the rattle of musketry and the roar of cannon, amid which, with bounding dashes here and there, the savages endeavoured to break our lines, but these brave endeavours only resulted in increased losses to the enemy, and after more than two hours of fierce fighting the Indians disappeared as mysteriously as they had swooped down upon us, leaving many dead on the field, but rescuing by acts of admirable daring most of their wounded, whom they bore away on their ponies. Lines were now reformed for the march, and the expedition covered a distance of over twenty-two miles over a difficult country before establishing camp. After the close of the morning engagement not an Indian was seen during the day's march.

When the expedition reached Big Mound, where the first engagement was fought, the Indians were in camp near the foot of the southwestern exposure of the "mound." When the battle was precipitated, and the Indians finally forced to retreat, this camp was hastily broken and movables packed for flight. As the running fight warmed up, the flying Indians began to sacrifice one impediment, then another, until the path of the fleeing savages was easily traced thence to the Missouri River; the greater quantities being sacrificed in the first forty or fifty miles of the eighty-mile flight. The Indians had spent the summer up to the time Gen. Sibley overhauled them in buffalo hunting. They had already obtained and dried their winter's supply of buffalo meat, and had accumulated and tanned great quantities of fine robes.

These products were surplusage on such an occasion as this, and as they impeded the progress of the retreating savages were sacrificed by degrees as necessity compelled, so that the ground was strewn for miles with the dried meat and valuable robes. The soldiers gathered great quantities of the dried but unsalted buffalo meat, which they carried in their haversacks for lunch on the march, not questioning its preparation by hands never washed except by accident. The dried meat was very nutritious, and, sailed, highly palatable.

Of the hundreds of robes many choice ones were gathered, but being cumbersome the soldiers, like the Indians, were obliged, sooner or later, to discard them. In packing for the flight, even the dogs had been loaded to the limit of their carrying capacity. One poor canine, late in the afternoon of our running fight of the 24th, fell out of the race with his enormous load, which contained, among other things, a heavy axe, lashed to his body. A soldier kindly cut the thongs with which his load was bound up and fastened to him, allowing him to escape and join his friends.

The Indians had thrown away their entire stock of provisions in their panic, and the last day or so of their flight were compelled to subsist on "bread root," which grew abundantly on the hills and which had been dug in great quantities, as the freshly-made holes, with some pointed instrument, attested.

Breaking camp early on the morning of the 29th, the command took up the pursuit. A numerous body of mounted Indians suddenly appeared on the right, left and front, but as suddenly disappeared without offering battle, and without leading the expedition a wild chase, as they had hoped to do, and were not seen again. The Sioux are skilled in the art of concealing their movements, even in a comparatively open country.

Striking the Missouri—Death of Lieut. Beever.

As we descended into the valley of the Missouri at about 9 in the forenoon we could see the massed savages climbing the hills on the opposite side of the river, they having reached and successfully crossed that great stream during the night and early morning by the aid of rafts of hasty and rude construction, and even by plunging frantically into the turbid river and swimming for life. Those who witnessed the scurrying mass as it ascended the hills beyond the river, a few miles distant, will never forget the spectacle. The slanting rays of the forenoon sun were reflected from hundreds of mirrors hung as indispensable personal trappings to the bodies of these strange, wild people, producing an effect of the occasion's own peculiar exclusiveness.

At about 11 o'clock in the forenoon, the expedition reached the Missouri River at the mouth of Apple Creek, about four miles below the present city of Bismarck. Above the mouth of Apple Creek, a mile or so is the point at which the Indians had made their crossing of the Missouri. The river bottom on the east side was here quite heavily timbered, and the Sixth Minnesota, under Col. Crooks, was ordered to explore the woods and place of crossing. Numerous warriors were concealed in the timber, and spirited skirmishing resulted from their presence, during which Lieut. Beever of Gen. Sibley's staff entered the woods with an order to Col. Crooks, which he delivered, but the lieutenant was ambushed and killed on his return.

★★★★★★

Lieutenant Beever was an Englishman who had secured a position on Gen. Sibley's staff at his own request, and on the recommendation of influential friends who knew him, and was not, it was said, a naturalised citizen and not an American soldier.

★★★★★★

His body was not found until the following day, when it was discovered where it had fallen, pierced with bullets and arrows. He wore his hair cropped closely or was slightly bald, and his murderers removed the skin from the lower part of his face, bearing the trimmed beard, instead of taking his scalp. His body was interred in a lonely grave within the camp-ground, hundreds of miles from civilization, as was that of Private Nicholas Miller of Co. K of the Sixth, who was also killed in the woods.

Col. Crooks found about one hundred wagons the Indians had abandoned in their hasty crossing during the night, together with camp equipage, all of which he collected and burned. On the night of the 29th, the Indians attacked our camp, but retired after firing a volley or two, and very properly, for the night was beautiful—such as would have set the heart of Tom Moore attune with its summer breath, full moon and floating clouds—too beautiful for this incivility.

Here ended the campaign of the Sibley Expedition of 1863. With barely rations enough left to make the return to Camp Atchison, and with animals in a state of collapse, further pursuit of the savages was out of the question. It had been arranged before leaving Camp Pope that Gen. Alfred Sully should meet Gen. Sibley on the Missouri, if possible, he to proceed from Sioux City, Iowa, at least a part of the way by river transports, with an army similar to that commanded by Sibley; but nothing could be learned of Gen. Sully, he, as was later known, having been detained at many points by low water. Rockets and the battery were used on the nights of July 30th and 31st in the hope that by this signalling communication might be established with the Sully expedition, but no response came.

On the Ground Where Bismarck Stands.

On the 30th and 31st, the cavalry and scouts reconnoitred the country up the Missouri, riding over the ground where Bismarck is located, but in a day when that city was not so much as a figment in the mind of any dreamer.

The Indians had been severely punished, while their property loss had reduced them to a state of destitution, and not the least of their losses was the exhaustion very largely of their supply of ammunition, for upon this they must depend principally for their subsistence.

Inkpaduta Not a Leader—Lean Bear Dead.

It has been said recently by a writer that Inkpaduta was the "Napoleon" who led the savages from the opening of the battle at Big Mound until the passage of the Missouri, and that Lean Bear was one of his lieutenants. Inkpaduta was never more than a horse-thief and cut-throat, dreaded and despised by the Sioux in general, who were never known to give him any following, except from among the outlaws and outcasts whom the Indians in general could not tolerate with patience. As for Lean Bear, he had been dead nearly a year when the Battle of Big Mound was fought, having been killed August 20, 1862, by a settler named Duly, at Lake Shetek, Minnesota.

180

It was one of Inkpaduta's outlaws who shot and killed Dr. Weiser, and brought upon the Indians the hardships, suffering and losses they sustained from that hour on, making Inkpaduta more despised than ever before, for without any doubt it was the purpose of the Indians as a body to surrender peaceably to Gen. Sibley and trust to his clemency.

They knew of his presence in the immediate country they occupied, but did not even move their families, meeting the approach of the general when within cannon shot of their great camp, not as warriors, but as spectators, and sending him word by the Indian scouts they wished to hold a council with him, which would no doubt have taken place but for the treacherous act of a follower of Inkpaduta.

Turning Homeward—Great Joy in Camp.

I find in my diary, under date of August 1st, 1863, this entry:

All is joy this morning, for we turn our faces once more toward civilization. At no time has there been such rejoicing before, and the boys manifest their pleasure in everything they do, and at every turn. Never again will the hills of the Missouri echo the strains of 'Home, Sweet Home' with all the emphasis, feeling and meaning they are wafted over the valley this morning. And how sad the thought so many have been deprived by death from sharing this jubilee and the fond hopes that have inspired it. It is now forty-seven days since we saw a mark of civilization, and with our well-nigh exhausted animals we can hardly hope to make civilization in less than another forty-seven days. Not once have we seen the face of a woman during the long summer's campaign, and it is the hope of greeting again, someday, the kind-faced mother, sister or sweetheart that has made so joyful the hearts of the soldier boys today.

We left camp on the Missouri this morning, our company, with another, acting as rear guard, thus lingering until the command had taken up the march. But for the lonely graves we were leaving the farewell would not have been a sad one.

Death of Chaska—A Really Noble Indian.

We made twenty-two miles on the first day of our return march, and fifteen on the second day. On the evening of the second day, that of August 2nd, Chaska, one of the valued Sioux scouts and a good man was taken violently ill and died. He had left a family in Minnesota which he

181

had fondly, and that we had turned back, reasonably hoped to see again.

Back at Camp Atchison—Capture of Little Crow's Son

At our camp ground on the 3rd, we found springs of delicious water—the best we had been permitted to enjoy since leaving Camp Pope. The Missouri River was not accessible to us, and the water of Apple Creek was the personification of moisture and alkali. There were no empty canteens when we left this camp on the morning of the 4th. We reached Big Mound on the 4th. On the 6th, we met a party of Chippewa half-breeds, who had been at Camp Atchison, and who informed us George A. Brackett, after a heroic struggle, had reached that camp on the 29th of July. This was occasion for general rejoicing, for there was little hope that Brackett had escaped death.

We got out of the *coteau* at 10 o'clock on the forenoon of the 7th, to our great relief, as henceforth we should traverse a comparatively level country. On August 10th, we marched into Camp Atchison, and were given a soldiers' welcome by our comrades, who served to us a royal supper of baked beans, fried hardtack and coffee, with cream from the milk of human kindness in it. This was a royal supper from the fact that we had been kept too busy to practice cookery in so high a style of the art. The men were impatient for the story of our adventures, swapping their stock of information, which consisted of that of the capture of Little Crow's son by them in our absence, for the tales of an adventurous campaign.

To us the news of the capture of the young Indian was equal in interest to any single event we could recount, for through the boy was gathered the first knowledge we had of the killing of his distinguished father by Lampson.

The boy was hunted up and curiously scanned. He was a youth of sixteen, wan and slender, and gave his name as Wa-Wi-Nap-a, which he pronounced very musically. His father had wearied of fighting the whites, and with a small party of Indians, fifteen men and one squaw in all, had walked all the way from the Devils Lake country to the Minnesota frontier, his father's mission being principally to steal horses, of which he was in great need.

The boy had accompanied his father to assist in carrying his "pack." Little Crow and his son were separated from the other members of the party. They were five or six miles north of Hutchinson, Minnesota, on the evening of July 3rd, and were picking berries, unconscious of the presence of white men.

Nathan Lampson and son Chauncey as was later learned were passing the spot, and discovered the Indians. Both Lampsons were armed, as were all who exposed themselves on the frontier after the massacre. Little Crow and son were in comparatively open ground, while the Lampsons were less exposed. The latter were in doubt as to the best course to pursue, not knowing how many Indians constituted the party, but the senior Lampson resolved to creep forward to a tree, and from its shelter kill, if possible, the older of the two Indians.

CAMP ATCHISON ABANDONED—HOMEWARD BOUND.

On the morning of August 12th, 1863, Camp Atchison passed out of existence, the entire command taking up its long march to civilization. Here came a parting of the ways, too, for those who had so long been associated with each other, Gen. Sibley returning with the main body of the expedition by our former trail as far as the big bend the Cheyenne, thence to Abercrombie and on to Fort Snelling, while Col. McPhail, with companies B, E, F, I, and M of the cavalry, was ordered to the southward, west of the Cheyenne.

This Lilliputian offshoot was given one piece of artillery and a scant supply of provisions, and worst of all, Col. McPhail, knowing the great anxiety of the men to again reach civilization, informed his officers and men, when camp was established at the end of the first day's march, that his orders were to make an expedition into the Snake River country, and that he felt he had been unfairly shunted for such a perilous undertaking with so small a force.

The colonel betrayed no sign of the fact, but he must have suffered in his endeavours to suppress his pent-up feelings when he discovered what a hit he had made, for the outburst of the wrath of the disappointed men pretty nearly set the prairie afire. He cautioned moderation and obedience. He expressed earnest indignation himself, but the personal feelings of a soldier was as nothing, he said, when an order to perform a duty had once been given. He then repaired to his tent

The men were furious. Where was Snake River—east or west of the Missouri? No one could tell, and fortunately for the colonel, no map of this region had ever been made. Twenty-eight hours of fighting was nothing as compared with this outrage, for it was supposed the season's campaigning was over, and there was to be a return to civilized life; and now this infamous Snake River expedition had been sprung, with five companies and a wheelbarrow load of provisions. The old earthen bed upon which the men had slept all summer was unusually hard that night, but the boys became resigned to their fate.

Capt. Allen Kills Buffalo Where Redwood Fall Now Stands.

On the 14th, we discovered and captured six head of cattle, of which we made excellent use. They were probably from Brackett's herd, though this fact could not be established. A buffalo was killed on the 15th, just as we were establishing camp about three miles west of the Cheyenne River. On the night of the 16th, we camped where in 1853, was held a monster Sioux council, attended by all the Dakotas east of the Missouri, and by many from beyond that stream. Our Indian guide could tell us little of the council, except that it had some reference to the treaty of 1851, with which the Missouri River Indians were dissatisfied.

On the 17th, we camped on the spot on the Cheyenne where Fort Ransom was afterwards founded. On the 20th, after completing our march, four buffalo passed along the outer edge of our camp. A party of men mounted their horses and gave chase, killing two of the fine animals, and returning to camp loaded with choice steaks. On the 22nd, we struck our old trail amid great rejoicing. The Snake River hoax now positively revealed itself, and for the first time really had a funny aspect.

The 23rd, we had our first wood fire since leaving the Missouri, bidding final *adieu* to buffalo chips. The 24th, we camped near Big Stone Lake, and were put on half rations. Fortunately, a party from Capt. Austin's company killed a buffalo just before going into camp. A team was sent out and brought in the entire carcass. The 25th, we camped on the Wheatstone River. The event of the 26th, was that of being put on quarter rations. A diary notation suggests that "this beats Snake River."

At the crossing of the Lac Qui Parle River, on the 28th, we found a great abundance of wild plums, the first fruit in any form we had been privileged to enjoy for months. The last important event before terminating our return march occurred on the 31st, when Capt. Dwight W. Allen, of Co. I, killed a buffalo near the site of the present little city of Redwood Falls; The country had been deserted for a year, and the excellent pastures of the region had tempted the "cattle of the plains" to repossess themselves of it once more.

Our camp was on the Redwood River on the night of the 31st. Capt. Allen and a companion brought in what steak they could carry, and a team was sent out to bring in the remainder of the animal, which, to the hungry men, was like a shower of manna. Passing the abandoned Redwood Agency on the morning of September 1st, we arrived at Fort Ridgely before noon of that day.

BEHOLD THE TRANSFORMATION—THE END.

Behold the transformation that followed restlessly in the wake of this campaign—the evolution of an empire from a wilderness in the life-time of hundreds of those who assisted in the onerous tasks of wresting from the idle and indolent savage, as fair a land as the sun ever kissed, or the breath of summer ever caressed, moulded now into the magnificent commonwealth of North Dakota, with its cities and its towns, its schools and its churches, its net-work of railroads, its thousands of rural homes, many of them in all respects modem, its vast herds that have displaced the buffalo and the antelope, and its golden fields—a great state in a word, subdued, beautified, glorified, and made rich from the fertility of its own matchless soil. What a privilege to have witnessed such a transformation, inconceivable in any but our own wonderful country, for such a transition one could not witness on the Continent of Europe were he permitted to live a thousand years.

Blessed is the memory when we ranged with free hand in the work of reclamation, amid scenes forever vanished, or now obscured by the stage-settings of civilization.

There was ever an inspiration in the vast, rolling plains—a spirit of freedom never to be purged from the blood when once taken into it. Oceans and mountains challenge our admiration, and no less do great treeless expanses of boundless green, that roll away like the bounding billows of an emerald sea, to kiss the bending skies of our horizon. So far as the works of man were concerned, all was desolation. Buffalo and antelope scurried over the great, wild pastures in herds and bands innumerable, while the Indian, in all his pride and glory, roamed as the undisputed master of the great region that to man was merely a solitude of limitless possibilities.

FORT RIDGELY MONUMENT.

Reminiscences of the Little Crow Uprising

By Asa W. Daniels.

(Read at the monthly meeting of the Executive Council, November 14, 1910.)

Considering the two thousand lives involved, largely women and children, the successful defence of New Ulm was the most momentous event of the Indian war of 1862-3. From that defeat the Indians turned westward and abandoned further combined raids upon the settlements. The active part taken by the citizens of St. Peter will ever be an impressive chapter in the eventful history of that city. Her immediate and generous response with volunteers, and their long and hurried march, enabled them to join in defending New Ulm in the afternoon, and later to participate in the uncertain issue of battle that held the besieged in its grasp for a whole day. The command of General Sibley would have reached the city too late to save it from savage fury, and had not the response been immediate from St. Peter, Le Sueur, and Mankato, its fate must have been too horrible to contemplate.

Some of the events of that battle have never been fully stated in the official reports, and others not mentioned came under the observation of the writer. Therefore, it will be of interest to learn, from one who had superior opportunities, the particulars of the battle as seen by him.

The news of the Indian outbreak reached St. Peter during the night of Monday, the 18th of August, 1862, it having commenced at the Lower Sioux Agency at seven o 'clock that morning. Major Galbraith, who had reached St. Peter in the evening before, on his way to Fort Snelling with a company of recruits, learning of the situation, at daylight started on his return to Fort Ridgely, which he reached in time to participate in its defence.

At four o'clock in the morning of Tuesday, the writer was notified of the outbreak and was asked by Captain Dodd to go to the

187

Rounseville and Briggs neighbourhood, six miles to the northwest, and notify the settlers, and he informed me at the time that messengers had already been dispatched in other directions. I was soon on the way, going from house to house, spreading the alarm, and sending others to more distant locations. On my return the refugees were already pouring in, and by noon the village became crowded with men, women, and children. Some had been attacked on the way, and bore their wounded with them.

All were in most pitiable condition, having in their fright and haste taken little clothing and no provisions, reaching their destination completely destitute. Every house was sympathetically thrown open to the refugees, and was soon filled from cellar to garret. The vacant Ewing House, a hotel of fifty rooms or more, and an uncompleted store building, were soon filled, and being of stone afforded safety and comparative comfort; but many were compelled to resort to sheds and barns, or to remain unsheltered for some nights, until better provided.

A little more than a year before the outbreak I had located in St. Peter, having left the Government service at the Lower Agency as physician and surgeon to the Sioux Indians, after a service of more than seven years. I had visited them a month before and heard from them many complaints, principally against their physician, Dr. Humphrey. My long service among them had been satisfactory to myself and the Indians, and I had made many warm friends in every band, among them being Little Crow, and I may say most of the other chiefs. Therefore, when the news of the outbreak came, I was in great doubt in regard to its being general, but thought it confined to a single band, and that the outrages had occurred when they were under the influence of whiskey sold them by the whites. But within twenty-four hours my confidence in my old friends was rudely shattered, and I came to realize, on seeing the dead and wounded, that the outbreak was general and of the most barbarous character.

As a government officer, I had observed for more than two years the close intimacy that was growing up between the Sioux and Winnebagoes. This was apparent from frequent visits of large parties of Winnebagoes to the Agency, intermarriages that took place, uniting in games, and tribal pledges of friendship. No doubt some of the Winnebagoes participated in the battles that took place, but were too discreet to have it known. Had success attended the Sioux at Fort Ridgely and New Ulm, there is little doubt there would have been a union of the tribes against the whites.

My brother, Dr. J. W. Daniels, had served for five years as physician to the Upper Sioux, at Yellow Medicine, thirty miles west of the Lower Sioux Agency, and resigned at the same time that I did, both of us expecting appointments in some of the regiments going south. A few months later he was commissioned as assistant surgeon in the Sixth Minnesota Regiment, and soon afterward he was promoted to be surgeon in the First Cavalry. I received an appointment, but from domestic conditions was compelled to resign.

At St. Peter, to which we return after this slight digression, Captain Dodd and Major Flandrau had enlisted about one hundred and forty men to march at once to the defence of New Ulm. Many of these volunteers fled from their country homes in the morning, hurriedly disposed of their families, and bravely responded to the call for a thirty miles march before the close of their eventful day.

I joined them as the surgeon of the command, and we were on our way about midday. The men were armed with double-barrelled shot guns, a few rifles, and some other arms of uncertain efficiency. Some were on horseback, and a few in buggies; having to carry my surgical and medical cases, I availed myself of the latter conveyance. On reaching Courtland, twenty miles, a heavy shower drenched the command, but the march was continued, all being enthusiastic to reach New Ulm, where, refugees informed me, there was a battle going forward and much of the town burned. We reached Redstone, two miles from the village, just as it was getting dark, and from that distance it did look as if the whole town was on fire; but, crossing the ferry, we pushed on and reached the vicinity of the Dacotah House about ten o'clock at night.

As we were leaving St. Peter, we were joined by a command under Captain Tousley, of Le Sueur, of nearly one hundred men, who continued with us on the march to New Ulm. With them as surgeons were Dr. Otis Ayers and Dr. William W. Mayo, father of the two distinguished surgeons at Rochester. It was midnight before we found quarters for the night, and then I shared my bed with Dr. Ayers, passing a comfortable night after a long and strenuous day.

Early on the morning of Wednesday, we were looking over the situation as left from the engagement the afternoon before. On a vacant lot near the centre of the town lay six dead, brought in from the scene of the engagement, and others had been cared for by their families. The physicians then visited the wounded and cared for them, and for some of the refugees who were ill from fright and anxiety.

During the forenoon of Wednesday, Captain Bierbauer came in with nearly a hundred men from Mankato, and a few men came from Nicollet, under the command of Captain Samuel Coffin. An organisation was formed on that day by the military, who selected Major Flandrau as commander, Captain Dodd as lieutenant, and S. A. Buell as provost marshal. Pickets were established on the outskirts of the town, and guard duty for the night. During the day quarters and the commissary departments were established for the different commands.

A company of sixteen mounted men from St. Peter, among whom were Henry A. Swift and Horace Austin, afterward governors of the state, had started to the front some hours before the command under Flandrau was ready to leave, and had reached New Ulm in time to participate in the battle of Tuesday afternoon.

Thursday morning, after guard mount and after a company had been selected to dig rifle-pits, a company of a hundred men, under the command of Captain Dodd, was ordered to go to the Little Cottonwood settlement, six miles south, to bury the dead and rescue any that might be hiding or wounded. Dr. Ayers and myself were detailed to accompany the command. The doctor invited me to have a seat with him on his buck-board, which I thankfully accepted. The command had hardly made half the distance to the settlement before they were fired upon from ambush, but none were wounded, and, after returning a volley, we continued our march. Three mounted Indians soon showed themselves, but at a safe distance, observing our course, and in derision waving their blankets, keeping in sight most of the time during the march.

On reaching the settlement, the saddest scene presented itself that humanity is ever called to witness. The massacre had probably taken place on the Monday before, and the dead were lying in all directions about the farm houses, in bed, in different rooms of the house, in the yard, near the grain stacks, and on the lawn. During the three days that the remains had been exposed the flies had done their work, and as a result the faces of the dead presented a revolting spectacle. Trenches were dug, and the bodies were gathered together and laid within, blankets were spread over them, and a prayer was offered; then earth to earth, ashes to ashes; and the command turned sadly away, having witnessed a burial scene that could never be forgotten. On our return we reached New Ulm late in the afternoon.

By the military the day had been passed in strengthening the defences of the town, providing themselves with ammunition, and fixing upon positions of advantage in case of an attack.

News came in during the day, of fighting at Fort Ridgely, and of Captain Marsh's defeat at the Agency, and many other alarming accounts from refugees.

The principal event of Friday was the detailing of one hundred and forty men, under the command of Captain Tousley, to go to Leavenworth, west and south of Fort Ridgely, expecting to find persons there unable to escape and that might be rescued, but nothing definite was known in regard to the situation there. Drs. Ayers, Mayo, and myself joined the command, I again having a seat with Dr. Ayers. The route was across an open prairie, and we had not proceeded far before we discovered three mounted Indian scouts to the north keeping in line with us and watching our course. Late in the afternoon we reached the vicinity south of Fort Ridgely and for the first time heard cannonading going on there, the sounds reaching us at short and regular intervals.

After its significance had fully impressed me, I said to Dr. Ayers that the Indians had attacked the fort in great force, and that, as scouts had been watching our course, in case we continued our march to Leavenworth they certainly would withdraw from the fort during the afternoon or in the morning and cut us off. We had expected to remain at Leavenworth during the night, returning the next day. Dr. Ayers agreed with me fully, and rode forward and consulted with Captain Tousley, who called a halt and gave his reasons for doing so, asking of the command to express their wishes by a showing of their hands. It was carried by those in favour of going forward by two or three votes.

We continued our march for another hour, the warning notes of the cannon coming to us regularly; the sun was nearly setting, night coming on, and fatigue was telling upon the command, when a second halt was called and another vote taken, which resulted in an order to return to New Ulm. We reached our return destination after midnight, thoroughly worn out and disgusted from this long and useless march, which might have resulted not only in the destruction of the command, but perhaps in the capture of New Ulm.

The morning of Saturday was warm and fair, and at first, we hopefully looked forward to an uneventful day. Much time had been taken in preparing for an attack, by burning outer buildings, digging riflepits, and loop-holing such walls as might be made serviceable. On that morning Colonel Flandrau gave me a dozen men and I barricaded the avenue a little west of the Gross hotel.

From the roof of the Erd building, a central business block, with a glass an extensive view was had of the surrounding country, and at this point of observation a watchman was on duty during the day.

The first surprise and alarm of the morning came when at guard mount, west of the town, Lieutenant Edwards was instantly killed by an Indian so concealed in the grass that danger was unsuspected.

About eight o'clock a.m., the watchman from the roof saw Indians collecting some two miles west of the town, and signal smokes from the northwest. His observations were confirmed by officers and others.

The certainty of a deadly conflict with a barbarous foe, when no quarter is expected, is a most trying test of courage, but, with few exceptions, the situation was heroically accepted. The women and children were hurried to places of safety, the command was got under arms, and the physicians selected rooms for receiving the wounded, Drs. Mayo and McMahon in the Dacotah House, and Dr. Ayers and myself in a store room on the opposite side of the avenue.

Within one hour the large body of Indians who had been forming on the west, were seen to be moving rapidly upon the town. The signals indicated a like approach from the north. When aware of their approach, Colonel Flandrau posted his men upon the slope of one of the terraces on the west, with a line of skirmishers in front. Little Crow was mounted and led his warriors, who were on foot. In a long line with flanks curved forward, they approached in silence within a quarter of a mile of the defenders, when they gave a terrific war-cry and rushed forward upon a run, holding their fire until they had received that of our men, and then delivering an effective volley at close range. The defenders fell back in a panic and the whole line retreated to the barricades. The assault was well executed, and had it been pushed to its limit might have resulted in the capture of the town. But our men soon rallied behind the barricades and buildings, which arrested the onward rush of the Indians and compelled them to seek protection of the outer buildings.

Lieutenant Huey, with seventy-five men, was ordered to the ferry to prevent the Indians from crossing from the north side. Either from a misunderstanding or over-confidence, he crossed his command to the north side of the river, there meeting a large body of the enemy, retreated to Nicollet, and was not seen again until the following day. This unfortunate event was a serious loss to the defence.

The firing from both sides became rapid, sharp and general, the Indians gradually pushing their way in surrounding the town, which they accomplished before midday. They fought with the utmost boldness and ferocity, and with the utmost skill and caution from every hollow and grass patch, and from behind every house and hillock or log.

The crisis came at two p.m., when the Indians fired buildings on both sides of the avenue in the lower part of the town. A strong wind was blowing from the east, and the conflagration threatened the destruction of our only defence. Colonel Flandrau rallied a sufficient force, and charging down the street, drove the enemy from the avenue. But just at this critical time the wind changed to the opposite direction, and clouds, which had been gathering for hours, shed upon our threatened locality a sufficient shower of rain to prevent the further extending of the flames.

The unfortunate incident in the day's battle that led to the death of Captain Dodd has never been correctly reported. In justice to the brave men that participated in that critical movement, a correct understanding should be had of the reasons that, at the time, seemed to make the undertaking imperative.

It will be remembered that Lieutenant Huey had retreated toward Nicollet in the morning, and all through the day we looked for his return with reinforcements, which really took place the following day.

About five p.m., there appeared beyond the Indian outer line, at the east, some forty or fifty men, marching in single file, under the command of an officer, carrying an American flag. They were dressed in citizens' clothing, and had all the appearance of the reinforcement so anxiously expected.

The Indians had again gained possession of buildings on the avenue east, perhaps five blocks from the Dacotah House, and from that position were delivering a galling fire upon our line.

Immediately, on discovering what all thought to be our reinforcements, Captain Dodd, in a short, impassioned speech, volunteered to lead any that would follow, to the clearing of the avenue of Indians and joining our reinforcements beyond. Rev. Father Sunrisen and Dr. Mayo both made brief speeches, urging all to unite in support of Dodd. Some twenty men fell into line, Dodd and Shoemaker being mounted, and proceeded down the avenue. It was a movement of only a few minutes consideration, and seemed to promise an important result. Captain Dodd leading, the small volunteer force rushed forward with a cheer, hardly coming within the Indian lines before receiving a deadly volley, which hurriedly sent them back to positions of safety. Captain Dodd wheeled his horse and reached a log blacksmith's shop, when the horse plunged forward and fell. Partially supporting himself, with others assisting, the fatally wounded leader was taken into the building. A temporary cot was provided, where he was made as comfortable as possible.

The building was loop-holed and a half dozen were firing from it, as it was one of the important positions on our outer line. Dodd had received three mortal wounds, two other slight wounds, and the horses ridden by Dodd and Shoemaker were both killed. The writer had witnessed from our hospital the whole movement, saw Dodd fall, and hurried to his assistance. There was little that could be done, as he was in a dying condition, surviving only about one hour. He appreciated his condition, and met it courageously, giving me messages to his wife and to Bishop Whipple, with the utmost coolness and consideration. Thus, passed a courageous and heroic spirit, a man of large mental endowments, and one whose life had been full of stirring incidents.

William B. Dodd deserves more than passing notice, as he was one of the most energetic, fearless and reliant, among the early pioneers of southern Minnesota. He contributed largely to the settlement and development of that part of the state. "Lest we forget," it may be well to remind the present generation of some of the services he rendered the state and his home town.

He was largely instrumental in securing from the government the appropriation for the building of the Dodd road, from St. Peter to Mendota. He superintended its laying out and construction. He located the townsite of St. Peter, and from the first had the most supreme confidence in its future. He lived to see his wilderness claim develop into a thriving city, and he would have succeeded in making it the capital city of the state had not his enemies resorted to the most infamous methods. He led two volunteer companies against the Indians, the first in pursuit of Inkpaduta after the Spirit Lake Massacre. (Vide *History of the Spirit Lake Massacre and Captivity of Miss Abbie Gardner* by Abbie Gardner-Sharp and *Sioux Massacre at Spirit Lake* by Thomas Teakle & R. A. Smith, also published by Leonaur.)

During the years of 1853-4, he was at times acting United States marshal. He volunteered for service in the south during the civil war, but was rejected on account of impaired sight. He was one of the delegates to Washington that succeeded in making his city a chartered point on the Winona and St. Peter railroad. He was a ready and impressive speaker, and had held several positions of trust from the state.

The party we had supposed to be reinforcements, upon the volley from the Indians and our men falling back, suddenly disappeared, and it proved to be a stratagem to draw out some of our men and cut them off. Had the Indians in the buildings held their fire until they had advanced a half block farther, it would have been successful.

In explanation of how the Indians became possessed of so many suits of citizens' clothing, it may be said that twenty-two months before one hundred and fifty suits were issued to them by the government, under the pledge of becoming farmers, much of this clothing having never been worn more than a few days.

The assault, commencing in the morning at 9:30, was kept up without interruption until dark, when the Indians withdrew in the direction of Fort Ridgely. During the evening all buildings outside of our barricades were burned. By ourselves and the Indians one hundred and ninety buildings were destroyed. We lost ten killed and fifty wounded, the small loss being accounted for by the fact that we were fighting from loop-holed buildings and barricades. The Indian loss has never been known. Both hospitals received and dressed the wounded, providing temporary cots for them. Some that were only slightly wounded returned and continued in the fight during the day.

Saturday night was anxious and disturbed with desultory firing by our guards, and perhaps by the Indians. Sunday morning it seemed from heavy firing that the assault was to be renewed, but it gradually lessened and by noon it ceased entirely. About noon Captain E. St. Julien Cox arrived with about fifty men, accompanied by Lieutenant Huey with part of his detachment, who had been cut off the day before.

During Sunday afternoon search was made for the recovery of the dead. Three or four were found that had fallen so far out as to be exposed to any indignity that the Indians might offer, but none were scalped or otherwise mutilated. Jerry Quane, a St. Peter volunteer, had the totem of Little Crow attached to the clothing over his breast. The totem was the skin of a crow, preserved in its natural form, symbolic of his family name. The parting with such a treasured emblem was to boastfully inform us from whom the brave defender had met his death.

Early on Monday morning, the order was issued for the evacuation of the village. Colonel Flandrau must have been wholly responsible for this move, as I am sure the medical officers were not consulted and were entirely ignorant of it until a short time before the movement commenced. We had received reinforcements the day before, our position was stronger than ever, the sanitary condition did not necessitate great urgency in moving, and the volunteers would have loyally remained. General Sibley was at St. Peter, and would have arrived within a very few days, therefore it was a mistake to retreat from New Ulm until relieved by him. The route was a part of the way through a forest, and had a few Indians attacked, a panic and massacre would have followed. It is an ungracious and unwelcome task to criticise the colonel, but a truthful statement seems to demand that it should be done, in this respect at least. Nearly two thousand men, women, and children, took up the march for Mankato, thirty miles distant, bearing the wounded in conveyances. Fortunately, the long march was uneventful and we reached our destination late in the evening, where we received a generous reception.

On Tuesday, the volunteers from St. Peter reached home and disbanded. The writer brought with him Rev. Mr. Saunders, severely wounded, who had volunteered with the Le Sueur company.

Some of the wounded were left at Mankato, but most of them came to St. Peter, and their care became most urgent. My brother, assistant surgeon with Gen. Sibley's command, assisting, we established a hospital in the court room of the court house. The room was large, well ventilated, and afforded space for twenty beds, sufficient for the most serious cases. The care of the hospital devolved upon me, as my brother left with his command two or three days later.

Of the cases that came under my care, the most serious were as follows: Mr. Summers, of Nicollet, shot through the spinal column, died. Rufus Huggins was shot through the knee joint, and, refusing amputation, died. A New Ulm volunteer, having a shot through the mouth, severing the tongue, recovered. A Sibley County volunteer, with a compound comminuted fracture of the arm bone near the shoulder joint, had amputation and recovery. Rev. Mr. Saunders, with an abdominal wound, recovered. Mr. Bean, a St. Peter volunteer, with a shot through the face, fracturing his lower jaw, recovered. A St. Paul volunteer, with a penetrating gunshot wound of the brain, lived two or three years and died insane at St. Peter.

From the time the news of the outbreak was received, the citizens of St. Peter were active in providing for the refugees and the protection of the city. They organised committees for the various duties, as care of the sick, supplying food and clothing, and fortifying. Night and day guard duty was kept up, earth-works were thrown up, rifle pits dug, and barricades erected.

In the early fall the hospital was removed from the court house to the Ewing House, a hotel building that had been vacant for some time until occupied temporarily by the refugees. In January, 1863, I was succeeded in charge by Dr. Charles W. Le Boutillier, who was assistant surgeon of the First Regiment, and was captured at the first Battle of Bull Run and paroled on condition of not again serving against the South. He died suddenly while occupying this position April 3, 1863.

During the fall and winter of 1862-3, St. Peter was garrisoned by two companies of the Sixth Regiment, and Kasota by a cavalry company. This period was marked by the unusual amount of sickness. A few cases of smallpox occurred, first at Kasota, and afterward in the hospital; and cases of typhoid fever, diphtheria, measles, and scarlet fever, were frequent. Much of the disease was the result of the overcrowded condition of the city and the lack of sanitary conditions.

Through the next winter, of 1863-4, St. Peter was the regimental headquarters of the Sixth Regiment, under command of Colonel Crooks. This added to the already crowded condition of the city and was a source of increased unsalutary conditions. The quarters were without proper conveniences for personal cleanliness, crowded, badly ventilated, and without sewerage. The water supply was from shallow wells and soon became polluted. The result was that typhoid fever, cerebrospinal meningitis, measles, diphtheria, and smallpox, soon became epidemic, all taking on a most malignant type. Dr. Alfred Wharton, surgeon of the Sixth Regiment, had charge of the hospital, assisted by Dr. Potter. They faithfully and efficiently performed their duties under the very trying and adverse conditions that existed. Nine deaths occurred from smallpox, with a sad mortality from other diseases.

These diseases were not confined to the military by any means but involved the whole city, resulting in many families being stricken, the cloud of disease and death hanging like a pall over many households.

The loss of life in the Sioux Massacre, according to an estimate by Agent Galbraith, which was made with deliberation and may be accepted as conservative, was 654.

The additional loss of life that was caused directly and indirectly by the outbreak, in the many settlements across the extensive frontier, has never been known, but must have been very large. From a somewhat careful observation, and from consultation with parties who had good means of judging, the writer is of the opinion that the loss from disease and battle, and that in the frontier settlements resulting from the outbreak, must have been as large as that suffered directly from the hands of the Indians in the massacre.

In closing this paper, the writer, who was so long and intimately associated with the Indians as a government official, desires to say that he found this people possessed of many of the virtues common to the human family, and that socially and morally their lives were of a standard quite as high as among many of the civilized races. The outbreak was induced by long-continued violation of treaty obligations on the part of the government, inflicting upon these unfortunate wards untold want and suffering. Like violent acts of mobs among civilized communities, the massacre was a barbarous and unreasoning protest against injustice. Had the government faithfully carried out the treaty obligations and dealt with the Sioux justly and humanely, the outbreak would not have occurred.

www.ingramcontent.com/pod-product-compliance
Lightning Source LLC
Chambersburg PA
CBHW021056090426
42738CB00006B/367